FAMILIA

ULSTER GENEALOGICAL REVIEW

Ulster
Genealogical
& Historical
Guild

NUMBER 34

2018

COVER IMAGE

Daylight Raid from my Studio Window, 7 July 1917
by Sir John Lavery, 1856–1951
Ulster Museum, Belfast, October 2017
© NATIONAL MUSEUMS NORTHERN IRELAND
COLLECTION ULSTER MUSEUM, BELUM U71

BACK COVER IMAGE

Brian Trainor
PRIVATE COLLECTION

Published 2018
by Ulster Historical Foundation
www.booksireland.org.uk
www.ancestryireland.com

ISBN 978-1-909556-70-6

Printed by Martins the Printers Ltd
Design and production by Dunbar Design

CONTENTS

REVIEWS

CONTENTS

EDITORIAL

The theme of Ireland and the First World War and, by extension, the events leading to the partitioning of the island of Ireland, is a theme that has recurred in recent issues of *Familia*. The dual commemoration in 2018 of the centenary of the ending of the Great War and of the work carried out by women as their contribution to the war effort, an achievement that secured the franchise for them, is effectively acknowledged in Sarah Paterson's account of the Imperial War Museum 'Women's Work' collections. The article is nicely enhanced on the front cover by the reproduction of Sir John Lavery's *Woman at the Window*, depicting a Zeppelin raid on London viewed from his studio window.

The mounting number of associated publications are included in Richard McMinn's thoroughgoing appraisal in three discrete review articles which have been such an distinctive feature of issues in the last few years. In the context of the war and its aftermath in Ireland, the story of Erskine Childers' graduation from true-British diplomat to committed Irish nationalist and eventual fate at the hands of the independent government he sought to establish, is recounted by Patrick Butler.

Richard Holmes's consideration of the several generations of the Drennan-Duffin family from the eighteenth to the twentieth centuries, all the time preserving their liberal Non-Subscribing Presbyterian ethos in dramatically different political and cultural circumstances, calls on one of PRONI's most extensive family collections. Linde Lunney provides a timely reappraisal of the establishment and development of Presbyterianism in Dublin. William Roulston traces James Hull's path as an exemplar of the fate of Presbyterian ministers associated, as a good number had been, with the 1798 rebellion in Ulster and their flight to and subsequent careers in the United States.

Don McCloy and Angus Annan reflect on two important aspects of educational provision in rapidly-growing Belfast in the nineteenth, twentieth and now in the twenty-first centuries. Professor McCloy charts the rise and outlines the importance of elementary education in the quickly-developing town and city; Angus Annan looks at the adaptation of one of the city's iconic educational buildings, the Belfast Technical College, into accommodation for the twenty-first century generation of third-level students.

Arthur Bell's family research in the overlooked TRANS 2A archive have brought to the fore a story of sea-borne enterprise over two generations in the coal trade. James Bartlett recounts the serendipity of coming across, while visiting a Melbourne tourist venue, the contemporary story of two second-generation Irish immigrants to Australia.

The dearth of pre-Famine sources is a constant deficit for historians and genealogists alike. Bill Macafee's detailed account of the 1831 County Londonderry 'census' is remarkable not only for the unrivalled access it allows to the source but because his research has made available some 40,000 names and, by linking the source to valuation records, it has the capacity to identify their precise locations.

In addition to his three comprehensive review articles on aspects of First World War events and the subsequent steps towards Irish independence, Richard McMinn reviews Leo Kehane's *Captain Jack White: Imperialism, Anarchism and the Irish Citizen Army*. Leslie Clarkson's review article renews the focus of attention on the steady stream of publications relating to the Great Famine and its memorialisation, a phenomenon that was set train nearly a quarter of a century ago with the sesquecentenary of the tragedy and which shows little sign of abating. Eull Dunlop's review of several books associated with the covenanting tradition in Ulster reflects one of his trademark interests and, poignantly, his widow Dorothy submitted the review after Eull's sad passing in August.

Anthony Malcomson's legendary knowledge of sources associated with 'big houses' in Ireland is very much in evidence in his authoritative review of John Kirwan's study-through-time of the Ormond(e) family, as it is in his review of Martin Sheppard's two publications, *For the Fourth Generation* and *Love on Inishcoo*. Dennis Kennedy is ideally qualified to evaluate Alan Parkinson's survey of crucial elections over the last century outlined in *Election Fever*. Patrick Fitzgerald assesses *Exiles of '98*, an account of those who fled Ulster in the wake of the 1798 rebellion, a research exercise with which, in the company of Peter Gilmore and William Roulston, I was very glad to have been associated.

Peter Roebuck considers Douglas Bartlett's resourceful, in every sense, publication on the history of the town of Limavady, County Londonderry. Gerry Cleary evaluates Tanja Poppelreuter's survey, through the eyes of architectural students, of a range of hitherto uncelebrated twentieth-century

Belfast buildings. Brian Walker's expertise on the history of the Church of Ireland is well to the fore in his review of Mark Empey, Alan Ford and Miriam Moffitt's history of that institution.

Brendan Fulton's review of Marianne Elliott's intriguing – and personal – account of an early mixed-housing initiative in post-war Belfast is informed by his role as a founding parent of the neighbouring Hazelwood integrated schools established in the mid-1980s. And it is always a pleasure to carry a review by Jonathan Bardon, this time of Mairèad Carew's *The Quest for the Irish Celt: The Harvard Archaeological Mission to Ireland, 1932–36.*

Trevor Parkhill's range of reviews takes into account Frances McGee's description of the archival material arising from the establishment and early development of that most comprehensive and valued of sources, the valuation of Ireland. On the theme of female emigration to Australia, something that has characterised the titles of Anchor Books, Jennifer Rushen and Kathlyn Gibson's assured use of immigration sources uncovers the absorbing success story of one impoverished female migrant from Famine Ireland, *Anastasia: From Callan to Stockyard Creek. Nurses' Voices from WW1: The Northern Ireland Connection* is a timely consideration of the several categories of the professional and volunteer nursing profession who contributed so nobly to the 1914–18 war effort. Jeffrey Dudgeon's well-researched and sensitive mini-biography, *H. Montgomery Hyde: Ulster Unionist MP, Gay Law Reform Campaigner and Prodigious Author* is enough to suggest that a full-scale biography would not go amiss. The review of the third edition of the *Scottish Clan and Family Encyclopaedia*, with a host of expert genealogical voices, completes the section.

The recent passing of Dr Brian Trainor is an inestimable loss for the world of Irish archives and genealogy. As Deputy Keeper of the Records of Northern Ireland and then as Director of the Ulster Historical Foundation he was at the forefront of developing the crucial understanding and mutual respect that currently exists between the worlds of historical and genealogical research. At the core of this were the archives that he curated and, in many, many instances, located and catalogued. A good number of the articles and reviews, and indeed the authors and reviewers, not least the editor, in this current issue of *Familia*, owe much to Brian's boundless enthusiasm for the preservation and research use of Irish archives.

TREVOR PARKHILL

NOTES ON CONTRIBUTORS

ANGUS ANNAN attended the Technical High School 1955–58. As an apprentice he followed the National Certificate and IEE Courses at the College of Technology Belfast. He retired as Director of IT and Libraries at the University of West London.

JONATHAN BARDON is an historical consultant, broadcaster and author whose most recent publication, *A Narrow Sea* (2018) has just been published. He is also President of the Belfast Natural History and Philosophical Society.

JAMES BARTLETT is a freelance journalist, broadcaster and author in Los Angeles who has published in *Familia* and elsewhere on topics of Irish historical and genealogical interest.

ARTHUR BELL held senior posts on major engineering projects in Belfast Shipyard, Shetland Isles Oil Terminal and overseas, before promoting exports and the commercial use of foreign languages through government and European Commission programmes.

PATRICK BUTLER is a Belfast-based barrister, presently specialising in public inquiry work. He was president of the Belfast Literary Society 2017–18.

LESLIE CLARKSON is Emeritus Professor of Social History, Queen's University Belfast.

GERRY CLEARY is a retired Assistant Professor in the International College, I Shou University, Kaohsiung, Taiwan. His PhD research, concentrating on Belfast's nineteenth- and early twentieth-century growth, inform his current 'Builders of Belfast' walking tours.

EULL DUNLOP, who sadly passed away in August 2018, was a retired teacher involved in researching and publishing local history, including regular contributions to *Familia*.

PATRICK FITZGERALD is Lecturer and Development Officer, Mellon Centre for Migration Studies, Ulster American Folk Park, Omagh, County Tyrone.

BRENDAN FULTON, a Queen's University Belfast history graduate and retired senior social worker, researched and co-authored *Making the Difference*, a history of probation in Northern Ireland (2009). He is a founding parent of the Hazelwood integrated schools.

RICHARD HOLMES has published mostly on eighteenth-century Ireland including *James Arbuckle Selected Works* (2014). He is currently researching Ulster writers in the period of the Home Rule crisis.

DENNIS KENNEDY, a historian who has worked in journalism in Ireland north and south, USA and Ethiopia, was lecturer in European Studies at Queen's University Belfast 1993–2001. Publications include Irish and European history and politics and 3 volumes of memoirs.

LINDE LUNNEY, born in County Antrim, was the first staff member on the Royal Irish Academy's *Dictionary of Irish Biography*, 1983. She has now retired after 777 biographies. Her research interests include Ulster emigration and family history.

BILL MACAFEE retired in 2000 from the Faculty of Education, University of Ulster. Much of his recent research on local and family history can now be seen on his website: www.billmacafee.com.

ANTHONY MALCOMSON, archivist and historian, was Director of PRONI 1988–98. His archival specialism is archives of the 'big houses' of Ireland and, as a historian, has published extensively on Irish politics and aristocratic society, *c.* 1725–1832.

DON McCLOY was Dean of Science and Technology at Ulster University, Rector of Belfast Institute for Further and Higher Education, and Chairman of NI Curriculum Council and Stranmillis University College.

RICHARD McMINN is a former Principal of Stranmillis University College, Belfast, where he also taught Irish history, and is a former Trustee of the National Museums Northern Ireland.

TREVOR PARKHILL is editor of *Familia* and former Keeper of History, Ulster Museum.

SARAH PATERSON is a Librarian at the Imperial War Museum, London. Her research interests include women in wartime, military families, prisoners of war and the British in Germany following both World Wars.

PETER ROEBUCK is Emeritus Professor of History at Ulster University and chairman of the Cumbrian Local History Federation. His latest book is *Cattle Droving through Cumbria 1600–1900* (2015).

WILLIAM ROULSTON is Research Director with the Ulster Historical Foundation. His latest book is a new and greatly-enlarged edition of *Researching Scots-Irish Ancestors* (2018).

BRIAN M. WALKER is Emeritus Professor of Irish Studies at Queen's University Belfast. His most recent book is *A History of St George's Church Belfast: Two Centuries of Faith, Worship and Music.*

Brian Trainor 1928–2018

BRIAN TRAINOR
AN APPRECIATION

Brian Trainor devoted much of his professional life and indeed his 30-year retirement to making good the almost-irreparable damage done to Irish archives by the destruction of the Four Courts during the Civil War in 1922. Initially as archivist from the mid-1950s, then Director of the Public Record Office of Northern Ireland 1970–87 and as Chairman of the Irish Manuscripts Commission and of the National Archives Advisory Committee, he was at the forefront of the campaign to improve the quality and awareness of historical sources whose availability and interpretation have played such a vital role in the improved understanding of the island's past.

Bernard Ignatius Trainor was born in 1928 in Coleraine, the son of a railway official and, although his father died when he was aged three, it was that mixed railway community which imbued him with a lifelong sense of the importance of cross-community relations in Northern Ireland. In 1939 the local church funded scholarships to St Columb's College in Derry for Brian and older brother Frank. He obtained a First Class honours history degree at Queen's University Belfast (to which he travelled daily by train) in 1949. After research in London at the Institute of Historical Research he was appointed assistant lecturer in history at Queen's in 1951. In 1956 he was appointed assistant archivist in the Public Record Office of Northern Ireland and from then until the late 1970s embarked on an extensive and energetic campaign throughout Northern Ireland of identifying and accessioning historical records from solicitors' office, businesses, linen firms threatened with extinction, together with thousands of individual family records.

Dr Trainor succeeded Ken Darwin as Director of PRONI in 1970, and seized the opportunity to realise his vision as the office moved to purpose-built premises in Balmoral Avenue. Now the major holdings of documents could be stored under proper conditions and accessed by students, academics, genealogists and casual researchers alike. An accrual of additional staff to locate, acquire and process new documentary collections, on an unprecedented scale, facilitated the dawning of a golden age as he oversaw PRONI becoming an outstanding source of academic riches, producing pioneering studies in the field of social, economic and political history. A programme of publications was launched (*Aspects of Irish Social History*, which he edited with Bill Crawford, went into several reprints and remains a classic), resource packs for teachers produced, seminars and exhibitions hosted, programmes of local history lectures undertaken, teachers seconded (this in liaison with the Department for Education Northern Ireland (DENI) History Inspectorate), links formed with universities and academic institutions throughout Ireland, and scholarship encouraged. With extraordinary application, he created an outpost which embodied his ideal of an institution where archives and documentary collections were made freely available for purposes of furthering an objective and evidence-based understanding of our shared past. The vision succeeded because it so strongly reflected Trainor's own work ethic and personal values. It was a vocation as much as a profession.

This mission was initially carried out with the minimum of intervention from officialdom in Stormont. That began to change, however, when collections of governmental records dating from the foundation of the Northern Ireland state began to be added to the PRONI holdings. The 30-year rule for access to these holdings, and the need to act in conformity with practice elsewhere in the UK, inevitably introduced constraints on the use to which some of these records could be put: controversy arose as academics were denied sight of what they suspected was information reflecting adversely on former Unionist administrations. Such constraints were contrary to Trainor's instincts. It was a world that he found frustrating and increasingly uncongenial.

He took early retirement in 1987 to devote himself to the work of the Ulster Historical Foundation, an independent historical and genealogical research and publication agency, formerly part of PRONI. Among his contributions to the Foundation's development were the annual lecture tours 1989–2013 in the United States (44 of the 50 states visited) and Canada, involving herculean travel by Greyhound bus and hired car, delivering lectures to audiences with an increasing appetite for information on sources that would inform their interest in Irish heritage. He also championed UHF's formative involvement in the landmark Irish Genealogical Project, an all-Ireland initiative (of the Irish Family History Foundation (IFHF) to which Ulster Historical Foundation is a significant contributor) compiling databases from church and civil birth, death and marriage records. He edited *Familia's* sister publication, *The Directory of Irish Family History Research*, until his retirement as Research Director in 2006. Following his retirement he continued with the famous lecture tours until the age of 85. He was closely involved in the 1980s in the campaigns to save the Linen Hall Library and Friar's Bush graveyard, both integral features of Belfast's heritage.

His archival vision incorporated a strong all-Ireland identity, something that was recognised by Dr Garret Fitzgerald in 1987 who appointed him chair of the Management Committee of the National Archives Advisory Committee. Throughout the 1970s he served on the Irish Manuscripts Commission and was Chairman 1976–77 and 1987–99. Among his publication initiatives was the first output from the Women's History Project (*The Drennan McTier Letters, 1776–1819*). He also ensured that the records arising from the very successful Irish Manuscripts Commission's business records survey were entrusted to the National Archives of Ireland.

Dr Trainor was awarded two honorary doctorates, in 1984 by the University of Ulster and in 1986 by the National University of Ireland. He is survived by his wife Pilar, originally from Madrid, his children, Rosana, Pancho and Katrina, and five grandsons, Santi, Milo, Jacob, Beni and Sami.

After his funeral, in accordance with his wishes, his remains were returned to Coleraine for burial among his own. An old friend from those days sketched a picture of the young Brian studying his books as he lay among the dunes on Portrush strand; after an hour or two he would set off to swim the full length of the bay as far as the bar mouth and then back again, to return to his books, applauded by the watching holiday-makers.

Brian Trainor, born Coleraine 26 May 1928 died at home, Belfast 22 August 2018.

Young female munition workers filling shells
in a factory at an undisclosed location.

The role of women in the First World War
The Women's Work Collection
at the Imperial War Museum

SARAH PATERSON

The Women's Work Collection (WWC) was compiled by
the Imperial War Museum (IWM) between 1917 and the
early 1920s as a national initiative to record the female
contribution to the Great War. The story of the Women's
Work Sub-Committee (WWSC) deserves greater
recognition for the monumental task of gathering this
material and making it available to the public.

Not all women chose to engage with the war effort; some were very
active in the Pacifist movement or saw the war as an opportunity
to challenge the established social order. The immediate pre-war period
had been volatile with two points of looming conflict in the shape of
Home Rule for Ireland and the campaign for women's suffrage. The
WWSC saw its remit as covering only the period between the outbreak
of war in August 1914 until the immediate aftermath, and included
either women's direct efforts to help the war effort or assist those
suffering as a result of the military conflict. The work of collecting
began in a period of dramatic expansion of the opportunities open to
women, and finished as these abruptly contracted and halted owing to
men returning home to take up their traditional work. They also
recorded what they wanted to be remembered, knowing they had
witnessed a unique and special, though challenging and turbulent,
period in history. It is therefore an extremely important source for
discovering more about the many roles women assumed during the

war, and has a great deal of material potentially helpful to those undertaking local history and genealogical research.

We now tend to look back on the First World War as a single historical event, and do not necessarily think about or appreciate how those living through it regarded it on a day-to-day basis, not knowing when or how it would end. The IWM was established in London on 5 March 1917, and was a response to the profoundly shocking impact the war had on British society. It was the first 'total war' that had affected just about everyone in the country and beyond. The war had been raging for 32 months, and would continue for another 21 – but the end was not in sight, and they had no idea when or what the outcome would be. Virtually every family had somebody, or knew somebody, who had been killed or afflicted with life-changing injuries, while air raids had brought the war to the Home Front, with women and children as well as men becoming casualties. The government exercised increasing control, with conscription introduced in 1916 in Great Britain and rationing in 1917. Every person who could be was mobilised for the war effort, with women playing an increasingly important role after 1916, while March 1917 saw members of the newly formed Women's Army Auxiliary Corps travelling to the Western Front in government-issued uniforms to support the army behind the lines, something utterly unimaginable in August 1914.

The Museum was set up to be both a memorial to those who had lost their lives and a place of record of every type of activity that had taken place as a result of the war. The intention had originally been to name the institution the 'National War Museum' but the name was changed at the request of the Dominion and Empire governments who wanted their contribution to the war effort to be recognised. Although there was an original intention that a bespoke building to house the museum would be created, there was a shortage of money, and it would not have a permanent home for nearly 20 years. It opened, on a four-year lease, in the Crystal Palace in South London on 9 June 1920. Sir Alfred Mond, chairman of IWM, spoke about the aspirations and origins in his opening speech:

> … A General Committee was appointed to elaborate and carry out the scheme; it was assisted by various Sub-Committees, each responsible for one branch of the Services or of civilian activity. The collection here

assembled thus comprises upwards of one hundred thousand exhibits illustrating the Naval, Military, Aerial and Civil labours of men and women throughout the Empire during the period of the War. It is hoped to make it so complete that every individual, man or woman, sailor, soldier, airman or civilian who contributed, however obscurely, to the final result, may be able to find in the galleries an example or illustration of the sacrifice he made or the work he did, and in the archives some record of it. The museum was not conceived as a monument of military glory, but rather as a record of toil and sacrifice; as a place of study to the technician in studying the course of development of armaments; to the historian as an assembly of material and archives to instruct his work; and to the people of the Empire, as a record of their toil and sacrifice through these fateful years.[1]

The WWSC was set up on 4 April 1917, led by Lady Priscilla Norman, who served as the chairman, and Agnes Ethel Conway, the honorary secretary. Lady Priscilla Norman and her husband had taken a hospital out to Wimereux in northern France in the autumn of 1914, which entitled her to wear the 1914 Star campaign medal. She was to become the longest serving trustee of the IWM, performing this duty until 1962. Agnes Conway was the daughter of Sir Martin Conway, the first Director-General of the IWM, and had been involved in caring for wounded Belgian soldiers and refugees who came to Britain in 1914. Other members of the Committee were Lady Haig, Lady Askwith, CBE, Lady Mond, Mrs Carey Evans, Miss Durham, CBE' and Miss Monkhouse, MBE.[2]

They set about their task with vigour and enthusiasm. Between them, the women had an enormous number of contacts, and they wrote hundreds of letters. The museum archive, which houses some of this correspondence and various minutes from their different meetings, provides some insight into their thought processes and how they went about achieving their aim. Not everyone replied, and there was a great variation in quantity and detail. They were particularly interested in organisations that had originated or developed during the war: for example, there is a great deal on the Voluntary Aid Detachments (VADs), a newly formed organisation in 1909 designed to be of use in a national emergency and which wanted its achievements to be recorded for posterity. The collection cannot, therefore, be regarded as totally comprehensive: roles that do not seem to have been sought out include, for example, schoolmistresses or stewardesses working with the Merchant Navy. There may also have been some overlap with other collecting committees – some women did not want to be included under the umbrella of women's work, presumably thinking that their own work had a greater significance. An example of this is Dr Flora Murray who declared to Agnes Conway in December 1917, 'Hands off our Hospital in the Women's Section' as she did not want the totally female-run Endell Street Hospital under the auspices of the Royal Army Medical Corps to be associated with hospitals run by non-professional or unqualified people.[3]

The development of women's activities and the opportunities open to them can be traced through the WWC, though these can be viewed with more detachment in retrospect. The initial roles open to women were in domestic, caring and nurturing spheres. Nursing was the principal area in which women were first seen as being vital to the war effort. Florence Nightingale and her experience in the Crimean War had had a profound effect on both military and civilian nursing throughout the latter half of the nineteenth century and early years of the twentieth. Queen Alexandra's Imperial Military Nursing Service (QAIMNS) and Queen Alexandra's Royal Naval Nursing Service (QARNNS) were both established in 1902, from predecessor organisations. In August 1914, the former had an establishment of 297, whilst the QARNNS had about 70 nurses. Both were supplemented to a great degree by civilian nurses volunteering to create a Reserve. The army also had the Territorial Force Nursing Service (TFNS), which was primarily set up to staff converted civilian hospitals on the Home Front to increase the medical capacity, although members could volunteer to serve abroad, and many did. The Regular QAIMNS and QARNNS were extremely sought after as career choices, and only took the best qualified women from the top training schools with respectable social backgrounds. The vast numbers of Reserve nurses required meant that they were no longer able to be so selective, though only trained nurses, and later in the war, Special Military Probationers, were taken.

However, in 1914 although professional training had been well established, anyone could call themselves a nurse. And although the

Royal College of Nursing was founded in 1916, there were sensitivities about the position of nursing and those for whom it was a career. The well-documented bad feeling that sometimes occurred between professional nurses and volunteer nursing assistants, usually in the shape of VADs, needs to be viewed in this light. It is also the case that the volunteer nurses have had a much higher profile – films and television frequently use the white-aproned VAD with a prominent Red Cross on her bib as the symbol of the 'First World War nurse'. Numerically there were more of them, and they were more visible. There were no recruiting posters for QAIMNS or QARNNS as they did not need to advertise because their nurses usually came either through nurse training schools or hospitals. Charitable organisations advertised both for volunteers and for donations – there was a constant demand for money to provide the assistance that was so badly needed. Many of the accounts of nursing published during and after the war were by VADs (arguably they had more free time and inclination as they probably did not have to work for a living as a professional nurse did).

Edith Cavell (1865–1915) is by far the best known female name of the war. She is remembered for being a nurse who was brutally executed by the Germans on 12 October 1915. But this is not quite the whole picture – her death was seized on by the British government as a propaganda gift showing the inhumanity of the German foe. She had trained as a nurse and was running a training establishment for nurses in Brussels, with the aim of professionalising this occupation. She was executed not for nursing activities but for being part of a resistance network aiding British and Allied soldiers to escape to Britain. The WWSC were keen to commemorate her, and acquired many items relating to her, as well as commissioning William Hatherell to paint, *The Funeral Service of Edith Cavell at Westminster Abbey, 15th May 1919* (Art.IWM ART 2624)[4] and a bust sculpted by George Frampton.

Another woman who the WWSC was keen to recognise was Dr Elsie Inglis (1864–1917), who was probably the most prominent face of the Scottish Women's Hospitals. She had qualified in medicine at Edinburgh University and was an ardent suffragist and prominent in the Scottish Federation of Women's Suffrage Societies. On the outbreak of war she went straight to the War Office to offer them her services, only to be told, 'My good lady, go home and sit still'. Instead, she offered the all-female hospital unit to the Allies, and France was the first to accept, with the hospital at Royaumont opening in January 1915. Other units served in Belgium, Corsica, Macedonia, Malta, Serbia, Romania and Russia. It should be noted that an extra challenge facing these women was communication with their patients who spoke in their own native tongue. Dr Inglis returned to Britain from Archangel following the outbreak of the Russian Revolution, and died of cancer in November 1917 after a very difficult journey home.

Medicine was not a role widely undertaken by women, and those who had the determination, money and ability to qualify often cared for women and children. More opportunities became available as the war progressed and, by 1916, female doctors were serving with the military, though often in less-visible places, such as Malta or Salonika. In May 1915 the all-women Endell Street Military Hospital was established by Dr Louisa Garrett Anderson and Dr Flora Murray, under the auspices of the Royal Army Medical Corps.

Nursing was undoubtedly the most instantly recognisable role, with the uniform being a key symbol – although it is evident that nursing is the most difficult First World War role to research as there were so many different organisations, each with their own uniform. The Voluntary Aid Detachment (VAD) movement had begun from 1909, and denoted both the local organisation and the individual within it. The VAD unit took the name of its county followed by a number – men served in odd-numbered units whilst women served in those with an even number. These, primarily British Red Cross Society and St John of Jerusalem, units were set up to assist the Army Medical Services in the event of an emergency. The volunteers did basic medical training and would be awarded first aid and home nursing certificates. VADs could be employed full time by the War Office once they had undertaken sufficient hospital experience, but the role was primarily undertaken in a voluntary capacity, and may have been something that was done in addition to a main job (for example, a school teacher might work as a VAD at weekends).

Another organisation that already existed on the outbreak of war was the First Aid Nursing Yeomanry (FANY). Established in 1907, the idea was that these women would gallop onto the battlefield on their horses, perform first aid and transport the wounded to safety. It was necessary to have your own horse, which provides some indication of the member's social class. They were serious about their training, and had a summer camp each year. In 1913 the FANY offered an ambulance column to serve in Ulster if conflict broke out in Ireland. It was recorded that: 'In September a large and enthusiastic Ulster camp was held, although the summer training had been held in July as usual. All through the winter and spring that followed, weekly drills and bandaging practices were held.'[5] The WWC also contains a large collection of press cuttings and has a few entries publicising this Ulster readiness. When war broke out they worked for the Belgians and French. The British authorities stated 'it was not considered practical to employ women to drive for the British wounded in France', but these objections were eventually overcome by their persistence and the increased need for manpower that could be redeployed. From January 1916 they were allowed to drive motor ambulances at British bases.[6]

The other initial main role undertaken by women was charitable work, often involving fund-raising. Middle- and upper-class women were used to running their homes and working in a voluntary philanthropic capacity, and they were, therefore, well suited to organising. Refugees flooded into the UK from Belgium, while the constant movement of troops around the country called for buffets on railway stations and other welfare facilities. The Ulster Women's Gift Fund was a good example of a welfare organisation set up to provide comforts for Ulstermen or those serving in Ulster Regiments. Between April 1915 and November 1916 (when prisoner of war parcels were centralised) it sent two parcels each month to POWs in Ulster Regiments and one parcel to Ulster POWs in non-Ulster Regiments. In this period it had 800 men on its books. It raised £120,000 from voluntary contributions over the duration of the war.[7]

Many women also wanted to do more. They had time on their hands, and realised that the war would have many far-reaching consequences. One of the first of these organisations was the Women's Emergency Corps. Established in August 1914, it set out to make itself useful in an enormous variety of different ways, setting up such sections as driving, foreign languages and providing work for women struggling as a result of the war (one of their activities was setting up a toy-making initiative, as Germany was responsible for producing many of the toys that were sold in the UK, and there was an awareness that their availability would stop). The Women's Volunteer Reserve was another of these initiatives. This was a khaki-uniformed organisation whose role was to be a disciplined unit capable of being useful in an emergency, and which practised military-type activities such as drill and signalling. Lady Londonderry was a leading light in this and in 1915 she set up the uniformed Women's Legion, which aimed to provide female workers in roles that could free up soldiers for front line service, primarily, though not exclusively, in the roles of cookery and driving. Their distinctive badge featured the figure of Victory holding a laurel wreath aloft, although this was often affectionately referred to as a frying pan. When the Women's Army Auxiliary Corps was formed in March 1917, the first members and many of the ideas came from this organisation.

Uniforms were a key marker of their wearer performing war service, and the streets of London were awash with them. A nurse's uniform was a clearly identifiable outfit, but women in other organisations wanted to signify their activities more visibly. No doubt stylish women gained an enormous amount of satisfaction from designing a uniform from scratch, but most were modelled on the uniform of a British army officer. Khaki, belts, military style pockets, jackets and ties proliferated. They would be purchased by their wearer, who had to be able to afford them, and would either be privately tailored or bought from upmarket shops. The *FANY Gazette* of October 1916 complained that 'for some months members have been more or less pleasing themselves' regarding their uniforms, which should all have been standard. It went on to say the 'chief points' were:

1 Khaki tunic to have four pockets, FANY buttons and badges to be made with plain sleeves, a red [sic] Cross circle on each sleeve, the centre of the cross to be seven inches from the shoulder.

2 Bottom of Khaki skirt to be 10 inches from the ground.

3 Khaki puttees and brown shoes *or* Boots *or* long brown boots to be worn.[8]

As more women entered the workplace they wore the uniform of their employing body, for example, the Post Office or the various different transport companies. As the opportunities for being paid for work in support of the war effort grew, more women became involved (and consequently those organisations relying on volunteers found it more difficult to recruit and retain people). Women were employed in munitions factories in growing numbers from 1915 and, following conscription in 1916, these increased enormously. They had no uniform, although as the war progressed and injuries and accidents caused by the dangerous environment increased, protective clothing began to be provided. Although there was some concern for the individuals – and a new job opportunity for welfare officers arose – the primary driver for this was ensuring that production continued at an ever increasing rate with no stoppages. A report on *Intramural Welfare Work in National Factories 1916 to 1917* observed, 'Without good welfare conditions there is bound to be bad work and consequent loss of time, and a worker's body may in one limited sense be likened to a machine and if a machine is not kept well oiled it cannot be expected to run swiftly and smoothly or turn out perfect goods'.[9] Protective clothing was increasingly worn in factories. A booklet entitled *How to Dress for Munition Making*, issued by the Ministry of Munitions in conjunction with the Factory Department of the Home Office in June 1917, recommended that each woman worker should have two caps and overalls issued (with arrangements for the 'necessary washing of these'), and this was a 'working expense' for the factory. Sizes ranged between small, medium and large and there were different outfits depending on the type of work undertaken, with the standard clothing being a khaki jean or brown drill overall (five shillings and one penny or five shillings and nine pence respectively). 'Outdoor or shipyard work or any dusty or wet occupation, or where skirts are unsuitable' merited a 'brown drill three-quarter coat and bib trouser suit' (nine shillings and eight pence), while 'a brown drill one-piece "boiler suit"' was available 'for women working among dangerous machinery or where close-fitting clothing is necessary for safety' (eight shillings and seven pence). A variety of different caps were sold at different prices.[10] The protective clothing was kept at the factory and changed into on-site; so to ensure it was visibly clear that munitions workers were doing their bit, they could wear a triangular 'On War Service' badge on their outdoor clothing.

Agricultural work was vitally important to maximise food production, especially following the call up of male farm workers from 1916 and increased enemy attacks on imports into the country. In March 1917 the Women's Land Army (WLA) was established, but this formalised and centralised various other initiatives such as the Women's Farm and Garden Union, Women's National Land Service Corps and Women's War Agricultural Committees. While most women worked on the land outside these organisations and were employed directly by farmers,[11] the WLA was a significant presence with a distinctive uniform featuring trousers and leggings, hat, and a green armband was awarded after 30 days of work.

The introduction of the women's auxiliary services marked the peak of female involvement in the war. The work they did was, in the main, 'typical' women's work, involving cooking, waitressing, cleaning and clerical work, with some driving. Formalising this within a military structure meant the authorities had control of this workforce. In all three services, women signed on for the duration of the war, although they were still effectively civilians in uniform. They 'enrolled' rather than 'enlisted', and they could elect to be 'immobile', meaning they would only serve in their home area, or 'mobile' where they would have to work wherever they were sent.

A War Office report in December 1916 recommended that women could work in many of the support roles performed by soldiers, which would consequently free up the men for front line service. The work of the Women's Legion paved the way for this, and in March 1917 the Women's Army Auxiliary Corps (WAAC) was formed, with the first contingent being deployed behind the lines in France. It was renamed Queen Mary's Army Auxiliary Corps (QMAAC) in April 1918, following their stalwart and stoic service during the upheaval of Operation Michael, the German offensive of the previous month. Some 57,000 women served with this organisation (although some moved on to the other services when they were set up), and the last members were demobilised in 1921 when it ceased to exist.

The WWC charts the development of the WAAC, and there are a variety of different types of documents, including details of all the members who died and inspection reports of various bases. On 22 April 1918 a petition was drawn up by the QMAAC Depot Hostel in Belfast, based in the Grand Central Hotel in Royal Avenue.[12] This complained that administrators [officer equivalents] were paying 15 shillings and sixpence per head per week for the same rations as the other women, who were being charged 12 shillings and sixpence. The various administrators all signed this, headed by Unit Administrator, A. M. Featherstone.[13]

There was a scathing reply from Chief Controller Florence Burleigh Leach in London to this petition, which was regarded as a breach of protocol. She wrote to the Area Controller of Irish Command in Dublin:

> Will you point out that to the Unit Administrator, QMAAC Depot Hostel, Belfast, that it is most irregular for her to communicate direct with Headquarters, and if she does not know the proper channels through which communications of this sort should be sent, she had better make enquiries, and find out what they are. You may also inform her at the same time that no alteration can be made with regard to the deductions for rations, quarters, fuel, light and attendance for Administrators. She does not seem to have read the Army Council Instructions with intelligence. Will you also point out that it is not usual to allow her subordinate officials to sign petitions of this kind, unless she has your sanction.[14]

The Women's Royal Naval Service (WRNS) was formed in November 1917 and disbanded in October 1919. It took time to establish a new organisation, and the copious documentation about the WRNS in the WWC is helpful for showing what was happening on the ground. The Irish Division opened on 10 April 1918 and closed on 28 August 1919.[15] In the Buncrana, Londonderry Sub-Division,

> The A P [Assistant Principal] only managed to initiate drill in September 1918. The Admiral and his Secretary thought it nonsense, and that hockey would be better for them, and the women themselves were shy about drill. Some of the women resented being marched back after the dancing class, but the A P insisted on this, because the roads are usually pervaded with tipsy sailors ashore from the patrols and drifters.[16]

One senses the Admiral was not quite taking the new organisation totally seriously, and similar attitudes can be seen in the same document, when 'No ledger clerks being available, an immobile from Larne was sent to Londonderry. The Paymaster said she was of no use. But when it was proposed to draft her to England, he refused to spare her'.[17]

The Women's Royal Air Force (WRAF) was formed on 1 April 1918, the same day the Royal Flying Corps became the Royal Air Force. It existed until the spring of 1920. Although there is some information about the WRAF in the WWC, there is much less than for the WAAC and WRNS.

The fact that the war was still going on as the WWC was collecting presented challenges. In May 1917 Dame Katherine Furse (1875–1952), at that time head of the VADs, replied to an appeal writing, 'Personally I should be very glad if this matter could be deferred until after the war because we are desperately busy and it would be very difficult to get people to work up an interest in a war museum before the war is actually won'.[18] She later became the Commandant of the WRNS, and deposited an extensive collection of documents relating to both organisations. In 1920 Agnes Conway wrote to her thanking her for 'just the type of material we think it is so important to preserve in the museum', especially as a great deal of it was from 1916 and pre-dated the start of the collection. She finished by saying 'I think you are the best friend our section has'.[19] Dame Katherine was also typical of many women who moved from one organisation to another as opportunities grew. It was quite common for women to have worked in several different capacities by the end of the war.

The WWSC was particularly anxious to have a record of the various types of uniforms that were being worn, and in the first year of collecting 69 outfits were acquired. Horace Nicholls was commissioned to take a series of photographs showing women dressed in different uniforms – some featuring two women, one wearing an indoor and the other an outdoor uniform, or depicting different grades. Nicholls was a photographer with the Department of Information from the summer of 1917, essentially taking propaganda photographs, and later went on to work at IWM for many years. These uniform photographs were mainly taken in December 1917 at the same location – the roof of the Department of Information building – and most share the distinctive white tile backdrop. When researching women who served in the First World War, a photograph of a woman in a uniform can be very helpful in determining which of the many possible organisations she worked for, and this series of images can be helpful in doing that. They can be found on the IWM website, and the catalogue numbers range between Q 30335 and Q 30395.

A second male photographer who also took many photographs of women at work was G.P. Lewis. He too worked at the renamed Ministry of Information from the spring of 1918. The WWSC commissioned the female photographer Olive Edis to take photographs of women on the Western Front. It took a long time to make the necessary arrangements, and by the time she was able to travel there in March 1919 the fighting had finished. She left an account of what was a rather gruelling four-week visit but the photographs she took provide an excellent glimpse into living and working conditions, and include cemetery shots showing women's graves, including that of Edith Cavell in Brussels. She took some portraits (for example, Dame Maud McCarthy, Matron in Chief in France of QAIMNS, at her desk) and many of her photographs contain names of individuals. These can be seen on the IWM website ranging between catalogue numbers Q 7951 and Q 8125.

The WWSC also commissioned artists to record women's work. In May 1918 they appointed the first British woman war artist who was tasked with drawing women in substitution roles on the Home Front. Victoria Monkhouse had been at university in Cambridge, as had Agnes Conway, and this was probably where the connection originated, as the former had a reputation for drawing caricatures. She created seven drawings showing women in roles such as a window cleaner, ticket collector and bus conductress.

Eminent artists were also induced to produce work for the WWSC. The most famous was probably Sir John Lavery, the Irish society portrait painter who travelled to the Western Front in early 1919 to depict a variety of typical scenes, for example, *The Women's Emergency Canteen, Gare du Nord, Paris, 1919* (Art.IWM ART 2890) and *The QMAAC Convalescent Home, Le Touquet, 1919* (Art.IWM ART 2885). He also painted scenes in Britain, including *Lady Henry's Crèche,*

Woolwich (Art.IWM ART 3084) and *Elswick, 1917: Messrs Armstrong, Whitworth and Company* (Art.IWM ART 2883). Money was always an issue for IWM and the WWSC would always try to obtain material as a donation, or negotiate to lower the price as much as possible; Sir John Lavery was persuaded to work for half his usual fee.

It was believed that three-dimensional coloured wood and plaster models would be helpful to enable the public to visualise and better understand the work undertaken by women. Now regarded as very old-fashioned with none currently on display (though most can be viewed online – with the catalogue number of either the model or photograph following in the paragraph below), they were the equivalent of digital media today, and they were employed right across the different galleries of IWM. Dioramas of battlefields and model ships were made for the galleries dealing with the Army and Navy, and the WWSC commissioned women artists to create scenes to show what women had done. There was much debate over the models to be made; a few feature individuals such as Dr Elsie Inglis performing an operation in a hospital tent in Serbia (MOD 34) and Sergeant-Major Flora Sandes standing boldly upright clutching a rifle in what is obviously a battle scene in Serbia (MOD 109), though most are generic scenarios.

Other models included a woman leading a blind Australian soldier from St Dunstan's Hostel by Clare Sheridan (Q 66143/Q 64019), packing food parcels in the Central Prisoners of War Depot by Miss Helen Frazer Rock and Kate Elizabeth Oliver (MOD 364), a crèche for Belgian refugees at Earls Court by Helen Frazer Rock (MOD 37/Q 31414), the first voluntary munition works canteen, Woolwich Arsenal, in 1915 by Helen Frazer Rock and Kate Oliver (MOD 1058/Q 31417), a scene from *The Merchant of Venice* performed by the Lena Ashwell Concert Party in Le Havre by Miss Ethel Pye (MOD 21), the Soldiers' and Sailors' free buffet at Victoria Station by Mrs Meredith Williams (MOD 366), the Almeric Paget Military Massage Corps by Ethel Pye, bandage-making by Queen Mary's Needlework Guild at the Central Surgical Depot at 2 Cavendish Square by Liebie Callard (MOD 1056), papier maché splint-making by Elinor Halle and volunteers at the Surgical Requisites Association in Mulberry Walk

(MOD 1045), Lady Helena Gleichen and Nina Hollings working for the British Red Cross in Italy with their portable X-Ray apparatus by Lady Feodora Gleichen (MOD 365/MOD 1060), women working in a leather tannery by Mrs Gilbert Bayes (MOD 970), the Women's Forage Corps, Royal Army Service Corps, hay-baling for the Army by Mrs Meredith Williams (MOD 53), timber-felling by Mrs Meredith Williams, women at Hayes Filling Factory working in an assembly shed by Mrs Meredith Williams (MOD 158), Lilian Barker, the Lady Superintendent at Woolwich Arsenal, overseeing women bagging TNT with gloved hands behind glass screens by Liebie Callard (MOD 1057), stacking tank chains at the Newbury Depot, Central Stores of the Ministry of Munitions, by Alice Meredith Williams (MOD 29), policewomen searching workers at an explosives factory by Mrs Gilbert Bayes (MOD 159), women lacing up an airship envelope at White City by Lilian Vereker Hamilton (MOD 518) and WRNS cleaning and testing depth charge pistols in the stern of a torpedo boat destroyer by Mrs O. Wallace (MOD 45).

The WWSC organised an exhibition of women's work, which was held at the Whitechapel Art Gallery in the autumn of 1918. This was the first opportunity to show the items they had acquired (and some that had been especially loaned), and would turn out to be the largest physical display space the WWSC ever had (although the idea of a gallery devoted to women was revolutionary, it was always rather regarded as a 'poor relation', and was allotted much less space than other subjects). It attracted 82,000 visitors including the Queen, and was very well received; the announcement of both the Armistice and the December 1918 election that offered eligible women the opportunity to vote or be elected to parliament for the first time may have contributed to its success.[20] Lady Priscilla Norman's letter inviting the Queen described it as:

> arranged with a view to its being the first comprehensive representation of the various aspects of women's war work. A shrine in the centre, with the photographs of those who have lost their lives, and a Roll of Honour, containing some five hundred names, has been prepared as a tribute to the memory of those women who have sacrificed their lives in the service of their country.[21]

This shrine had an enormous impact, and was much commented on in the press coverage of the exhibition. Although men were expected to lose their lives in war, there was something profoundly shocking about the fact that women too had been killed. There was an inconclusive debate about whether women who had died of disease or natural causes should be included in this – especially pertinent with the deadly influenza pandemic of 1918 – but men who were serving with the forces would automatically have been eligible for a military burial and Imperial War Graves Commission (IWGC) headstone.[22] IWM appealed widely for photographs of men and women who had died – or who had been decorated – and an advertisement even appeared in the ration books that would have featured in every home. Seeing the photographs on display also prompted families to send in images. An example of this was the photograph of Betty Stevenson who had been killed in an air raid in Étaples in Normandy on 30 May 1918, while working as a driver for the Young Men's Christian Association (YMCA), which provided a service to enable the relatives of dangerously ill and wounded servicemen to visit them in hospital.[23] This was sent in – along with her memorial book which came to the library in 1920 – because her aunt was disappointed not to see her niece featured in the shrine. These photographs are now available online, having been digitised to form an essential part of the ambitious IWM 'Lives of the First World War' centenary project to create an online permanent digital memorial of all those who served in the conflict.[24] The male photographs, originally known as the Memorial for the Fallen, and now as the Bond of Sacrifice, were kept separately, with the WWSC having full responsibility for the female portraits of 397 women which formed an integral part of the collection.

An estimation would conclude that there are photographs of about one in three women who died. A quick survey of the names on the QAIMNS memorial in Saint Anne's Cathedral in Belfast reveals seventeen names, with a slightly better result: there are photographs of seven of the women who appear here, notably, Matron Martha Farley, Sister Margaret Hessie Johnston, Staff Nurse Rachel Ferguson, Staff Nurse Elizabeth Grace Stewart, Staff Nurse Elizabeth Wallace and Sister Eileen Mary O'Gorman and Staff Nurse Hilda Garlick of the Territorial Force Nursing Service. The WWSC knew that their lists of women's deaths was incomplete – this was particularly the case when it came to those working in munitions and industry – and they went to great lengths to make them as comprehensive as possible. These were the names that appeared on the women's national war memorial screen and Five Sisters Window in York Minster dedicated in 1925.

The WWC also appealed for photographs of women who were decorated. Women who served abroad under the auspices of the War Office were eligible for campaign medals. Some women received medals for bravery or service, such as the Military Medal (MM), a gallantry decoration introduced in 1916 for other ranks in the army. This was the only decoration that the British gave to women for bravery under fire; it was mainly issued to nurses or other women who were caught in air raids, and coolness in those situations and setting an example to the men seemed to be a key qualification. This was typified by the award to Staff Nurse Annie Rebecca Colhoun from Londonderry, who had been working as a matron in a hospital in Vancouver, British Columbia, before she joined the QAIMNS in June 1916 (and took a 'demotion' in order to serve). Posted to the 37th General Hospital in Macedonia, she was caught in an air raid on duty on 12 March 1917. Although she was seriously wounded, she cared for her fatally wounded colleague and helpless patients.[25] Mentions in Despatches could also be awarded. The Royal Red Cross (RRC) was a medal instituted in 1883, specifically for female nurses tending military or naval patients. In November 1915 a second class of this award was introduced – the Associate Royal Red Cross (ARRC). Standard Civilian orders and decorations were also given. Photographs sent to the WWC sometimes feature full details of what people did: for example, the reverse of the portrait of Mrs Dehra Chichester, OBE, leaves one wondering where she found the energy to be involved with all her activities:

> Vice President of the St John's VAD for East Belfast. Commandant of St John's VAD at Castledawson (Londonderry /22) and Organiser of Castledawson St John's Work Party in connection with the latter. Member of the Belfast Local War Pensions Committee. Hon. Sec. in charge of E. Belfast (Dependants) Branch of the SSFA [Soldiers' and Sailors' Families Association] and subsequently of the War Pension's Office for the same area (Dependants Section). Member of the Co.

Londonderry Local War Pensions Committee. Hon. Sec. of the Bellaghy War Pensions Sub-Committee. Chairman of the Magherafelt Area Committee (War Pensions). On the Executive Committee of the Ulster Women's Gift Fund as representing and looking after the comforts for the 14th Royal Irish Rifles'.[26]

The WWSC had no idea how the role of women would change in the twentieth century, but they were aware they had witnessed a remarkable period in history. Their dedication and determination that this should be recorded led to an outstanding archive and collection of material. When the new First World War galleries opened in the IWM in 2014 the Home and Battle fronts were intertwined showing how inter-dependent they both were. The objects gathered by the WWSC are now dispersed around the museum, according to their medium. The paper documents and news cuttings are held by the Library, and were digitised by Gale Thomson in 2005. They are now available on subscription, and can be accessed in university or other reference libraries.[27] The work that the WWSC did – and especially that done by the women they were recording – deserves to be remembered and celebrated. Women played an integral part in keeping the Home Front running, providing munitions for the army, growing food to enable the country to eat, supporting the armed forces, nursing the wounded and civilians who also needed care, and providing comforts and support to help ease the misery inflicted by the conflict. Although women's working opportunities shrank after the war, their horizons had been widened, and in 1939, when another 'total war' broke out, there was no question that women would play their part again. There was no need to create another WWC because they had proved their worth, and women were factored in as an integral part of the war effort from the start.

NOTES

1   *Third Annual Report of the Imperial War Museum, 1919–1920* (London: HMSO, 1920) [Cmd. 844].

2   *Report of Imperial War Museum 1917–1918* (London: HMSO, 1918) [Cd. 9061].

3   Women's Work Collection/Women, War and Society, 1914–1918 (WWC); B.R.C.S. 24.1/1; *Account of an interview at Endell St. Hospital, 1917.*

4   Catalogue references are given to enable the item to be found on the IWM website at www.iwm.org.uk – the search box can be found under 'Collections Online'.

5   WWC; B.R.C.S. 20/9; *Report (Typescript) on work and organisation of the FANY,* 1 Nov. 1917.

6   Ibid.

7   WWC; L.R. 416/2; *Ulster Women's Gift Fund* L.R. 416/2.

8   WWC; B.R.C.S. 20/51; *FANY Gazette,* Oct. 1916.

9   WWC; MUN. 18 9/4; *Intramural Welfare Work in National Factories 1916 to 1917: Various Reports received from the Welfare Section of the Ministry of Munitions, 1916–1917.*

10   WWC; MUN. V/1; *How to Dress for Munition Making.*

11   Mary Ingham in *Tracing Your Service Women Ancestors: A Guide for Family Historians* (Pen and Sword Family History, 2012) provides the figure of 15,500 WLA members in 1918 compared with a general figure of 300,000 women working on the land.

12   WWC; Army 3 23/3; *Petition. Irish Command, Controller-in-Chief, Army.*

13   The National Archives at Kew has an extensive service record for Ada Maria Featherstone in WO/398/74/23 which contains no reference to this incident, which is quite surprising considering the sharp reprimand. Of the 12 women listed on the petition, hers is the only record to have survived enemy bombing in 1940. The other Administrator signatories are H. Haller, F. Edith Seller, Katherine Grange, Florence Moore, E.J. James, M. Fitzherbert[?], M. Lanigan-O'Keeffe, Gladys Phillips, D. Chippendell, Amy M.H. Lloyd and Constance A. Bowler.

14   WWC; Army 3 23/2; *Notice re proper channels of communication. Irish Command,* 27 Apr. 1918.

15   WWC; W.R.N.S. 8.2/32; *Statement re Belfast Sub-Division.*

16   WWC; W.R.N.S. 8.2/34; *Statement re Buncrana, Londonderry Sub-Divisions.*

17   Ibid.

18   IWM, Museum's Administrative Records (MAR), EN1/3/SER/15/3, Letter from Katherine Furse to Lady Norman, 28 May 1917.

19   Ibid., letter from Agnes Conway to Dame Katherine Furse, 17 Jan. 1920.

20   Katy Deepwell, 'Women War Artists of World War One', in *Women's Contributions to Visual Culture, 1918–1939* by Karen E. Brown (ed.) (Routledge, 2008).

21   IWM, MAR, EN1/3/EXH/3, letter from Lady Priscilla Norman to Sir Edward Wallington at Buckingham Palace, 11 Oct. 1918.

22   Women serving overseas with the War Office would have been covered by this too, but strict criteria for IWGC burial and the fact that most women did not serve beyond the British Isles, and would have had a family home burial means that the Commonwealth War Graves Commission (as it later became) does not cover all female deaths in the First World War.

23   Generally speaking, the YMCA and Salvation Army looked after the families of Other Ranks, while the Red Cross catered for officers families.

24   The current website address is https://livesofthefirstworldwar.org/ but this is due to freeze in March 2019, with the data being migrated to the IWM website at www.iwm.org.uk in July 2019.

25   WWC; DEC. 7/2; *Roll of Women of the British Empire to whom the Military Medal has been Awarded: Military Medal; Decorations, 1914–1918.*

26   WWC; DEC. 2/83; *Mrs Dehra Chichester OBE.*

27   The database is called *Women, War and Society 1914–1918* and is available through Gale Cengage.(Sources of historical materials are held at the National World War 1 Museum and Memorial's archives and research library. Direct quotes are designated.)

Coal laden for Belfast

ARTHUR BELL

Throughout the eighteenth and nineteenth and indeed well into the twentieth century the only source of news for most people was the daily morning newspaper and, in Belfast, one such source, founded in 1737, was the *Belfast News Letter*. Its broadsheet pages contained a vast range of subjects – petty sessions reports of larceny, woundings and notorious drunkards were mixed with local cricket matches, theatrical productions, trade and commerce, church services, society meetings together with court, parliamentary and international news. For a people connected to the wider world by trade, family ties and the burgeoning empire it was essential reading. These reports were arranged under a series of headings – sporting intelligence, legal, political, foreign and Ulster intelligence and, on each day – shipping intelligence.

Shipping intelligence – news of the arrival and departure of vessels – reflected the importance of shipping at a time when world trade was growing rapidly and goods were still brought and distributed on water – by sea, river, lake and canal. The boilers of the mills in Killyleagh were powered by coal brought to the harbour owned by the local coal merchant. Ships sailing from the Quoile Quays connected the citizens of the county town of Downpatrick to Liverpool, Dublin and Belfast. Coleraine, on the Lower Bann was a busy port despite the difficulties caused by sandbanks at the river bar mouth. The lime, tile and brick works at Castle Espie at the shallow northern end of Strangford Lough were dependent on schooners to deliver coal and ship out the manufactured products from a jetty at the end of a clay embankment which reached out over the shallows to the relatively deeper water of the Comber River estuary. In 1860 there were over 5,530 vessels registered in ports around the Irish Sea and while the majority of them were in the main ports – Liverpool registered 2,171, Belfast, Greenock, Glasgow and Dublin together registered 1,888 – there were also another 1,470 registered in smaller ports such as Londonderry, Coleraine, Drogheda, Dundalk, Newry and Strangford. There were many smaller boats and fishing vessels that were not registered and thus did not appear on the Mercantile Navy List.

A very substantial subsection of the 'Shipping Intelligence' column was entitled 'Coal Laden Vessels', recording the daily arrival and departure of ships that carried this essential fuel and reflecting its prime importance as a source of energy. Coal fired the boilers that drove spinning machines and looms in factories, fuelled steam trains and agricultural equipment and was used in domestic fires and kitchen ranges. Gas, distilled from coal, lit the streets, homes and public buildings in many towns and coke – a byproduct of coal distillation – was essential for the iron and steel industries, fuelling blast furnaces, blacksmiths shops and riveters braziers alike.

Coal from the west coast of Scotland and from Cumberland in northern England was essential to the life of Ulster's towns and was the lifeblood of Belfast's extensive development. Many seamen were involved in bringing it to Ulster. We can see this in the 1871 English census which records some 53 Ulster vessels in three of the five Cumberland ports. One in Workington, seven in Whitehaven – in addition to five from Dublin – and 45 in Maryport. Ulster vessels made up 38 per cent of the total vessel count. Many of the other vessels, English registered, had received their census forms in advance in Irish ports; suggesting that they were also involved in the Irish Sea coal trade. In fact there were 226 Ulster seamen in Maryport on census night, no doubt dominating the town. There were 35 Ulstermen in Whitehaven. My great-grandfather, Captain William Bell, was one of them and this is his story. It is a story of changing technology as wooden sailing ships gave way to iron hulled steamers. A story of social change as the small coastal harbours gradually fell into disuse, faced with competition from railways, and also as the port and city of Belfast grew rapidly into dominance in the nineteenth century. But, above all, it is a story of hardship and danger.

THE SHORT SEA CROSSING

William and his father Samuel were both born and raised in Donaghadee, County Down, which was a major port on the Irish Sea for several centuries. The Irish Sea both separates and connects the two islands, Ireland and Great Britain. One hundred and fifty miles separate the coasts of England at Morecambe Bay and Ireland at Dundalk. However, much further north the coasts of west Scotland and east Ulster almost touch across the North Channel; the long fingers of the Scottish highlands and islands reaching south and west towards the hills and glens of County Antrim. The Mull of Kintyre is only 12 miles from Torr Head and only 19 miles separate Galloway from Island Magee. Throughout many centuries a voyage across the sea was much less arduous than a journey through bog, briar and forest, the haunt of wolves and outlaws. Short sea voyages have sustained close family, cultural and commercial connections between Ulster and Scotland.

The Gaelic over-kingdom of Dalriada in the sixth and seventh centuries encompassed parts of western Scotland – Argyll and Lochaber – and County Antrim in Ulster and was held together by sea voyages in curraghs. There is evidence of voyages much older than these. A neolithic axe factory near the summit of Tievebulliagh in the Glens of Antrim worked an outcrop of an uncommonly hard rock – porcellanite.[1] This heavy dark blue-grey rock with its distinctive pale flecks made exceptional axes which were essential tools for making clearings in the forests to grow crops and for working timber. Porcellanite axes from County Antrim have been found in the Shetlands and southern England, brought there along exchange routes as tribute, trade or trophy – their dispersal starting with a journey across the North Channel around 5,000 years ago.

Donaghadee was not part of Dalriada or the trade in stone axes. It does not appear in Baptista Boazio's 1599 map of Ireland although Knockfergus, now Carrickfergus, the centre of the northern Pale and of Norman power in Ulster, together with the 'Baie of Knockfergus' now Belfast Lough and Olderfleete Haven – Larne Harbour – where the Vikings built a stockade and winter anchorage, are all marked.

Donaghadee owed its prominence as a port to a chain of events that started just four years after the publication of Baptista Boazio's map.

The story of the settlement of parts of counties Antrim and Down by Ayrshire men Hugh Montgomery and James Hamilton in the early seventeenth century is reasonably well known. It triggered the migration of Scottish settlers into their new estates.[2] For many of them the point of entry was Donaghadee only 22 miles from Port Patrick – the shortest sea crossing from this part of Scotland. Hugh Montgomery obtained possession of Donaghadee and then exchanged lands near Ballymena for lands near Portpatrick. By 1616 he had obtained a Royal Warrant limiting travel between the Rhinns of Galloway and Ards to the Portpatrick-Donaghadee route, giving him a monopoly of the crossing and ensuring Donaghadee's prosperity for over two centuries.

The first harbour was a timber landing jetty built in 1610 and improved several times before being replaced by a curved pier 400ft long and 22ft wide built of uncemented stones.[3] At a time when pirates and sudden storms posed a considerable threat to travellers, there was a real advantage to a short crossing which was clearly visible from land. In 1662 an act of the Scottish parliament established a mail service from Edinburgh to Donaghadee via Portpatrick. It appears to have operated sporadically and was re-established in 1677 and again in 1695 by a further act of the Scottish parliament. In 1718 the route was established for mails from London and as well as from Edinburgh. Ferry services from Donaghadee were also popular with wealthy travellers who preferred the short sea crossing to the longer routes out of Belfast. Donaghadee was a thriving port with mail, passenger and freight services. The poet John Keats, the author James Boswell and the actor David Garrick are known to have travelled this route.

Acts of Parliament in 1710 and 1755 ordered further improvement and in 1774 a larger harbour, designed by John Smeaton, a leading marine civil engineer, was built at a cost of £10,000.[4] In 1790 the French aristocrat and travel writer Jacques-Louis de la Tocnaye noted 'the number of cattle taken from here is something inconceivable ... on the day I crossed there were 400 horned cattle taken over to Scotland, and in the six weeks previous there had been transported nearly thirty thousand'.[5] However, by the end of the eighteenth century it was apparent that both ports had limitations and each required repairs. The government would have to invest in improvements. The leading civil engineer of the time, Thomas Telford, was commissioned to determine the best possible route. Although his 1809 report advocated the alternative Bangor-Port Nessock route, which had been supported by petition of some 240 ships' captains and owners, strong lobbying by the Donaghadee Packet Company ensured that the government continued with Donaghadee. This decision was endorsed in 1815 and Sir John Rennie was engaged to design and construct a new harbour.

Work commenced in 1821 and the new harbour, which exists to this day, was opened in 1825. Although this was one of the last harbours in British and Irish waters built for sailing vessels, the Donaghadee Packet Company replaced its sailing cutters with steam vessels in the same year. Sadly, despite the new harbour and the switch to steam, Donaghadee's history of two centuries as a mail and ferry port would eventually end. In 1849, despite considerable local lobbying, the packet service switched to the sheltered deep water ports of Belfast and Greenock on the River Clyde.

LEARNING THE ROPES

Two years later, in 1851, William Bell started work as a ship's boy. He was 15 years old and he had, quite literally, to learn the ropes. He would have to know about the standing rigging, tar coated permanent ropes that held the masts, spars and booms in position – and the running rigging that attached, raised and controlled the sails. He also would have to learn all the variety of knots – hitches, bends, bowlines – which joined and attached all these ropes, together with the wooden masts, booms, spars which framed the rigging and supported the sails; a great deal to take in before he even began to understand the art of sailing and then of navigation.

Nineteenth-century society's dependence on waterborne transport meant that there were a great variety of sizes and types of vessels on the seas for a great many purposes, all with different rigs and characteristics. There were, however, two main rigs: fore and aft where the sails followed the principal axis of the ship; and square rigged, where they were set at right angles to that axis. Fore and aft rigged vessels, such as sloops and schooners, required only a small crew and could point higher into the wind; ideal for the variable winds of coastal sailing. Square rigged vessels were more suitable for long ocean passages with large vessels that required a greater spread of canvas. The brigantine, frequently used on the Irish Sea, was a hybrid; square rigged on the foremast with fore and aft sails on the mainmast. It was a rig adapted from earlier vessels on the Mediterranean where both speed and manoeuvrability were particularly valued by pirates. The name is derived from the Italian *brigantine* – brigand.

William would have to know how schooners, smacks, brigantines and barques handled, how they responded to different sea conditions and then he would have to get to know the waters of the Irish Sea. There was much to learn and, even at 15 years of age, not much time to learn it. We can see how he acquired and then used his knowledge and skills through a unique set of government records – Registers of Seamen, Crew Lists and the Mercantile Navy Lists which were set up just after William was born and developed throughout his lifetime.

The Battle of Trafalgar on 21 October 1805 all but destroyed the Spanish and French fleets and heralded a century of British dominance of the seas. Trade with a far-flung empire grew at an astonishing rate. However, supremacy of the seas could not be guaranteed. Trade routes and overseas possessions had to be defended, the seas had to be patrolled and overseas bases had to be supplied and maintained. Britain needed a peace time navy and a wartime reserve. This reserve would come from the Merchant Navy and the Register Office of Merchant Seamen[6] was created to identify experienced seamen who could be called upon in time of war. The Merchant Shipping Act of 1835 required the masters of ships to file Agreements and Crew Lists with this office and Registers of Seamen were created. Accumulated over more than a century, these documents are now held in the National Archives at Kew, in the National Maritime Museum, local archives such as PRONI, and in the Maritime History Archive at Memorial University in Newfoundland.

Governments also require additional vessels during wartime and the Mercantile Navy List published yearly from 1857 records details of vessels throughout the empire, allocating an Official Number (ON) to each vessel which would stay with her even when renamed by new owners. Registers, Crew Lists and the Mercantile Navy Lists are an invaluable source of information which have enabled me to trace much of my great-grandfather's sailing career.

Crew lists record the crew and voyages for merchant ships and, as they also record the previous vessels of each crew member, they provide a means of tracing them from vessel to vessel. Although they are a rich source of information they have some limitations. They can only be traced backwards and require a starting point. William Bell became master of the *Franklin* on her return from Whitehaven on 25 March 1871. After discharge of her cargo and taking on ballast she left Ballywalter on 5 April arriving in Whitehaven on 6 April just in time for William and his crew (including his father Samuel) to be recorded in the English census of 1871 under Vessels. I have been able to find crew lists in PRONI, National Maritime Museum and the National Archive which have enabled me to trace him back from that starting point.

William Bell was registered in Belfast on 5 March 1851 starting his career as a (ship's) boy. The Register records that he was born in 1836 in County Down and was 4 feet 10 inches tall. Sadly the opportunity to record the colour of his hair and eyes and his complexion was not taken. The Register also shows that he served as an ordinary seaman from June 1851 to December 1852. The next Register from 1853 to 1857 identifies three ships on which he served.

In 1853 he was on the *Mary Dunville*. There is no record of this vessel as Mercantile Navy Lists only started in 1857. However the Dunville family were prosperous whiskey distillers and tea importers. John Dumvill (the original version of the name) had joined Napier & Co. in 1801 at the age of 16 becoming a partner in 1807. The firm became Dunville & Co. in 1825 and in 1837 his son John junior married Mary Grimshaw, daughter of the Deputy Lord Lieutenant. Perhaps the *Mary Dunville* was named after her. Dunvilles VR was a very popular whiskey in America but the business never recovered from the effects of Prohibition and was liquidated in 1936. All that remains is (Lisburn) Distillery Football Club founded by the workers in 1880[7] and Dunville Park on the Grosvenor Road, Belfast.

In 1855 William was an able seaman sailing on the *North Star* of Exeter between Belfast and Bridport in Dorset. Bridport was an ancient

Saxon settlement and, since the Middle Ages, had been a major centre for the making of rope and nets. Although Belfast, in the late nineteenth century, would have the largest ropeworks in the world, it was not founded until 1876. Until then, while there were small ropeworks in many coastal towns, including Donaghadee, large supplies of rope and nets would come from Bridport to meet the demand for shipbuilding, ships maintenance and for fishing.

In 1856 he was an able seaman on the *Vortigern* of Quebec, a 900-ton vessel which was engaged on the North Atlantic routes. *Vortigern*, named after a fifth-century warlord and ruler of Britons, was registered in Quebec 1856–7, Greenock 1858, Melbourne 1864 and Adelaide 1867. She then disappears from the Mercantile Navy List; however, there is a later record of her, renamed *Fanny*, owned in San Francisco and carrying coal on the Pacific coast of America.

William Bell took no part in these later adventures and served with *Vortigern* for a short while gaining valuable experience and no doubt earning useful money before the next major event in his life.

COASTING TRADE

On 16 September 1857, aged 21, William married Elizabeth McCartney in Donaghadee parish church. She was 19 years old; the daughter of Robert McCartney who lived in a house on Meeting House Street, a short distance from Bow Street where William lived with his father Samuel Bell. The McCartney house had gardens extending down Salt Works Street[8] and Robert McCartney was a bailiff with responsibility for executing court decisions and administering the manor estates and buildings; he was also a grocer. The marriage record shows that William's father Samuel was also a mariner and the Register indicates that in 1853 he served on the *Marys* – a 64-ton vessel registered in Belfast in 1837. In 1856 he was on the *Margaret Gibson* a 148-ton brigantine registered in Workington and carrying coal to various ports. There are no records for 1856 but in 1861 – the first year for which crew lists are available – she sailed from Workington and Maryport on the Cumberland coast to Liverpool, Cardiff, Dublin and Londonderry.

William's marriage was short lived: Elizabeth died in 1859. There were no children and she may well have died from complications during pregnancy and childbirth – an all-too-frequent cause of death for otherwise healthy young women. Elizabeth was only 20 years old. Two years later in 1861 William, a widower of 25, married Mary Jane McConkey[9] in Shore Street Presbyterian Church. She was 20 years old and the daughter of Robert McConkey, a joiner and boat builder. He set up home in Railway Street, renting a house from his father-in-law.[10]

William Bell's arrival in Whitehaven on 6 April 1871 ensured that he was recorded on a vessel in the harbour on census night and provided the starting point for a trace back through crew lists to their start in 1861. His first ship in this sequence was the *John Alexander*,[11] a 35-ton sloop owned by George McQuoid, a Donaghadee coal dealer and ship owner living on the Parade. The crew were: William Bell master, his father Samuel mate, and his young brother Hugh – ship's boy. Between July and December 1861 they made three voyages carrying coal from Ardrossan and Troon to Donaghadee, Runcorn Docks on the River Mersey and Carrickfergus. In 1862 he served as mate on the *Mary Jane*,[12] an 88-ton schooner owned by John Neill of Belfast, carrying coal to Belfast.

On 26 March 1862 he left the *Mary Jane* and on 5 May he joined the *Commerce*[13] a 47-ton sloop, as master. *Commerce* was built in Belfast and owned by a Donaghadee coal and timber merchant, Peter Smith of Back Street (now Manor Street).[14] She was engaged in the coal trade and her four man crew, all Donaghadee men, included Hugh Bell, 16, as ship's boy and William John Neill, 19, as able seaman. William John Neill was the son of Captain John Neill and Grace Jamison, who had been given the King's Arms on High Street by her father as a wedding present. The family lived on Sandy Row (now Shore Street). Grace would eventually live in the King's Arms. She died there in 1907 at the age of 99. It is now known as Grace Neill's and claims to date back to 1611.

The *Commerce* carried coal from Whitehaven and Troon mainly to Donaghadee with occasional trips to other ports such Liverpool, Cardiff and Douglas on the Isle of Man.[15] By 1864 William and his family had moved to Back Street and at the end of December he had left the *Commerce* and was the mate of a much larger ship, the 143-ton brig *Milton*[16] owned by Hugh Craig, a Belfast coal merchant. Hugh Bell has joined him as ordinary seaman.

My researches have shown that many of the ships that William served on were built in North America. The extensive tidal mud flats, known as the slob lands, around the port of Belfast limited the size of ships that could be built during the first half of the nineteenth century. The River Lagan did not follow its present line straight towards the centre of Belfast Lough. Downstream of the Long Bridge the river took a wide swing towards the South Shore, then east again before flowing into deep water at the Pool of Garmoyle 'which is used as a harbour for ships trading to Belfast on account of the shallowness of the water at Belfast Bridge … this pool which can float twenty ships at low tide lies a mile from the South shore near Hollywood [sic] and about five miles south west of Carrickfergus.'[17] An act of parliament in 1831 empowered the Ballast Board to 'divert, deepen and improve the channel of the Lagan between the Long Bridge and the Pool of Garmoyle'. This work commenced in 1841. The excavated material from the channel created Queen's Island, eventually the site of the shipyard of Harland and Wolff. The old channel of the river was used to form the Abercorn Basin, a timber pond and a ladies' bathing pool. The timber pond and the bathing pool later became the Musgrave Channel – the latter now the site of Harland and Wolff's shipbuilding dock.

Shipbuilding in Belfast was also limited by a shortage of suitable timber. Much of Ulster's extensive forests had been felled to finance the Plantation and suitable timber had to be imported from the Baltic countries and from North America. This led inevitably to shipbuilding throughout North America

Vortigern had been built in the port of Quebec which mainly produced larger three-masted vessels such as barques, barqentines and ships, whereas Prince Edward Island specialised in two-masted schooners, brigs and brigantines using native forests of spruce, yellow birch, tamarack, beech and pine.[18] The extensive forests of the Canadian Maritime provided the raw material for many ships to be built on Nova Scotia, New Brunswick and Prince Edward Island during the golden age of Canadian shipbuilding.

William served on *Milton* for over a year, from 2 January 1865 to 1 March 1866, learning the ropes on a much larger ship, square rigged on both masts and bringing cargoes of coal from Maryport to Belfast.

During the first half of 1866 he made this voyage nine times.[19] *Milton* had made the same trip 16 times in 1865 under the command of John Tomelty of Portaferry.[20]

This experience enabled him to secure another command as master of the *Rock* (ON 8127), a 58-ton sloop built in Belfast in 1837. *Rock* was owned by James Duffy of New Street, Donaghadee, a ship owner and a coal, lime and iron merchant who also manufactured bricks and tiles.[21] She had paid off her previous crew in Belfast at the end of 1865 and had been under repair there until 9 March when William took command. William would serve as her master for five years until 11 March 1871. *Rock* left Belfast the next day and then brought three cargoes from Troon to Donaghadee before 30 June. She made seven further voyages from Troon, Ayr and Maryport to Donaghadee and one from Troon to Ramsey, Isle of Man during the second half of the year.[22]

Hugh Bell and William John Neill served with him as mate and seaman during the first half of 1867. During the year *Rock* brought coal to Ballywalter and Donaghadee from Ayr, Troon. Whitehaven and Maryport.[23] She also sailed from Donaghadee to Larne possibly carrying bricks and tiles manufactured by James Duffy. *Rock* was laid up in Donaghadee for the first three months of 1868. On 2 April she sailed for Ayr with William Bell as master and William John Neill as mate. She made eight coaling trips from Ayr, Troon and Maryport to Donaghadee and was then laid up from 6 November. She had sailed seven months in the year.[24]

Rock sailed again in the spring of 1869 with William Bell as master and this time with Thomas Neill as mate; the crew being made up with an able seaman and a boy. In 1869 she sailed mainly between Ayr, Troon and Donaghadee but also made return trips to Black Head and Larne from Donaghadee and on one occasion supplied coal from Troon to Rostrevor.[25] She was laid up again on 6 December. In 1870 *Rock* continued to supply coal from Ayr, Troon, Whitehaven and Maryport mainly to Donaghadee although single voyages from the coal ports to Greencastle, Howth and Whitehead are recorded. William John Neill was mate at the end of the year.[26] *Rock* continued to trade across the North Channel. However, on 11 March 1871 William Bell was discharged and on 25 March he joined the *Franklin* (ON 34719) as master. *Franklin* was a 72-ton schooner built in Cranville, Nova Scotia in 1843 and owned by William Gibson of Ballywalter, ship owner and general merchant.

William Bell had left the *Rock* in March 1871, quite fortuitously, as it turned out. Her next crew list records that she was 'wrecked on the Scotch coast on Wednesday, 26 July 1871,' just 20 weeks after William had left. *Rock*'s crew survived her stranding but are recorded as having been discharged on the same day at Ballantrae, several miles north of Stranraer. They were fortunate as many sailors did not survive shipwrecks. Her loss was not exceptional. *Marys* (ON18407) on which Samuel Bell had served was burnt in Port St Mary Bay, Isle of Man in July 1875. *Franklin* lasted much longer but on 30 December 1907 she dragged her anchors in Larne Lough during a storm. She was driven ashore, a lantern was upset and *Franklin* was burnt out.

SHIPWRECKS AND STORM WARNINGS

> Eternal Father, strong to save!
> Whose arm doth bind the restless wave,
> Who bidd'st the mighty ocean deep
> Its own appointed limits keep!
> O hear us when we cry to Thee,
> For those in peril on the sea!
>
> W. WHITING, 1860

William Whiting's hymn, 'For those in peril on the sea', was inspired by Psalm 107 and his own experience of delivery from a storm. Published in 1861 it was popularised by the Royal Navy and the United States navy in the late nineteenth century. A century earlier a similar experience of a fierce storm off Donegal in 1748 set in motion the religious conversion of John Newton, then a slave trader. He wrote the first verse of 'Amazing Grace' while repairing his vessel in Londonderry and completed the hymn when curate of Olney, Buckinghamshire, in 1773.

In 1873 Samuel Plimsoll published *Our Seamen, An Appeal* in which he recorded the appalling loss of life at sea, outlined the causes and made the case for reform. His publication was the first instance of photo-journalism, as he used many illustrations, and was the start of a public campaign that would eventually lead to improvements in safety at sea.

He quoted Board of Trade statistics for lives lost on the English coast within ten miles during 11 years from 1861 to 1871. The number ranged from 516 in 1864 to 1,333 in 1867 and averaged 800 per annum over the period.

The nineteenth century had seen considerable reforms. The trade in slaves had been abolished in 1807 and slavery itself in 1833. Factory Acts of 1833, 1844, 1847 and subsequent had regulated hours of employment and brought in safety regulations. The Mines Act of 1842 had improved conditions and safety in coal mines. Similar regulation of the merchant navy was long overdue but would take a determined campaign against vested interests.

Although there were considerable deficiencies in the way that shipping was organised, much was being done to reduce the loss of life due to shipwreck. The Royal National Lifeboat Institution was founded as the National Institution for the Preservation of Life from Shipwreck in 1824 in response to the loss of life of crews and also passengers. The first lifeboats were rowing boats – a far cry from today's self-righting motor-powered vessels – nevertheless they saved many lives through their skill and courage. However, many shipwrecks occurred on rocky coasts or far from lifeboat stations. In those cases the Rocket Brigade was called on. From the early nineteenth century Rocket Apparatus Stations were established around the coastline using a system invented by Henry Trengrose after he had witnessed the loss of the frigate *Anson* in Mounts Bay, Cornwall, in December 1807 with the loss of over 100 lives despite being very close to the coast and safety.

The rocket was fired from shore and carried a light line out to the ship. This was used to pull a hawser and a looped rope running through a block. The hawser is made fast to the mast or a funnel as high as possible and similarly raised above the waves at the shore end. A breeches buoy – a lifebelt with a pair of canvas breeches attached – was then suspended from the hawser on a travelling wheel. This was pulled to-and-from the shore by means of the looped rope running through the block. The 1861 crew list for the *Margaret Gibson* (on which Samuel Bell had served) has the following statement from the master: 'I hereby certify that I have on board a copy of the Instructions issued by the Board of Trade for the use of Mortar & Rocket Lines for the Preservation of Lives in the event of Shipwreck'. The instructions were printed in English, French, Norwegian and German. Many lives were saved using this method until it was superseded in the late twentieth century by the use of Sea King helicopters.

Shipwrecks were a regular occurrence during the storms of the winter months. *The Belfast News Letter* of 5 December 1867 devoted more than a column to an account of a storm – the worst since January 1833. It records several vessels ashore between Bangor and Donaghadee, a schooner ashore opposite the Skerries at Portrush. Several vessels were wrecked near Holyhead, including a French barque which had sought safety in the harbour but broke her moorings and was wrecked against the harbour. The crew and passengers of a full-rigged ship which could not make the harbour were saved by the lifeboat.

The brig *Margaret* was wrecked at Heysham with the crew saved by the rocket apparatus. A crew was lost when a steam tug was overwhelmed at the bar of the Tyne. Two vessels were wrecked at Berwick and their crews perished. A brigantine *Amor* was wrecked on the Goodwin Sands and a brig was reported ashore at Dungeness and expected to go to pieces. The paper also reports that immense damage was done to shipping along the Welsh coast and St George's Channel and further losses as far apart as Malton Island, County Clare and Robin Hood's Bay, Yorkshire. Many of these vessels and their crews would have survived if they had been forewarned of the approaching storm and had stayed in harbour. Ironically such a system had been in widespread use a year before.

The development of accurate barometers and thermometers had led to the creation of detailed records of the weather and to the growing realisation that the weather was not a random and capricious system. International interest in the new science of meteorology had led eventually in Britain to the appointment in 1854 of Robert Fitzroy as Meteorological Statist (statistician) with a remit to 'collect and collate data from ships at sea to build a database which could be used to develop an understanding of weather patterns'.[27] The position was jointly funded by the Board of Trade and the Admiralty.

Fitzroy, an experienced Royal Naval captain,[28] soon established the system of collection of these records and then turned his energies towards more practical use of the data. As a ship's captain he had already devised rules of thumb for predicting weather from wind direction and barometric movement. On 6 June 1860 he was given permission to establish a storm warning system and he set up 13 centres with meteorological instruments in the charge of telegraph operators and devised a system of signals using large black cylinders and cones hoisted on a prominent mast to warn mariners of impending storms. Launched on 6 February 1861 the system was, with a brief hiatus, in use up until 1 June 1984. Fitzroy also devised a system to develop weather forecasts and started to issue these daily. Both the storm warnings and the weather forecasts were well received especially in maritime communities. However, like any innovation they had their detractors.

In April 1865, overcome with exhaustion, worry and profound depression he took his own life. Fitzroy's enemies in the Royal Society and the doubters within the Board of Trade soon established a committee to review the effectiveness of storm warnings and weather forecasts and by rather dubious use of statistics they cast doubt on both. Storm warnings ceased on 7 December 1866 and despite numerous petitions and protests were not resumed until 10 January 1868 – a month too late for those who had perished or suffered material loss in the great storm of December 1867. Weather forecasts did not resume until 1879.

COASTING IN DECLINE

William Bell served on the *Franklin* from March 1871 to March 1872 making a total of eight crossings of the Irish Sea to bring coal from Maryport, Whitehaven and Cardiff to Ballywalter. However, the coasting trade was in decline. The railway had been constructed from Queen's Quay to Holywood in 1848 and extended to Bangor in 1865. A line to Downpatrick through Comber was established in 1859 and a spur line from Comber reached Donaghadee through Newtownards, Conlig, Ballygrainey and Millisle Halt in 1861. This enabled the Donaghadee importers to supply Newtownards and Comber but they faced stiff competition from Queen's Quay at the other end of the line – a much larger operation, unimpeded by the tides and increasingly mechanised. The spread of the railways had enabled Belfast to grow as a redistribution hub. The port now received goods to be supplied to many towns along the growing network of railways as well as those required to meet the constantly increasing demands of its rising population and fast growing industry. Merchants in the smaller ports no longer needed to have capital tied up at risk in a sailing vessel and this reflected in the ownership of vessels. Around 1860 there were six shipowners in Donaghadee;[29] by 1880 there were only two and one of these was the tender of a local diving company.

For Donaghadee seamen there was a steady decline in opportunities in the smaller coastal ports. William Bell (born 1836) cannot be found in crew lists immediately after 1872, although another William Bell, born in Donaghadee in 1843, appears in the records. He had progressed as an able seaman on a series of sailing vessels until 1878 when he became master of the *Ohio*[30] a 177-ton brigantine. All of these vessels brought coal to Belfast however after leaving the *Ohio* in 1884 he became master of the *William Bell*[31] a 124-ton brigantine. She was owned by Robert Dunn of Newtownards and brought coal to Donaghadee. He left this ship in December 1886, a curt note on the crewlist by John Gunning, the new master, relates that he was 'discharged – own fault'. The coasting trade was very insecure and as sailing vessels aged – it was also very dangerous.

In 1874, the *Commerce,* a Donaghadee vessel we have previously encountered, was wrecked. The sole survivor of the crew of three, Thomas Neill, gave a deposition to the Receiver of Wreck at Whitehaven,[32] providing a detailed and vivid account of a shipwreck. (Thomas's brother William John Neill had previously sailed on the *Commerce* with William Bell.) The *Commerce* was rigged as a sloop, built of wood in Montrose in 1822 (52 years sailing already behind her) and was carrying coals from Whitehaven to Donaghadee for her owner Peter Smith. She left harbour on 19 March at 2:00am in clear weather with a moderate breeze from the south. At 6:00am the weather became squally with heavy rain and hail from the west. At about 10:00am, four miles north of the Point of Ayr on the Isle of Man, while under topsail, jib, foresail and double-reefed mainsail, the mast broke off four and a half feet from the deck and to save life was cut away together with ropes and sails. The crew then put the vessel before the wind, to make for Whitehaven and came off the harbour about 9:30pm. At 10:00pm, the tide being four hours' flow, the weather thick, and the wind blowing a gale from the north-west, the sloop dropped both her anchors when about 400 yards off the West Pier Head. The anchors held for about half an hour after which the chains parted and the vessel drifted ashore; shortly after midnight broke up and became a total wreck. The *Commerce*'s boat was unshipped, with a view of making for the shore, but became swamped and unserviceable.

The captain of the Life Brigade reported that attempts to get a line to the *Commerce* by rocket were delayed as the cart was too large to pass under the railway arch and the gear had to be carried to the beach. One of the legs of the stand gave way and had to be repaired causing further delay. Two rockets were fired and the second line reached the vessel, was secured to the mast but fouled and could not be worked. The crew of the sloop had battled hard and long to save their vessel and their own lives. There was only one survivor, Thomas Neill, a non-swimmer who clung to the stump of the mast and was washed ashore exhausted. He lived to the ripe old age of 83 and was buried in Donaghadee. The body of Captain James Gunning washed ashore at Harrington and was interred in Workington, that of William John Neill washed ashore at Parton and was buried at Moresby church.[33]

DONAGHADEE DIVERS

Although Donaghadee declined as a port and many of its citizens turned their attention to providing hospitality to the growing numbers drawn to its beach and to bathing in its clear waters, there were some who retained their involvement with the sea and ships. A diving bell had been used during the construction of the harbour and is mentioned in progress reports from 1827 to 1829.[34] About this time Donaghadee men used diving bells to recover silver coins, bullion from the slave trader *Enterprize* which had been wrecked off Mew island several decades earlier. When diving suits were invented in the 1830s they were soon adopted by the Donaghadee men.[35] This appears to have established Donaghadee as a centre of expertise and there is frequent mention in the press of the authorities 'sending to Donaghadee for divers'.

In 1850 they searched the wreck of the steamship *Orion* off Portpatrick recovering silver plate, money, luggage and valuables.[36] They searched for the body of a crewman missing from a Groomsport fishing smack in 1865.[37] In 1866 they searched for the bodies of the crew of the yacht *Pearl* which capsized and sank off Greypoint. When the yacht *Tana* struck the Skullmartin Rock off Ballywalter in 1867, James Duffy of Donaghadee, in charge of the search, employed several divers to search for bodies.[38] In 1871 John McConkey & Sons were employed to search the River Mourne for the weapon used in a murder in the Northern Bank in Newtownstewart; the search was unsuccessful.[39] In 1878 John McConkey & Sons used dynamite to remove the wreck of the schooner *Old Harry*, a Workington vessel, from the Carrickfergus Bank on the approaches to Carrickfergus Harbour.[40] The expertise gained in this salvage brought, in 1881, a call from an unexpected quarter – the European Commission of the Lower Danube.

Much of the corn consumed throughout Europe was grown in the central European plains and the Danube was one of several routes for its export. The Danube was a vital international trade route and was supervised by this European Commission. In June 1879 the screw steamer *M.Moxham* was proceeding downstream with a full load of Indian corn when it came into collision with the screw steamer *Intrepid*, going up light. *Intrepid*, slightly damaged, continued on its voyage. *M.Moxham*, cut into for a distance of 20 feet, sank some 2,000 feet farther down the river with its stern in 9 feet of water and its bow in 30 feet. Very little of her cargo was salvaged due to the depth of the water and the strength of the current, caused by the spring land-flood. Over the next three days the swelling of the corn sprung the deck and bulged the sides of the steamer. Two more collisions with the wreck rendered her unsalvageable and it was decided that the Commission should remove her.

While the staff of the Commission had considerable experience of destroying the numerous wrecks of wooden vessels originally found in the river using gunpowder, they had never removed an iron wreck using dynamite. Messrs John McConkey & Sons of Donaghadee were requested to send out an expert, thoroughly acquainted with the use of dynamite in the removal of iron wrecks and Mr Robert McConkey came out and superintended the work. This was a complex task using several large charges to lift the wreck, breaking her back and dislodging a very large build-up of silt. Chains of explosive, old boiler tubes driven into the silt and packed with explosive and large bags of dynamite to break up heavy forgings such as the stern post were all deployed and the work was completed without accident.[41] Robert McConkey returned to Donaghadee and the firm was still in business as builders, contractors and divers on the Parade in 1910.[42]

MOVING TO BELFAST

We lose sight of William Bell (b. 1836) in crew lists after he left the *Franklin* in 1872. He appears to have decided to leave Donaghadee and move to Belfast. He and his wife Mary Jane baptised Sarah – their last child – in 1875 when the family was living in Baltic Street, just off Bridgend and a short walk from the coal quay. The river fogs and the smoke of industry were different to the clean air and water of Donaghadee – now relaunching itself as a holiday destination. The family moved to 23 Sherbrooke Street, off the Old Lodge Road, where new housing, connected to the city centre by horse-drawn trams, offered the fresher air of the Antrim Hills.

While the port of Donaghadee declined, the city of Belfast grew rapidly as its industry and population expanded. With 19,000 inhabitants in 1801 the population increased by 458 per cent to 87,062 in 1851 and then quadrupled to 349,180 by the end of the century. The tonnage of shipping through Belfast Harbour, which stood at 50,000 tons in 1801, doubled and redoubled every 15 years throughout the nineteenth century. This reflected the growing population, the growth of industry and the redistribution of goods along the Lagan Canal and through the growing network of railways. However, the growth in tonnage was not reflected in the number of vessels handled, which grew steadily from 1800 to 1860 but only increased by 30 per cent from 1860 to 1914 despite a four-fold increase in tonnage. This is also reflected in the number of vessels registered in Belfast. From 393 in 1857 at the start of records, it rose to a peak of 430 in 1870 and then steadily declined to just over half that figure – standing at 221 in 1900. It was only 227 in 1930. The growth in shipping was not matched by increased opportunities for the captains of sailing ships, particularly as steam ships, which were larger and less dependent on wind, tide and sea conditions, were becoming increasingly common.

The coasting trade out of the small ports brought together seamen and ship owners who were neighbours, who worshipped in the same churches, whose children attended the same schools. There was a much greater sense of a community. Shipping out of Belfast appears to have been different with much more casual employment and more remote owners. The brief snapshot of William's life that I have managed to glean from PRONI's collection of crew lists demonstrates the insecurity of a seaman's life. He joined the SS Bickley[43] as an able seaman in Barrow on 2 June 1880 but left her three weeks later in the same port. He is recorded as joining from SS Magnetic[44] but does not appear on that vessel's crew list; perhaps his service was too short. On 7 July 1880 in Workington, he joined the Mary Jane[45] of Belfast, a vessel on which he had previously served. He left her in Belfast nine days later and spent some time at home before joining the Busy[46] in Belfast as an able seaman on 13 August 1880. He served on Busy for three and a half weeks before leaving her on 6 September 1880 in Maryport to join the crew of SS Italia[47] in Workington, on the following day. His brother Hugh had already joined the crew of this vessel in Belfast three weeks earlier. The crew agreement for this vessel was for voyages to St Nazaire in western France and thence to any port on the Mediterranean, France, Spain, Portugal or the Baltic Sea from 29 June to 31 December. William was discharged in Belfast on 28 October 1880 and Hugh followed suit on 1 November. Thirty seamen served on this vessel during this six month period with two changes of crew. William and Hugh then joined the crew of SS Irishman[48] and he is recorded as continuing as bosun (a corruption of boatswain, a rank above able seaman) on 3 January 1881. However, he left the Irishman on 25 January 1881 in Barrow. Hugh remained until 2 May 1881. It seems very likely that this was the pattern of employment for most Belfast seamen. It will have been William's way of life until late in 1886.

MINNIEHAHA

As the American War of Independence drew to a close a substantial number of North American Loyalists, who had supported the Crown and had not been persuaded of the rightness of the Patriot cause, chose to leave the new republic. Many of those from the northern states chose

Canada as their destination and received land grants to settle there. Among them was John Morehouse, born in 1761 in Redding, Connecticut, who left New York in 1783 and settled in Sandy Cove, Digby. John was a member of the United Empire Loyalists. Morehouse and his family prospered and in 1864 the brigantine *Minniehaha* was built for his son Gershom Morehouse at Sandy Cove and launched into the Bay of Fundy on the west coast of Nova Scotia (famous for the greatest tidal range in the world). She was one of many Canadian ships named after the lover of Hiawatha in Longfellow's epic poem which had been published to immediate success in 1855. Her name, translated from Dakota as 'laughing water' by Longfellow, was to prove cruelly ironic in the case of vessel ON 49484.

Minniehaha remained in the Morehouse ownership after Gershom's death in 1867, passing to the joint ownership of Nicholas and George. In 1879 she was in home trade, presumably in Canadian waters. In 1881 and 1882 she was in foreign (Atlantic) trade.[49] In 1882 she was owned by John Barr of Ardrossan and in home trade in 1883. On 25 March 1886 she passed to James Kingsberry of 15 Queens Quay, Belfast, a well-known coal merchant. At that time a representative of the late owner stated that she had been 'lying up in Ardrossan Harbour from 30 December 1883 to present date': some two and one quarter years out of use. She carried coal to Belfast from various ports sporadically and William Bell served on her between April and 25 June when he joined the SS *Black Diamond*, a steam ship, as second mate. He was serving with his brother Hugh, able seaman. *Black Diamond* shuttled between Troon and Belfast very frequently. However, at some stage William made the fateful decision to return to a sailing ship and to take command of *Minniehaha*. It was an understandable choice. As second mate on the *Black Diamond* he was paid 25 shillings a week, the first mate received 35 shillings but the Master was paid £3-0-0. The financial advantages of command were obvious. However, he was taking charge of a ship that was approaching the end of its working life, retired from Atlantic service and laid up in Ardrossan Harbour for over two years.

Minniehaha departed Belfast on 23 October, discharged her ballast, took on a cargo of coal in Ardrossan, and left that harbour on Thursday afternoon, 4 November, bound for Belfast. The weather records show a depression forming in the Atlantic just north of Ireland. Over the next two days this would deepen and track eastwards with the wind direction changing from south-west to north-west and then north. *Minniehaha,* faced with adverse winds on Thursday and unable to make any headway, then found herself in the grip of a force 9 gale on Friday. The centre of the North Channel is 200 metres deep and this allows the Atlantic waves to carry well into the confines of the channel before they break: it is a dangerous place in a storm. A survivor of the schooner *Eclipse* which left Maryport for Belfast and foundered three miles off Donaghadee on Friday night described that vessel being 'the sport of every wave, driven hither and thither as if we had neither rudder or crew ... making no headway'.[50] Two men from her crew of four were rescued by the steamer *Optic.*

Minniehaha, in the grip of the same storm, was driven off course towards the County Down coast. The wide seaway of Belfast Lough presents few dangers to ships; however, close to the coast the rocks and reefs have claimed many ships. The Briggs reef runs out to sea near Orlock Head from the eastern side of Sandeel Bay. It was clearly marked on charts from the late eighteenth century,[51] a hazard to be noted. A red can buoy warns ships to keep clear of these submerged rocks. However, the Briggs also had teeth: the sternpost of the *Emily,* a 500-ton iron steamship wrecked in 1884 en route to Bordeaux from Glasgow with 1,200 tons of coal, lies only a few feet below water.[52] Witnesses saw the *Minniehaha* founder so suddenly that no assistance could be offered. Wreckage, papers from the ship and four bodies were washed ashore. They were mutilated by being beaten against the rocks. Reports at the time noted that Captain Bell had the reputation of being an able and experienced sailor, perfectly acquainted with both sides of the North Channel. Captain Gunning of Donaghadee said that a better sailor than the mate Richard Murphy could not be found. 'It must, therefore, have been owing to the dreadful nature of the weather that these experienced seamen were beaten so far south of their course as the Buoy of the Briggs'.[53]

William Bell's body was brought back to his sister's home in Meetinghouse Street, to be buried in Donaghadee on Monday, 8 November. His death notice[54] requested that members of LOL 941 should attend the funeral of Br Captain William Bell wearing the regalia of the Orange Institution. It was reported that his funeral 'was largely attended by not only the brethren of the district, but a large concourse of the inhabitants of Donaghadee'.[55] The Orange Hall LOL 941, on Back Street, was at the heart of Donaghadee's seafaring community; its members well acquainted with the hardships and dangers of their trade.

William's brother Hugh had not accompanied him when he left the *Black Diamond* to take command of the *Minniehaha*. He was, however, to meet a similar fate three years later when the *Zuleika*, a 212-ton brigantine owned by William Mulholland, Princes Street, Belfast, was cast onto a reef in Dingle Bay off the County Kerry coast on 7 October 1889. She broke up on the rocks and the entire crew was drowned. *Zuleika* (ON 55981) had been engaged in the coasting trade and had been in Cork a few weeks earlier. The ship's cabin did not break up and in it was found a letter to William Mulholland from his father John dated Belfast 15 April 1889.[56] Hugh was recorded as an able seaman, aged 37, born Donaghadee and living in Baltic Street, Ballymacarrett.[57]

A short distance from Groomsport, along the A2 to Donaghadee, there is a small car park on the seaward side of the road, the start of a National Trust coastal walk. It is very pleasant in summer; crossing a rocky foreshore and then climbing steps to the top of Orlock Head. There are fine views of the nearby Copeland Isles and, on a clear day, the coast of Scotland can be seen – a range of blue hills low on the eastern horizon. Sea birds nest on the cliffs and bottlenose dolphins are seen near the Briggs reef. The walk descends to the soft beach of Sandeel Bay and a rock cut archway, the remains of an eighteenth-century coast road, supposedly used by smugglers. During winter storms it is quite different. When the north wind howls around chimneys and roof tops, when curtains are drawn and the heat is turned up, Orlock Head is a dangerous place. Wind and tide combine to pile great waves onto the shore and even turbo-engined ferries shelter in their harbours. This onslaught of tide and waves reaches down and scours the deeper water around the reef and, in the calm of the morning after the storm, beach combers may still find lumps of coal washed ashore. They are reminders of voyages that were never completed, cargoes that were not delivered and men who did not return to the warmth of hearth and home.

Hugh appears to have been the last seaman in my family. My grandfather, Robert Bell, had wanted to go to sea and had stowed away at the age of 12. Discovered and returned to his family in Baltic Street, he was dissuaded from seafaring and trained as a riveter, eventually becoming a foreman at Harland and Wolff shipyard. He was a keen amateur cyclist and lived to the age of 94. He married Margaret Kennedy, the daughter of Denis Kennedy, a blacksmith,[58] on 11 July 1888. He and Margaret had seven children. In 1911[59] the three eldest girls were shop clerks in drapery, grocery and dairy; the eldest son, William, was an apprentice fitter. The fourth daughter was at school as was my father Robert. James, the youngest child, was 11 months old. The family prospered and James attended the new Stranmillis Training College becoming a primary school headmaster. He was an excellent sprinter, setting the Northern Ireland record for the 100 yards at 10.0 seconds on a cinder track in 1938. It stood for 20 years until broken on a new Olympic standard track made using sophisticated surfacing and much more effective running spikes.

My father left St Enoch's National School at 14, started work in a bank and attended night school to further his education.[60] In 1925 at the age of 22 he emigrated to the USA,[61] initially to his aunt Bella in Hartford, Connecticut. He worked in the Chase Bank on Wall Street until news of his mother's illness brought him back to Belfast in 1928 after 3 years.[62] He never returned to New York as the Wall Street Crash followed in 1929. However, his experience of banking in New York secured him the position of Secretary of the Belfast Stock Exchange. He held this post for 40 years and was able to buy his own house and provide me and both my sisters with the opportunity to go to grammar school and then university in the 1960s – a very different life from his grandfather's and one which reflects the profound social change during the century from William Bell's birth in Donaghadee to mine in Belfast.

NOTES

1   This is an unusual rock which also outcrops and was worked at Brockley on Rathlin Island. It is the result of volcanic activity where a layer of basalt was weathered, then overlain by further basalt layers and then baked at high temperature in contact with an intrusive dolerite plug. This produces a very heavy, fine-textured rock that was ideal for the axes and adzes used in forest clearance and wood working.

2   Scotland was by then a stable kingdom with a rising population. They were a people on the move and in fact more Scots went to settle in Poland at this time than in Ulster.

3   Report to Institution of Civil Engineers Resource Panel for Historical Engineering Works 2012.

4   Institution of Civil Engineers/panel for historical engineering works.

5   Chevalier De Latocnaye, *A Frenchman's Walk Through Ireland, 1796–7*, translated by John Stevenson (new edition by Blackstaff Press, 1984).

6   This office would eventually become the Registrar General of Shipping and Seamen and the form, style and contents of the documents would evolve over time.

7   See www.dumville.org/whisky.html for more detail.

8   This led to Salt Pan Beach where salt had been made by the simple expedient of trapping seawater in metal pans at high tide and boiling off the water when the tide fell.

9   McConkey is a variant of Mac Dhonnchaidh – son of Donagh.

10   Griffith's Valuation for Donaghadee Town Parks.

11   ON 1793, built Inverness 1834, National Maritime Museum.

12   ON 1125, 88-ton schooner built *Clare*, Nova Scotia 1842, National Maritime Museum.

13   ON 8056, 47-ton sloop, built Belfast 1854.

14   *Belfast and Province of Ulster Directory*, 1870.

15   Crew lists from National Maritime Museum and PRONI, TRANS 2A/1/71A&B and 2A/68A&B.

16   ON 37417, 143-ton brig, built *Liverpool*, Nova Scotia 1854.

17   Rev. G. Hansbrow, *An Improved Topographical and Historical Hibernian Gazetteer* (Dublin, 1835).

18   David Sobey, *Shipbuilding and the Forests of Prince Edward Island* (PEI, 2011).

19   PRONI, TRANS 2A/3/3328.

20   Crew list for 1865, National Maritime Museum.

21   *Belfast and Province of Ulster Directory*, 1863.

22   PRONI, TRANS 2A/3/87 A & B.

23   PRONI, TRANS 2A/4/75 A & B.

24   TNA, BT99/426.

25   TNA, BT99/539.

26   PRONI, TRANS 2A/7/70 A & B.

27   John and Mary Gribbin-Fitzroy.

28   Earlier in his career he had mapped the Pacific coast of South America, producing charts which served the Navy for many years. He had taken Charles Darwin as a companion on this voyage. A visit to the Galapagos Islands was to transform our understanding of the origins of life.

29   *Belfast and Province of Ulster Street Directory* and crew lists.

30   ON 34713, 177 tons, built Sandy Cove, Nova Scotia, 1864.

31   ON 39142, 124 tons, built Prince Edward Island 1856.

32   *Cumberland Pacquet* quoted at length in the *Belfast News Letter*.

33   http://graceneills.com/about-us/ (accessed 8 Dec. 2018).

34   Sir John Rennie's reports, Archives of the Institution of Civil Engineers.

35   Harry Allen, *Donaghadee: An Illustrated History* (White Row Press, 2006).

36   *The Lancaster Gazette*, Saturday, 20 June 1850.

37   *Belfast Morning News*, Friday, 6 Oct. 1865.

38   *Dublin Evening Mail*, Saturday, 14 Sep. 1867, from *Northern Whig* of same date.

39   *Dublin Evening Mail*, Friday, 18 Aug. 1871 and Thursday, 24 Aug. 1871.

40   *Belfast Newsletter*, Monday, 29 Apr. 1878.

41   Charles Henry Leopold Kuhl, 'Breaking up a Wreck by Dynamite on the Lower Danube', Paper No. 1841: https://doi.org/10.1680/imotp.1882.219549, Archives of the Institution of Civil Engineers.

42   *Belfast and Province of Ulster Street Directory*, 1910.

43   ON 76970, *SS Bickley*, an iron steamer, built Sunderland 1877, owned by the Ulster Steamship Co.

44   ON 45125, *SS Magnetic*, an iron steamer, built Glasgow 1863, owned by the Belfast Steamship Co.

45   ON 1125, *Mary Jane*, schooner, built Clare, Nova Scotia 1842, owned by John Neill, Queens Quay, Belfast.

46   ON 37594, *Busy*, brigantine, built Luneburg, New Brunswick 1857, owned by William Pollock, Ballymacarrett.

47   *SS Italia*, iron steamer, built Greenock 1869, owned by Robert Brown of Antrim, Iron Ore Co., PRONI, TRANS 2A/16/3030.

48   *SS Irishman,* Iron steamer, built Paisley 1854, owned by William Pirrie of Ballymacarrett. PRONI, TRANS 2A/17/12 B.

49   Maritime History Archive.

50   *Newtownards Chronicle*, 13 Nov. 1886.

51   Master Williamson's 'Chart of Belfast Lough Late 18th Century', Admiralty Library Manuscript Collection, MS 358; John Blake, *Sea Charts of the British Isles: A Voyage of Discovery Around Britain & Ireland's Coastline* (Conway Maritime Press, 2005).

52   Board of Trade Enquiry into the 1895 loss of the *Ranger*, a 16-ton wooden paddle steamer tug which had become impaled on the sternpost of the *Emily* and sank when going to the assistance of the steamship *Davaar* which was stranded on the reef. The wreck of the 850-ton iron steamship *Orator* had joined *Emily* on the reef in 1890.

53 *Belfast News Letter*, Monday, 8 Nov. 1886.
54 Ibid.
55 *Newtownards Chronicle*, Saturday, 13 Nov. 1886.
56 *Belfast News Letter*, Wednesday, 9 Oct. 1889.
57 TNA, Register of Deaths at Sea, Registrar General of Shipping and Seamen, see http://discovery.nationalarchives.gov.uk/details/r/C478 (accessed 8 Dec. 2018).
58 Denis, then aged 15, appears in a rare surviving page from the census of 1851 at his father Patrick's house and smithy on Main Street, Larne, County Antrim,
59 Census of Ireland, 1911.
60 He was eventually a Fellow of the Institute of Chartered Secretaries.
61 Manifest of Alien Passengers for the United States, *SS Baltic*, June 1925.
62 Passenger manifest *SS Celtic*, March 1928.

The riddle of Erskine Childers[1]

PATRICK BUTLER

INTRODUCTION

In a non-historical context, Erskine Childers is perhaps
most famously remembered now as the author of *The
Riddle of the Sands*, a story of intrigue and spying on the
seas and islands around East Frisland on the North Sea
coast of Germany in the years leading up to the First
World War. In addition to being a great boating adventure,
the novel is considered by many to be the forerunner of
the modern genre of espionage thrillers.

However, the intriguing question remains – how did a true son of
the British Empire and the author of such a patriotic novel end
up as director of publicity for the IRA, fighting against king and
country? And why, when a form of the Irish independence for which
he struggled was achieved, did he reject it and was ultimately executed
by the new Free State government?[2]

EARLY LIFE

Robert Erskine Childers was born on 25 June 1870 in the fashionable
Mayfair district of London, the second of five children, with one older
brother, Henry, and three younger sisters, Constance, Sybil and
Dulcibella. The name Robert came from his father while the name
Erskine came from Thomas Erskine, an ancestor on his mother's side,
who had been Lord Chancellor 1806–07, in the reign of George III.
His parents' marriage appears to have been happy, as was Erskine's early
childhood.

Erskine's father, Robert Caesar Childers, was an academic whose specialism was the Pali language. His interest in this language had been sparked while working as a civil servant in what was then Ceylon, now Sri Lanka. Pali was used across much of southern Asia since the seventh century BC and was the literary language of that part of the world. All of the great Buddhist works of literature were written in Pali; however, it was practically unknown in Europe and no Pali dictionary was available. This was a lacuna that Robert Childers senior was determined to fill and a task at which he worked obsessively, to the point where he seriously compromised his health. Extreme obsession is a theme that would also assume greater significance in his son Erskine's career.

Erskine's mother was Anna Henrietta Barton, from an old Irish Protestant family in County Wicklow. Her family home was Glendalough House, near Annamore. The family had lived there for over three hundred years, having been granted the surrounding lands in the reign of Elizabeth Tudor, for loyal service in perilous times. Over more than three centuries the Bartons had established deep local roots and considered themselves unquestionably Irish. As members of the Ascendancy they were somewhat set apart from the general population, being educated in England and marrying within their own social bracket, but as landlords they appear to have been viewed with some affection by their tenants.

In addition to the marriage of Robert and Anna Barton, the bond between the Childers and Barton families was further strengthened in 1875 by the marriage of Robert's youngest sister Agnes to Anna's brother Charles.

Another significant family figure to mention was his father's cousin, Hugh Childers. Hugh had made something of a name for himself in the rambunctious world of Australian politics and was even more successful as a Liberal politician upon his return to Britain. Between 1868 and 1892 he served as First Lord of the Admiralty, Secretary of State for War, Chancellor of the Exchequer and Home Secretary.

However, the happy serene days of Erskine's early childhood were not destined to last long. In the spring of 1876, his father Robert contracted consumption, having never fully recovered from his physical breakdown in Ceylon and, despite the devoted ministrations of his wife Anna, he died in July 1876 at the age of 38. Worse news was to follow – it soon became clear that Anna too had contracted the much-feared disease. She was removed to a sanatorium in the autumn of 1876 and, although she lingered painfully for a further seven years, that was the last time Erskine or his siblings saw their mother. Having been effectively orphaned at the age of six, Erskine and his siblings were taken in and adopted by Charles and Agnes Barton and given a home in Glendalough. One can only speculate as to what Charles and Agnes might have thought married life held for them, but they can scarcely have imagined that they would inherit a ready-made family of five children immediately after their honeymoon. Whatever the emotional consequences of this upheaval, Erskine and his siblings were well catered for in all material ways; there was a governess and plenty of servants in Glendalough and over the coming years, they quickly acquired five Barton cousins to keep them company. Indeed the appearance of ten children meant that an extra wing had to be added quickly to Glendalough.

At the age of ten Erskine was sent to a preparatory school in Hertfordshire called Bengeo [*Ben-jo*] and progressed from there to Haileybury School and from there he won a place at Trinity College, Cambridge. He was part of a circle of friends at Cambridge which included Bertrand Russell, Lytton Strachey, Charles Trevelyan, Walter Runciman and, perhaps most notably, Eddie Marsh. Marsh went on to become Winston Churchill's long-time Private Secretary and confidant. Churchill, perhaps inevitably, is an important player in this story of Erskine Childers, as will become apparent. Having graduated at Cambridge, Childers stayed on a further year to read law, adding the law degree to his BA in 1893. He then undertook the Civil Service entrance exam and finished in an impressive third place, which allowed him to choose his Department. Perhaps on the advice of his father's cousin Hugh, he chose to become a Committee Clerk in the House of Commons.

Childers slipped easily into the role of parliamentary clerk and the precision required in the endless drafting and re-drafting of clauses seems to have been well-suited to his mindset. In addition to the starting salary of £100 per year and sense of being close to the centre of government, the other great perk of the job was the long parliamentary recesses. These facilitated Erskine's pursuit of his new passion – sailing.

Along with his brother Henry, Erskine bought his first boat just before Easter 1893. It was a former racing yacht called *Shulah* – with an enormous mainsail and boom and a long keel of over 8.5 feet. It was an entirely unsuitable boat for two inexperienced mariners and was equally unsuited to the purpose for which it had been bought, namely to explore the little coves, ports and inlets of the Irish and Scottish coasts – most of these places are inaccessible to a boat with such considerable draft. Nonetheless the brothers enjoyed their explorations and appear to have quickly attained a certain level of seamanship. *Shulah* was subsequently sold and replaced by an 18-foot clinker built half-decker called *Mad Agnes*, in which he explored much of the south coast of England and the north cost of France. *Mad Agnes* was then sold and replaced by *Vixen,* a 30-foot cutter, and a former lifeboat. She was not an attractive boat to the eye, but was undoubtedly the most sea-worthy craft he had yet acquired. August 1897 found him on board *Vixen* in the port of Boulogne. His plan was to sail down the English Channel and make his way into the Bay of Biscay and down to Bordeaux before entering the Languedoc canal system to ultimately reach the Mediterranean. However, a succession of south-westerly gales rolling in off the Atlantic made it impossible to make much headway so instead he sailed up along the French, Belgian, Dutch and German coasts, before passing through the Kiel canal and into the Baltic. Clearly, this trip was to provide the inspiration and much of the detail for *The Riddle of the Sands*. However, in the midst of all this pleasant 'messing around on boats', another chapter of Childers' life was about to begin.

BOER WAR

In late 1895, Cecil Rhodes and a number of accomplices launched an unsuccessful attempt to seize Johannesburg and to bring its newly discovered gold and mineral wealth under British control. This was to become known as the Jameson Raid, one of the events which led to the second Anglo-Boer War. What is clear is that by 1898, war was likely if not inevitable and as a consequence Erskine restricted his sailing to the south coast of England so that he would not 'miss it'. It is also clear that the 28-year-old Erskine Childers was a totally committed imperialist, a completely loyal subject of Queen Victoria and a strong believer in the righteousness and *raison d'être* of the British Empire. When the British attempt to lift the Boer siege on Ladysmith in March 1900 was repulsed with 1,200 casualties, there was a strong clamour in the media for Britain to take this war seriously.[3]

A few days after Christmas 1898, Erskine made his way back from Glendalough to London in great haste and went straight from the train to the barracks of the Honourable Artillery Company and applied for service. The Honourable Artillery Company was part of the City Imperial Volunteers, which was the force raised by the City of London for service in South Africa. Erskine was lame in one leg, but as a consequence of his fondness for long walks and his constant sailing, he was in better physical condition than most young men of his age and was accepted by the HAC. On 3 February 1899, he set sail from the Royal Albert Dock for South Africa, on board the *SS Montfort*. Sailing via the Canary Islands, the *SS Montfort* dropped anchor in Table Bay on 26 February 1899. As they were financed by the City of London rather than the Treasury, the HAC were one of the best equipped units in the army. After the early embarrassments of the war, the British had appointed new and aggressive commanders, particularly Kitchener and Roberts. They also poured an enormous amount of men, artillery and ammunition into South Africa. By the end of the war there were over 450,000 British troops on South African soil. Erskine served in South Africa until September 1899. He was clearly frustrated by the fact that his unit was generally held in reserve and was not involved in much front line fighting, except for the period from June to August 1899, although these encounters were more in the nature of skirmishes as the Boers resorted to guerrilla tactics, particularly under their legendary commander Christiaan De Wet. There is no particular evidence of which I am aware that Erskine was anything other than a loyal and committed soldier of the British Army in South Africa, nor that he doubted that the British cause was just, although there is some indication that his attitudes towards the Boer enemy shifted. Erskine had come to South Africa with his head full of the British press depictions of the Boers as a cruel and brutish race, but he found them to be courageous, stoic and resourceful farmers. His friend Basil Williams's description reads, 'Both of us, who came out as hide-bound Tories, began to tend towards more liberal ideas, partly from the jolly democratic company we were in, but chiefly I think, from our discussions on politics and life generally'.

An interesting observation, but hardly the stuff of revolution. There is also an interesting paragraph in Erskine's subsequent book on the Boer War, entitled *In the Ranks of the CIV.* It describes an encounter he had with a number of wounded soldiers from the Royal Munster Fusiliers. He records: 'It was pleasant to hear the rich Cork brogue in the air. It seems impossible to believe that these are the men who Irish patriots incite to mutiny. They are loyal, keen and simple soldiers, as proud of the flag as any Britisher.'[4]

So in late September Erskine, with the rest of the City Imperial Volunteers arrived back in London to great pomp and ceremony. They marched down the Strand and along Fleet Street before attending a thanksgiving service in St Paul's followed by a great banquet and reception in the Guildhall.

MARRIAGE, ETC (MARY ALDEN OSGOOD – MOLLY)

In 1903, Erskine was promoted in the House of Commons to become Clerk of Petitions receiving an additional £60 per year in salary. By this stage he had successfully published two books achieving reasonable sales with both – the first, *In the Ranks of the CIV*, was essentially a personal account of his time in South Africa based on his diary entries. The second, entitled, *The HAC in South Africa*, was the official account of the company's experience in the second Boer War. He had been encouraged to write this by Lord Denbigh, who had been Colonel of the HAC. It was also under the encouragement of Lord Denbigh that Erskine agreed to go on a tour of North America, which can only be described as something of 'a jolly'. It was sponsored, paid for and hosted by the extremely well-heeled Ancient and Honourable Artillery Company of Massachusetts, a sister organisation of the London HAC. In September 1903, Erskine sailed to America along with 165 other members of the HAC. As an aesthetically minded tee-totaller, he might not have gone on the tour had he known what lay in store. In Boston alone the budget was for some $251,000. This included $30,000 on a banquet, $15,000 on wine, $8,000 on cigars and $50,000 on what is simply described in the accounts as 'other private entertainments'. In addition to Boston the tour also included visits to New York, Washington, Rhode Island, Buffalo, Niagara Falls, Toronto and Montreal, with the Company being formally presented at both West Point and the White House. However, amidst all the feasting and hoopla, Erskine, rather impressively, found time to meet, court and marry a young Bostonian lady by the name of Mary Alden Osgood, known as Molly. He met her while riding around the suburbs of Boston on a motorbike he had hired. They were married on 6 January 1904 by the bishop of Massachusetts, honeymooned in Italy and settled down in a house on the Chelsea Embankment in the spring of 1904.

THE RIDDLE OF THE SANDS

1903 had also been a significant year for Erskine's literary career. After a difficult gestation of almost five years, his first novel, *The Riddle of the Sands,* was published in May 1903 to immediate acclaim and massive sales. By the end of the year it had gone through three editions, as well as a special cheap edition, something akin to a modern paperback, which alone had sold several hundred thousand copies. It was the literary sensation of the year and Erskine became a sought after figure by society hostesses. The instant success of the book was probably down to a mixture of luck and serendipitous timing. The experiences of the recent Boer war and the increasing bellicosity of anti-British German nationalist sentiment meant that the central message of the book did not fall upon deaf ears. It is interesting to consider that Erskine had a considerable row with his publisher about the exact nature of the book and how it should be described. To Smith Elder, the publisher, it was plainly a novel. Erskine however, did not see it as such. He saw it as an allegorical tale, or in his own words, 'a story with a purpose, written from a patriot's natural sense of duty'.

From Childers' point of view, the key point of the book was the message about British naval unpreparedness for war. Leonard Piper, in his excellent book *Dangerous Waters* states that:

the difficulty really was that, at the time, most novels in English were being written for women. The great improvement in the education provided for girls, combined with the lack of employment opportunities for them, created an enormous market for suitable books for them to read. Novelists such as Arnold Bennett and John Galsworthy eagerly met that requirement. The very word novel had come almost to mean a book for women.

In any event, the publisher won that battle, the book was substantially edited and shortened and was sold as a novel, which, to this day, continues to sell impressively. It was by no means the first male orientated book, owing as it does, a debt to the adventure stories of Rider Haggard and the detective stories of Arthur Conan Doyle. Nor was it the first spy story, Rudyard Kipling's *Kim* having been published in 1901, but it unquestionably elevated the genre to new heights of respectability and inspired subsequent writers such as Buchan, Fleming and Le Carré.

There has been some debate about the extent to which *The Riddle of the Sands* actually influenced government policy. In the epilogue of the novel Childers writes: 'We have a great and, in many respects magnificent navy, but not great enough for the interest that it insures, nor built or manned methodically, having an utterly inadequate reserve of men. We have no North Sea naval base, no North Sea fleet and no North Sea policy.'

Churchill himself subsequently credited the book as being the major reason why the Admiralty decided to establish new naval bases, but the timing of this does not seem to quite fit. The novel was published in May 1903, some two months after the purchase of the land for the new Rosyth naval base had been announced in parliament. However, Childers' call for the formation of a proper naval reserve, was indeed shortly after enacted in parliament, with the setting up of the Royal Navy Volunteer Reserve.

The press reaction to the book was largely enthusiastic, although the critic in the *Times Literary Supplement* found it tiresome and stated that 'it could only be read with the aid of large maps, railway guides and special information about things nautical'.[6] He was in the minority, however. It was described by the *Westminster Gazette* as 'a literary accomplishment of much force and originality' and continued:

this is a book with a purpose, clearly stated and strongly enforced. It is meant to secure our national safety. Mr Childers is no panic monger; he does not install suspicion or hatred of Germany, but simply accepts statements repeatedly and deliberately made by the German authorities, and indicates how the danger might be met.

Lord Rosebery, the former Prime Minister, was a fan. He made a point of meeting Erskine in the House of Commons to discuss the book and to congratulate him. Childers also met Winston Churchill, through his association with Eddie Marsh. It is an interesting historical note that, despite Churchill's Cassandra-like predictions in the years leading up to the Second World War, in 1903 he was very much in thrall to Lloyd George. Churchill's primary interest at this time was actually in social reform and he was opposed to increased defence spending. This was a position which he continued to hold until the Agadir crisis in 1910.

MARRIED LIFE

To get back to boats, before leaving for South Africa, Erskine had sold *Vixen* and replaced her with *Sunbeam*, a 15-tonne yawl. Now, in early 1904, he was placed in a most enviable position, when his new father-in-law offered as a wedding present to have a yacht of the couple's choosing designed and built for them. After much thought, the legendary half-Scottish, half-Norwegian boat builder, Colin Archer, was chosen. In his yard in Larvik, he produced a spacious and weatherly 51-foot gaff-rigged yacht, which was called *Asgard*. Asgard, in Norse mythology, was the home of the gods, but the similarity with Molly's maiden name Osgood, may also have been a factor in the decision. In December 1905 Molly gave birth to a healthy boy, named Erskine Hamilton Childers, who was to become the fourth President of the Irish Republic. Further books and articles, mostly of a military nature, were published over the next few years, and two further sons were born, although the second, Henry, died in infancy. By 1907 Childers had probably drifted a little further to the left politically, although he appears, at this stage, to have been more of a liberal than a radical. In the summer of 1908, Erskine and Molly, along with his cousin Robert Barton, went on a motoring tour of western Ireland.

They were particularly interested in visiting the rural co-operative societies, then being organised by Sir Horace Plunkett. What precisely happened on the trip is unclear, but the result was a most significant change of attitude by Erskine regarding the future of Ireland. He wrote to long-time friend Basil Williams, 'I have come back finally and immutably a convert to Home Rule, as is my cousin, although we both grew up steeped in the most irreconcilable sort of Unionism'. Erskine, had discovered a new and powerful obsession, one which was to prove ultimately fatal.

GUNRUNNING

By 1910, Erskine had reached the position of Senior Clerk to the Chairman of Committees in the House of Commons and was on a salary of £800 a year. He had long been bored with the job and in 1910 his finances received a major boost when sales of *The Riddle of the Sands* went dramatically through the roof as a result of real life events on the Frisian Islands. Life was starting to catch up with art, with the arrest by the Germans of two amateur British yachtsmen, Brandon and French, on charges of spying. This financial boost, combined with the urging of Molly, led to Erskine resigning from his position to pursue a political career, hoping to take a seat as a Liberal. For social reform and other liberal policies, he cared little – the only political issue that he was truly interested in was Home Rule. However, he failed to win a nomination for a constituency for the general election of December 1910, and refused to accept the constituencies subsequently offered to him (including Devonport, St Pancras and Kidderminster), as he came to realise that his potential English constituents had little or no interest in Home Rule. He spent the next two years giving speeches and lectures, writing books, touring Ireland north and south and sailing to the Baltic and Scandinavia.

Then, in April 1914, the Ulster Volunteer Force (UVF) succeeded in landing 25,000 rifles and over three million rounds of ammunition from the *SS Clyde Valley* at Larne. One of the repercussions of this was to inspire the setting up of a committee of nationalists with a view to conducting a similar venture. The committee consisted mostly of liberal-minded Anglo-Irish Protestants, including Sir George and Lady Young, Lord Ashbourne, Sir Alexander Lawrence, Roger Casement and of course Erskine Childers. The idea was to purchase guns in Hamburg and load them from a German barge onto the *Asgard* off the Dutch coast. As a result of the Larne gunrunning and pressure from the British, the Germans had introduced a ban on the export of weapons to Ireland. This led to the rather bizarre scenario where Erskine Childers and his companion Darrell Figgis introduced themselves to the German arms dealers as Mexicans. It is probably safe to assume that no-one was fooled by this ploy, but it provided the Germans with a veneer of legality that satisfied them. Then, with an astonishing lack of security, given the highly illegal nature of the operation, Childers invited two British army officers to join him. Gordon Shephard accepted the offer, but Colonel Robert Pipon declined, as he considered Childers to be a crackpot. The crew of the *Asgard* therefore consisted of Childers, Molly, Gordon Shephard, Mary Spring-Rice and two Donegal fishermen. Despite unfavourable weather, the rendezvous was made and the *Asgard*, complete with her cargo, appeared off Howth Head on 26 July 1914. She was met there by hundreds of Irish Volunteers and the guns were quickly unloaded and marched back to Dublin. The *Asgard* then slipped across to Bangor in north Wales and Erskine and Molly returned to London. Erskine then returned to Ireland to await the upshot of his rather public foray into gunrunning. In the event, British eyes were not focussed on small yachts in the Irish Sea. Larger events were afoot. On 28 July 1914, the Austro-Hungarians declared war on Serbia setting in train a series of events that quickly brought about the beginning of the First World War. The British had been on the lookout for Irish gunrunners, but had been watching for a trawler, not a yacht. In terms of quantity the Howth gunrunning did not measure up to the Larne effort, with only 1,500 guns being landed. In terms of quality, they were similarly not a match for what was landed in Larne – Childers' guns were old fashioned, black-powder Mausers.

There is a further interesting postscript to the gunrunning saga: in early August 1914, the headquarters of the Irish Volunteers in Dublin were flabbergasted to receive a telegram from London asking them if they knew the whereabouts of Mr Erskine Childers and, if so, could they ask him to contact Admiralty Intelligence as a matter of urgency? The question mark about Childers' loyalty that this telegram placed in the minds of many in the Irish Volunteer leadership did not augur well for Erskine Childers.

THE GREAT WAR

For a man who had spent the first half of 1914 planning and executing the illegal smuggling of arms to Ireland for the Irish Volunteers, in plain defiance of the British government, Childers has an impressive, near downright outstanding, war record. At this point we need to step back briefly to October 1911, when Churchill was appointed First Lord of the Admiralty. He was not content with the purely defensive contingency plans he inherited and strongly desired offensive options which, in the event of war, could be deployed to either bottle up the German navy or force it to come out and fight. He had plans developed for the seizure of Borkum, Sylt and Helgoland, but these were rejected by the Prime Minister Asquith. However, Churchill bided his time and on the outbreak of war in 1914 he resurrected the plan and this time sent it straight to the War Office. The War Office said the plan needed more detail from someone with local knowledge. The first name out of the hat was Gordon Shephard who, as it happened, had just returned from the gunrunning expedition on board the *Asgard*. However, he was unavailable as he had just taken up a new post with the Royal Flying Corps. The second name picked was that of Childers himself. No-one was quite sure where Childers was – hence the plethora of telegrams sent out by Admiralty Intelligence (under pressure from Churchill), including the fateful one to the Irish Volunteers HQ. When Childers showed up at the Admiralty a week later, he half expected to be arrested. Far from it, a few hours later he was a First Lieutenant of the Royal Naval Volunteer Reserve, and set to work drawing up invasion plans. Ultimately the plan was stifled by naval planning staff, who resented Churchill's meddling, which they saw as political interference in their affairs.

His planning task complete, Erskine then joined HMS *Engadine,* a channel ferry, which was converted into a prototype aircraft carrier, carrying three seaplanes. The term 'aircraft carrier' is a literally correct term for what the HMS *Engadine* did – there was no flight deck – it literally transported three seaplanes, which could only be deployed by lowering them into the sea, from where they would take-off and land, conditions permitting. Childers' role was to teach the pilots how to navigate their aircraft and to act as an observer on board, when flying over enemy positions. Warfare of this kind truly was in its infancy and this was tricky and extremely dangerous work. Childers absolutely loved it. By October 1914, the navy had three ships converted to aircraft carriers, under the command of Commodore Tyrwhitt and Commodore Keyes based in Harwich. Tyrwhitt and Keyes were two of the most audacious and aggressive officers in the navy, definitely in the mould of Nelson, and unsurprisingly Churchill was one of their biggest supporters.

It was decided that they should attempt to use the prototype aircraft carriers in an attempt to strike a telling blow against the centre of German Zeppelin activity, which was based around Cuxhaven on the north German coast. After various weather delays, the raid finally took place on 24 December 1914, with Childers on board one of the seaplanes. The actual damage caused by the raid was fairly minimal, but the psychological impact was considerable. The Cuxhaven Raid certainly improved British morale and went some way to undermining the public dread of attack from Zeppelin airships. It also meant that both sides had to begin to re-think their tactics for dealing with this novel type of combined aerial and naval power.

For the first time, Childers was mentioned in dispatches. Lieutenant Commander Robertson commended the 'nerve and coolness' of Childers and his pilot when flying through an anti-aircraft bombardment at a height of 200–300 feet with a failing engine. In early 1915 Erskine was transferred to another ferry converted to aircraft carrier, the *Ben-My-Chree*. In May 1915, the *Ben-My-Chree* sailed for the Mediterranean. Childers was about to be caught up in another of Churchill's forays into military adventurism – the Dardanelles campaign.

By the time the *Ben-My-Chree* arrived in the Aegean Sea, the infantry campaign had already settled into the familiar bloody stalemate that existed in Flanders. It was bitterly ironic that the Dardanelles campaign, which was designed to break the stalemate on the Western Front, had in fact simply extended it to a new arena. The arrival of the *Ben-my-Chree* was timely – the only aircraft carrier already there was the abysmally slow *Ark Royal*. Childers quickly settled into a routine of reconnaissance work, bombing raids, anti-submarine work as well as acting as a spotter for the big naval guns. As an experienced officer, 46 years old, he was chiefly meant to be there to teach the skills of reconnaissance and navigation. The reality, however, was that he could not resist the thrill and danger of going on the sortie raids himself. The more dangerous the mission, the more likely Childers was to be on it. His commanding officer remarked that on two separate occasions when Childers was rescued from aircraft which had crashed in the sea, it was subsequently discovered that he should not even have been on board, and had either swapped places or pulled rank over men less danger-loving than himself. The *Ben-my-Chree* served with distinction at Suvla and oversaw the evacuation from Gallipoli, ensuring that no submarine could be launched against the waiting ships. He then served several months patrolling the south-east Mediterranean and the North Coast of Africa. He was then summonsed home to take up a new posting at the Admiralty.

The role here was primarily a planning one, and Erskine found it desperately dull. He constantly pestered his superiors to transfer him somewhere closer to the action. While Childers was based in the Admiralty, a number of events started to unfold in Ireland. On Good Friday 1916, Sir Roger Casement was captured as he landed from a German submarine and a ship carrying 20,000 German rifles to Ireland was scuttled as she was intercepted by the Royal Navy. The basic problem for the Irish was that the British had broken the German naval code and knew exactly what was planned. Despite these inauspicious omens, the Easter Rising went ahead on Easter Monday 1916. Casement's fate was sealed. He sought to argue that he was not a British traitor because he was not British but Irish. However, his argument was somewhat undermined by his knighthood from the King, his Foreign Office pension and his many years in the British consular service. Despite the petition signed by Molly and many of her literary friends, including Conan Doyle, Arnold Bennett, G.K. Chesterton, John Galsworthy and Jerome K. Jerome, Childers' accomplice in the Howth gunrunning was executed. By autumn 1916, the constant pestering of his superiors paid off and Erskine was transferred to the Coastal Motor Boat Squadron, as a Lieutenant Commander. These boats carried a torpedo and sought to sink enemy destroyers whenever the chance arose. In April 1917, Childers was awarded the Distinguished Service Order, primarily for his services in the Mediterranean. Then in July 1917, he was told he was to be transferred to Dublin as Assistant Secretary to the Convention on the Future of Ireland.

The background to the Convention on the Future of Ireland was that, by April 1917, the USA had entered the war on the Allied side. This was a great relief to the British Prime Minister, Lloyd George, but it came with an added complication in that his new ally was constantly pressing him to do something about Ireland. Lloyd George responded with a favourite manoeuvre of British governments under pressure and playing for time – he set up an inquiry and gave it the grand title of the Convention on the Future of Ireland. It had 101 members, 52 of Redmond's Nationalists, nine Southern Unionists and 24 Ulster Unionists. Sinn Féin refused to take up its seats. The chances of it agreeing anything, let alone the future of Ireland, were remote. But it bought Lloyd George time. Unsurprisingly it collapsed eventually, without agreement. By this stage Childers was now becoming increasingly sympathetic to the position of Sinn Féin. He wrote:

> The collapse of the whole Convention, and the attempt to enforce conscription, convinced me that Home Rule was dead, and that a Revolution, founded on the Rising of 1916, was inevitable and necessary. I only waited until the end of the war, when I had faithfully fulfilled my contract with the British, to join the Movement myself.[7]

After the Convention, Childers was promoted to become a major in the newly formed Royal Air Force. Molly meanwhile had been awarded an MBE for her outstanding services to the Belgian refugees who had fled to London during the war. Erskine was now based in Norfolk and his squadron was given the first two Handley-Page aircraft off the production line. These were huge four-engine bombers, the first of their kind in the world. Erskine planned to use them on a first-ever bombing raid against Berlin. However, before the plan could come to fruition, the Armistice was signed on 11 November 1918.

THE TREATY

After the war, Erskine appears to have come home mentally and physically exhausted. In March 1919, he fell prey to the 'Spanish flu' epidemic that swept across Europe, killing as many people as the war had done. For a month he lay in hospital, seriously ill, between life and death, but in the end pulled through and eventually returned to Glendalough to recuperate. In Ireland, the 1918 elections saw a dramatic swing towards Sinn Féin which won 73 of the 103 seats contested, and the old Irish Parliamentary Party was virtually wiped out. Sinn Féin declared a Republic with Eamon de Valera as its President. The Home Rule Bill that had been suspended before the war was to be put forward for Royal Assent, although Lloyd George was more pre-occupied with the Versailles peace conference negotiations in Paris. In the meantime, Childers had been introduced to Michael Collins, Eamon de Valera and Arthur Griffith. Collins liked him, though Griffith was deeply suspicious of him and thought he was probably a spy. In any event, he was sent off to Paris in May 1919 to plead Ireland's case at Versailles, although without much success. In the meantime, the Irish Volunteers, now the IRA, had been carrying out attacks on the British army and the Royal Irish Constabulary (RIC). Things came to a head when they attempted to assassinate Viscount French, the Lord Lieutenant. This led to the introduction of the Black and Tans, who were soon deeply despised. Meanwhile, Childers started to sit as a judge in the republican court for County Wicklow and had become increasingly involved in propaganda work on behalf of Sinn Féin. In the elections of April 1921 he was returned as the member for Wicklow West.

On 12 July 1921, de Valera went to London for negotiations with Lloyd George. His team consisted of Arthur Griffith, the Vice President, Austin Stack, Robert Barton and Erskine Childers. One evening, Erskine met up for dinner with his old friend Basil Williams, who gives an interesting description of the transformation which had come over the Erskine Childers he had known before the war. He writes:

> He was a very changed Erskine from the one we had known. Physically he looked almost a wreck; thin and deadly pale and

with quite white hair. His mind was as alert and bright as always, but it seemed a hectic brightness, with almost all his old sense of humour and proportion vanished, at least when he spoke of Ireland. I say almost, for when we got him for a few odd moments to talk of the old loved things, or of joys we had shared in former days, then the old Erskine seemed to flash out with that dear smile of his. But it was not for long, for he could not keep off Ireland for many minutes and when he spoke of her he would accept no compromise and could not for a moment see that, for example, Dominion status might mean all and more in substance than the name of a Republic would give. And when it came to means of achieving his end, he had become almost ferocious and pitiless.[8]

Lloyd George and de Valera met four times and did not take to one another at all. The negotiations ended without agreement and the Irish left with British proposals which in effect amounted to Dominion status. A further conference was arranged to begin in Downing Street on 11 October 1921. The British negotiating team consisted of Lloyd George, Churchill, Chamberlain and Lord Birkenhead. The Irish side consisted of Collins, Griffith, Robert Barton, Gavan Duffy, Eamon Duggan and Erskine Childers as secretary. Eamon de Valera deliberately did not attend, presumably to allow himself room to manoeuvre, depending on the outcome. There is no doubt that he had deliberately put Childers on the team, as Childers was the most extreme and uncompromising of all of them. Whether Childers was secretly reporting back to de Valera is unclear, but it was certainly the suspicion of Griffith. One way or another, Childers seems to have been fated to have always been suspected of spying for someone. Of the rest, Griffith was the most anxious to reach a settlement and Collins, like Lloyd George, was an arch pragmatist.

The negotiations dragged on for over two months, with Childers consistently taking the hardest line and trying to stiffen the resolve of others to resist and generally trying to reject any deal short of independence and British withdrawal. In the end, after various concessions by the British, Collins, Griffith and Duggan were prepared to sign, but Duffy, Barton and inevitably Childers were holding out. Collins lost patience finally and asked Barton how many more young men he wanted slaughtered in a new war in Ireland. Eventually Barton gave in and signed, as did Duffy. Lloyd George wrote an account of the signing ceremony.

> Outside in the lobby sat a man who had used all the resources of an ingenious and well-trained mind, backed by a tenacious will, to wreck every endeavour to reach an agreement – Mr Erskine Childers. A man whose slight figure, and kindly, refined and intellectual countenance and whose calm and courteous demeanour gave no clue to the fierce passions which raged inside him.
>
> At every crucial point in the negotiations he played a sinister part. He was clearly de Valera's emissary, and faithfully did he fulfil the trust put in him by that visionary. Every draft that emanated from his pen – and all the first drafts were written by him – challenged every fundamental position to which the British delegates were irrevocably committed. He is one of those men who by temperament are incapable of compromise. Brave and resolute he undoubtedly was, but unhappily for him he was also rigid and fanatical.[9]

There was one further telling postscript. On signing the document, Lord Birkenhead is reported to have turned to Collins and commented that he might well have signed his political death warrant that night. Collins replied that he may have signed his actual death warrant. As it transpires, both men were right.

THE CIVIL WAR

News of the Anglo-Irish Treaty was broadly welcomed in Ireland, but not by de Valera, who rejected it outright and, some say, without actually reading it. The Treaty was however ratified, albeit narrowly, by both the government and by the Dáil. Eamon de Valera resigned as President and this led to a further debate in the Dáil on the Treaty, during which there were bitter exchanges between Griffith and Childers. Griffith said he would not reply to any Englishman in the Dáil. Childers responded that his nationality was a matter for him and for the constituents that had sent him and that they had known his nationality since his boyhood days. Griffith said 'I will not reply to any damned Englishman in this Assembly'.[10]

He subsequently went on to accuse Childers of having spent his life in the English Secret Service. The Treaty was again ratified after this debate, although only by two votes. Civil war was in the air, and this intensified as the British troops began to withdraw. Dick Barrett, Joe McKelvey, Liam Mellows and Rory O'Connor seized the Four Courts for the anti-Treaty Republican forces and there were increased outbursts of fighting. Further elections were held on 22 June 1922, returning a large majority of pro-treaty candidates. On 28 June, the Free State forces began a bombardment of the Four Courts using field guns borrowed from the British. Civil war erupted across the country. Childers took up a position as staff captain in the southern Brigade of the IRA. He was primarily involved in producing a weekly newsletter for the republican forces. On 12 August 1922 Arthur Griffith died of a heart attack and on 22 August Michael Collins was killed in a skirmish at Béal na Blágh, County Cork. By the end of August, the rebel forces were effectively fighting a guerrilla campaign, based mainly in the south-west. Childers was there, fighting with a rebel group based in the Derrynasaggart mountains in west Cork. In late October, he received a summons from de Valera to meet him in Dublin. He set off on foot and made his way north, via Waterford, Wexford and Wicklow. He stopped off in the friendly sanctuary of Glendalough, but was almost immediately betrayed there, probably by a maid. He was arrested and charged with possession of a revolver. The revolver was small and pearl handled. It had been a gift from Michael Collins. The Free State Government had made it a capital offence to possess an illegal weapon. On learning of his capture, Churchill wrote:

> I have seen with satisfaction that the mischief making murderous renegade, Erskine Childers, has been captured. No man has done more harm or shown more genuine malice, or endeavoured to bring a greater curse upon the people of Ireland than this strange being, actuated by a deadly and malignant hatred of the land of his birth. Such as he is, may all that hate us be.

This was an accusation that Childers felt deeply and rejected. In a letter to Molly he wrote:

> I hope one day my good name will be cleared in England. I felt what Churchill said about my hatred and malice against England.

66

Don't we know it isn't true and what line have I ever wrote or spoke that justifies that charge? I die loving England and passionately praying that she may change completely and finally towards Ireland.[11]

He was court-martialled in Portobello barracks. His plea for belligerent rights as a prisoner of war was rejected and he was sentenced to death. His sentence was stayed for three days on foot of writ for habeas corpus which had gone to the Master of the Rolls. However, the Master of the Rolls washed his hands of the matter.

Now, whatever else you might think of Childers, he certainly died bravely. Molly was not permitted to visit him, but he wrote to her regularly from the condemned cell. His eldest son, Erskine who was then 15, was given compassionate leave from his English public school to visit his father. Erskine asked the boy to promise him two things. Firstly, to shake the hand of every minister in the Provisional Government responsible for his death and, secondly, that if he ever went into Irish politics, not to ever speak in public of his father's execution.

Erskine's last letter to Molly included the lines, 'Beloved wife, I am told that I am to be shot tomorrow at 7am. I am fully prepared. I have had 19 years of happiness with you. No man could ever claim so precious a blessing as that'.

As his last request, Erskine asked for the execution to be delayed a short while to allow him to see the sun rise. He spoke to the officer in charge and strolled down the line shaking hands with each man in turn. He tried to refuse the blindfold, but the officer insisted. When the time came, his last words were 'Take a step or two forward lads. It will be easier that way'.

And so he died, to the British, a traitor and to the Irish, a spy: a curious end for someone who considered himself to be an honest man of principle.[12]

ANALYSIS

A number of hypotheses have been put forward to explain Childers' transition from a man of empire to an armed revolutionary fighting a guerrilla campaign in the hills of west Cork and Kerry.

1) The first of the popular theories put forward and perhaps the easiest to dismiss is that there was no such transition, because all along Erskine Childers was operating as a British undercover agent. The principal problem with this theory is that there is practically no evidence to support it – in fact, all of the available evidence weighs to the contrary. It seems that this theory emerges most strongly after the telegram sent by the Admiralty to the HQ of the Irish Volunteers in 1914. If you think about it, it would be a most peculiar way to go about protecting the identity of your secret agent. Secondly, whatever you might think about Childers's views, there seems little doubt that he was a most extraordinarily honest and forthright about them, regardless of whose nose was put out of joint. Perhaps if he had been less doggedly honest about expressing his opinions, he might have lived longer. Basically, I find it difficult to envisage a man whose personality rendered him less well-suited to be a double agent. Furthermore, if he had been a British agent, one would have thought that some form of pressure might have been brought to bear by the British, on the Provisional Government, to save one of their own. Perhaps the one factor that has fuelled this enduring myth is the fact that Erskine came across as English. He had an English accent. He had an English demeanour and an English bearing. I believe that at a basic level, Griffith and others simply could not see past this and could not bring themselves to accept that someone so quintessentially English was in fact on their side, and I believe that the fact that he adopted much more extreme nationalistic positions than they did angered them at a deep and visceral level – which goes some way to explain the rancorous exchanges between Childers and Griffith in the Dáil '… I will not reply to any damned Englishman …'.

2) The second theory that is often put forward is that Erskine's rather fanatical personality was a direct consequence of emotional trauma caused by his parents' relatively-early deaths and the long enforced separation from his mother when she was in the sanatorium. I am no psychologist, and certainly have no expertise in childhood or developmental psychology, but I would put forward the following layman's analysis of the evidence of which we are aware. It is clear from

Erskine's letters that he was deeply attached to his mother, missed her greatly and that he was a somewhat intense and introverted boy during his early teens. However, on the other hand, it must also be said that he was extremely fortunate to be adopted by Charles and Agnes Barton and to benefit from the settled family life and support that they provided at Glendalough. Furthermore the education experience which he enjoyed was excellent and did not appear to have been marred by bullying and harsh discipline. In a time when infant and indeed early parental mortality was much more commonplace than it is today, he fared considerably better than most. Undoubtedly our formative adolescent experiences contribute to the adults that we become, but frankly I cannot confidently put more weight on this theory than that.

3) The third theory put forward regularly is that Erskine's cousin Robert Barton was the man chiefly responsible for the political transformation of Erskine Childers. There is some evidence to support this. Certainly the two men were extremely close friends and Robert Barton accompanied Erskine on the motoring tour of the west of Ireland in the summer of 1908 which appears to have been a key point in Childers' political awakening. It was also Barton who introduced Childers to Michael Collins in 1919 and through him that he met de Valera. I think therefore it can be fairly said that Robert Barton was a key friend and political colleague who nudged Erskine along the road that he went down and was certainly responsible for some important personal introductions. However, this must be balanced against what we know of 1921 negotiations at Downing Street, where, as we have seen, both men were part of the Irish delegation. Lloyd George described Childers as ingenious, tenacious, brave, resolute, fanatical, rigid and sinister. His description of Robert Barton was somewhat less glowing, calling him 'a pipsqueak of a man, who I would not make a private secretary to an Under Secretary'. It is difficult to imagine such an individual having much influence over someone as determined and implacable as Childers undoubtedly had become by this point in his life.

4) The next theory is that Molly was a key influence in persuading Childers to adopt the Home Rule cause. It seems that Molly did indeed cross the Atlantic with certain pre-conceived notions of the British occupation of Ireland and with a degree of sympathy for the Irish position. However, I think it would be wrong to overstate the significance of this. There is equally no doubt that Molly was a very bright, determined and independent woman, and had her own particular interests for which she advocated strongly. Furthermore, she was perfectly capable of refusing to do what Erskine wanted, if it did not accord with her own wishes. A good example of this was her refusal to move to Ireland and set up home in Glendalough, when she was still heavily involved in her Belgian refugee work, although she did eventually move to Ireland. However, there is little evidence to show that she (or indeed anyone else for that matter) could dissuade Erskine from a particular view or course of action once he had determined upon it. Thus Molly is undoubtedly an important influence, but not one that, by itself, would account for the Damascene scale of the transformation of Erskine Childers.

CONCLUSION

I do not think that Childers' behaviour can be properly explained by simply pointing to a single event or a single person. It is manifestly more complicated than that. We have to start with Erskine's nature and personality. He ended up an extremist and fanatic, but the shadow of that fanaticism was always there. His father's obsession with his study of the Pali language led more or less directly to him working himself to death, or at least being so obsessed by work that he did not look after his health. There is also the element of his character that was not uncommon in young men of his generation – a romantic fetishism for danger and adventure. We see it regularly in his sailing exploits and in his diary accounts of them. He enjoyed the thrill of battling into the teeth of a gale and taking on the elements and had a totally careless approach to his own safety. However, I think that the somewhat foolhardy adventuring that we see before the Great War, moves up several notches in intensity during and after that conflict. Childers appears almost incapable of existing without danger and peril and is endlessly thrusting himself in its path.

Whether this is the result of some effect on the nerves, or what might now be described as some form of post-traumatic stress disorder, I would not venture to say, but what I can say with confidence is that he came back from the war a changed man. His closest friends, including Basil Williams, could see this and another, H.A.L. Fisher, wrote about the vein of recklessness that ran through Erskine, but went on to say, 'I suspect that element was an essential part of his character, but there is something too in an explanation given to me by one of his English friends, that he was thrown off balance by the nervous strain of aviation in the War'.[13]

Even Churchill in the end came round to a more balanced view of the man whom he had previously been so critical, describing Childers as 'a man of distinction, ability and courage' who had 'shown daring and ardour against the Germans in the Cuxhaven raid ... and who had espoused the Irish cause with even more than Irish irreconcilability'.

Perhaps in the end the real mystery is not why this strange, romantic and intensely driven man moved inexorably from one end of the political spectrum to the other, but that a man who energetically sought out danger at every turn actually lived as long as he did.

NOTES

1   An original version of this article was read as the President's address presented to the Belfast Literary Society in 2017.

2   *Oxford Companion to Irish History* (OUP, 1998), p. 86 says: 'Thoroughly disliked by the Free State government he became one of the first republicans to be executed during the Irish Civil War.'

3   The garrison at Ladysmith, which endured a siege of more than four months, was commanded by Lieutenant General George White, born in Portstewart County Londonderry. White had won the Victoria Cross as long ago as the Indian Mutiny, 40 years before. Curiously, and not entirely unrelated to the Childers narrative, his son Captain Jack White also fought in the Boer campaign, won the DSO and later developed anarchist tendencies, joining the Irish Citizen Army and participating in the 1913 Dublin Lockout with Connolly and Larkin: *Oxford Companion to Irish History*, p. 591.

4   Erskine Childers, *In the Ranks of the C.I.V: With the City Imperial Volunteer Battery (Honourable Artillery Company) in the Second Boer War* (originally published 1900, new edition Leonaur, 2008).

5   Leonard Piper, *Dangerous Waters: The Life and Death of Erskine Childers* (Hambledon Continuum, 2003), p. 72.

6   *Times Literary Supplement*, 14 Aug. 1903.

7   Piper, *Dangerous Waters*, p. 187.

8   Ibid., p. 207, footnote 11.

9   *The Daily Telegraph*, 23 Dec. 1922.

10   Jonathan Bardon, *A History of Ireland in 250 Episodes* (Gill and Macmillan, 2008), p. 471. 'Troubles North and South' relates in some detail the debate in the Dáil. The main characters are Childers and Arthur Griffith, as they debate whether or not to accept the treaty: (Griffith) '... I will not reply to any damned Englishman in this house ...', (Childers) '... I am not going to defend my nationality ...'.

11   Andrew Boyle, *The Riddle of Erskine Childers* (Hutchinson, 1977), p. 23.

12   Bardon, *A History of Ireland in 250 Episodes*, p. 47 also makes the useful point, in the context of Childers' execution that 'Executions continued – seventy-seven in all before the [civil] war's end.'

13   Piper, *Dangerous Waters*, p. 234.

The 1831 'census returns'
online database

BILL MACAFEE

This article will serve as an introduction to the 1831
'census returns' database which is now available on my
website: www.billmacafee.com. It is assumed that the
reader will read it while using the website. Since much of
what I have to say is also available – word for word, in
many cases – on the website, some readers may go straight
to that resource.

A copy of the Home Page is overleaf. Click on *1831 'Census Returns'
for Co. Londonderry* at the bottom of the Home Page and that will
take you to the web page shown on page 75.

The 1831 'Census Returns' for Co. Londonderry page contains four main
components:

1 A background paper that introduces the user to the 1831
   'census' and my experiences with it.
2 A separate note on religion data in 1831 'Census'.
3 The database for the entire county.
4 Working with 1831 'census returns' at townland and street level.

BACKGROUND PAPER ON THE 1831 CENSUS

I was introduced to this source in 1967. At that time I was teaching in
Rainey Endowed School, Magherafelt. During the winter of 1967/68
I attended a course on local history in Maghera run by Dr Brian
Trainor and Dr W.H. (Bill) Crawford from the Public Record Office
of Northern Ireland (PRONI). I knew very little about local or family
history and I had no knowledge, whatsoever, of sources such as the

Family and Local History
[Bill Macafee's Website]

Sources	## Home Page	**My Databases**

Sources

PRONI

Births, Deaths, & Marriages

Census Records

Valuation Records

Tithe Records

Estate Records

Other Records

My Databases

Sperrins

Databases compiled from 19th Century Census Substitutes

Databases compiled from 18th Century Census Subtitutes

Databases compiled from 17th Century Census Subtitutes

Maps & Photos

Home Page

The purpose of this website is to to provide a research tool for anyone interested in researching their ancestors and the localities where they lived within the area of Ulster covered by Co. Londonderry and North Antrim - read more. See, also, my paper - Some thoughts on researching families and localities. The website is organised through three menus.

The left-hand menu covers the sources that you will need to consult when researching your ancestors or studying a locality. Clicking on the *Sources* link at the top of the menu will give you some idea of how I see the process of researching ancestors and localities and how this has influenced the way that I have constructed this website. There is also a *Further Reading* link at the bottom of this page where you will find a bibliography of some books and publications [both hard copy and electronic] relevant to the study of Family and Local History and a list of useful addresses. Note that because there are so many PRONI documents now online I have included a link to PRONI in this menu.

The right-hand menu concentrates on databases that I have created from census substitutes that relate to Co. Londonderry and North & Mid Antrim. My databases cover the period c.1630 to c.1860. There are separate links in the menu to those covering, the seventeenth century, the eighteenth century and the nineteenth and early twentieth centuries [1800-1911]. Recently, I have added a new *Sperrins* link which contains links to databases [in Excel format only] that cover the Sperrins area of Co. Tyrone and parts of Co. Londonderry.

The top menu contains a link to *Administrative Divisions* where you will find details of the administrative divisions that you need to be aware of when using sources. The *Case Studies* link will provide some working examples of the process of researching families and localities in North Antrim and Co. Londonderry, particularly in the nineteenth and early twentieth centuries.

Most of the records on this web site have been sourced from the Public Record Office (PRONI), Belfast and are reproduced with the kind permission of the Deputy Keeper of Records, Public Record Office of Northern Ireland.

Note that, recently, I have revised the database of the 1831 "Census Returns" for Co. Londonderry.

About the Author   Further Reading

1831 'census returns', the tithe applotment books or the Valuation books with their maps, etc. However, the enthusiasm and expertise of these two men (sadly no longer with us) opened a new window into the past for me.

The **Excel** database is primarily sorted by Barony, Parish and Townland. The names of each head of household within each townland are sorted by House Nos. - not alphabetically - as they were in my earlier databases. For those of you who do not have access to Excel I have included two **PDF** files. **PDF1** is a duplicate of the Excel file and **PDF2** provides an index of names sorted by Standardised Surname, Barony, Parish & Townland. Unfortunately, any search of a PDF copy of a database is more limited.

Excel	PDF 1	PDF 2

Working with 1831 "Census Returns" at Townland and Street Level.

Since 1967/68 I have studied many Localities within the County - probably around twenty Townlands in Rural Areas and a number of Streets in Derry/Londonderry, Coleraine, Limavady and Magherafelt. These Locality Studies have also generated associated Studies of Families.

In order to highlight the important role that the 1831 "Census Returns" often play in a Locality Study or a Family History Study, I have selected the Townland of Gorteade - Church Street in the Town of Coleraine - and William Street in the City of Londonderry.

Gorteade	Church Street in the Town of Coleraine	William Street in the City of Londonderry

1831 'census returns' database for County Londonderry

The course was very much hands on. All members of the class actually studied the sources that I mentioned above. I teamed up with another man, the late Joe Doherty who lived in the townland of Gorteade, located just outside the village of Upperlands in south Derry. We concentrated on his townland and both of us were amazed at what we were finding out about the place where Joe lived. Joe and I walked around his townland with copies of the 1831 'census' for Gorteade and the Griffith's Printed Valuation of 1859 and the accompanying Valuation map and we re-peopled that landscape with the occupiers of land listed in the source. We were also able to locate their houses and land within the townland during the first half of the nineteenth century. I then acquired other sources and the story of that townland and the surrounding townlands began to take shape. This study provided me with some of the evidence that I needed for my academic studies, but it also showed me how such work was of interest to anyone who wanted to know about life in their area in earlier times. Furthermore, people could identify with such studies – these were real people whom they knew, or whom their parents had known.

During the 1970s and the 1980s I gave talks to local history societies in various parts of the province and I was very much involved in local history both as an academic study and an important part of the schools' history curriculum. These different audiences meant that I was coming into contact with new townlands and streets. By the 1990s, for a variety of reasons, I became less involved in local history.

After I retired from university life in 2000, I became involved in the Glens of Antrim 'Clachan Project' *c.* 2003. This project rekindled my interest in local history and at the same time I became more interested in family history. This project, which ran until 2007, was followed by a CD-ROM – *Researching Derry and Londonderry Ancestors: A practical guide for the family and local historian.* This CD included Excel and PDF databases created from the microfilm copy of the 1831 'Census' in PRONI. That particular CD provided an index of names and places for the entire county, but did not include any of the statistical information on population and religion. Later, I included a copy of my CD database on this website. This meant that I could revise and update the database online. The early corrections concentrated on family names and placenames. The next step was to add all of the statistical data to the database. This final project, which took some three years, was finally completed in October 2018.

The inclusion of statistical data in the database means that the names and houses in each townland and street are now in numerical order. I already knew that the numbering of households within each townland and street was very important. Working with individual townlands and streets over the years it became clear to me that the numbering usually followed a geographical order which reflected the route that an enumerator took around a townland or street. Because of this, it is usually possible to match the names in the 1831 'census returns' with the *c.* 1830 tithe applotment books. Unfortunately there are no accompanying maps available for the tithe book locations in rural areas. However, it is often possible to match many of the 1831 names and locations with the 1858/59 Griffith's Printed (Tenement) Valuation and its accompanying maps. These maps and the printed pages of all of the Griffith's Valuation for Ireland are now available at www.askaboutireland.ie/griffith-valuation/. This means that, for some households, you might be able to get some idea of where individual houses and families may have been located within a townland or street in the first half of the nineteenth century.

However, a word of warning: it is not a 'perfect science'. There are times when the numbering in a part of a street or townland seems to be out of order because the enumerator may have forgotten a particular house and it is included at the end of a list. At this point I would need to say something about the religion data in the 1831 'census'.

NOTES ON RELIGION DATA IN 1831 'CENSUS'

Certainly, in the 1970s, when I first used the 1831 'census returns', I assumed that both the population data and the religion data in each townland were enumerated at the same time. However, I was surprised that religion data were not included in the *Abstract of Answers and Returns from the Population Acts, Ireland – Enumeration 1831*. This publication provided statistical data at parish, barony and county level. It also provided data on towns and villages, but not for townlands.

In the 1970s most of my use of the 1831 'census' was at townland level where I found the population figures and the religion figures always came to the same total. So, to be honest, I did not question whether or not the population and religion data were enumerated at the same time or at different dates.

This same question arose again during the later period when I was working on my database for the entire county. Even as early as the 1970s I was aware of the fact that the religion data from the 1831 Census was used in a religious census in the 1830s. Again, I had never really investigated this later religious census. I simply assumed that the creators of the 1834 Religious Census simply used religion data from the 1831 Census. I now know that was not the case. To be honest it made little difference when I was working with individual townlands and streets.

When I began to add the statistical data to my database I became more aware of the fact that the religion data did not always match the population data. I found 86 entries in the database where the numbers did not tally. In many cases this was due to discrepancies between the religion numbers and the population numbers. This, in turn, played havoc with totals for the entire county. Also, there are 55 entries in the database where no religion was given. The 55 entries totalled 642 persons but only 19 families. 50 of the 55 entries were in the city of Derry/Londonderry. The gaol, the asylum, the infirmary, a military barracks and 14 boarding/lodging houses made up the greater part of the 642 figure. Given the transient nature of the persons in these institutions and boarding houses, it is understandable that they were excluded from the later religion count.

A letter to *Irish Geography*, vol. XIV (1981) by Stephen A. Royle (published online 4 August 2009) confirmed that the enumerators had not recorded any religion data in 1831.

It now appears that the religion data in the 1831 'census returns' were used in a religious census which was part of the *First Report of the Commission of Public Instruction* (1834/35). You can read a copy of this report at the Dippam website (www.dippam.ac.uk). When you arrive at the website click on Open Document, then go to scanned page 5 (which is page 1 of the actual Report). Continue with scanned pages 6 to 12 (pages 2–8 in the actual document). These pages will explain how the details on religion were 'collected' and used. Look out for the following: how they gathered the information on religion (which was the main purpose of the exercise) and how they made use of the 1831 enumerators as well as the local clergy. Also how they caused tables to be framed showing the proportionate increase or diminution of the population of such rural districts and towns respectively, which, according to that assumption, might be estimated to have taken place between the years 1831 and 1834 (page 4 of the *First Report*).

Note also, that when I began to database the entire statistical data I had to look more closely at the microfilm pages, particularly those pages that indexed the townlands within each parish. There are 47 parishes in County Londonderry. Eighteen of them had later corrections to their religion data; three example pages include: Bovevagh, Killelagh and Killowen. Most of the corrections involved reallocating numbers across the various denominations. Rarely, was the total changed – and if it was it did not amount to much.

It is now a fact that the 1831 Census was transcribed into a new document that could be used by the persons associated with the enumeration of religion data for the religious census included in the *First Report of the Commission of Public Instruction* (1834/35).

THE COUNTY LONDONDERRY DATABASE

Turning now to the database, this resource (created within Excel) has 24 fields listed as Columns A to X. The paragraphs below explain the contents of each of these.

Column A or Field A lists a Record No. for each entry in the database. There are 41,787 records or entries in this database. Most of the entries are inhabited houses. I have also included 1,407 uninhabited houses, plus various public buildings such as churches and schools, and a number of industrial buildings, bringing the total of 'uninhabited' buildings to *c.* 1,531. In most of these cases these entries do not include any data on the occupants.

Columns B to D give details of the householders' names. With regard to the names of each head of household, I cannot guarantee that the surnames listed in the database are all correct. There are many variant spellings of certain surnames. To help overcome this problem I have used a system of 'standardised' spelling (Column B) to group together variant spellings of a name, thereby making it easier to see patterns in the distribution of surnames. In some cases I have added [?] at the end of a surname indicating that I am unsure about a particular spelling. For more details on surnames and townland placenames, read the article on my website – 'The Spelling of Townland Names and Surnames in the Databases'. At the end of the day, if in doubt about a surname you will need to consult the microfilms in either PRONI or in the Ballymena and Coleraine Libraries or the National Archives in Dublin.

Columns E, F and G provide the information on where each household was located (barony, parish and townland). Note that in 1831, in the barony of Loughinsholin, the townlands of Beagh

Temporal, Culnagrew, Knockoneill & Swatragh were part of Maghera parish. By the time of the Griffith's Valuation in *c.* 1860 they were part of Killelagh parish. Also, by *c.* 1860, in the barony of Keenaght, a new parish of Carrick had been created consisting of townlands taken from the 1831 parishes of Balteagh, Bovevagh and Tamlaght Finlagan. Likewise, by the late 1830s a new parish of Learmount had been created consisting of townlands taken from the 1831 parish of Cumber Upper and the parish of Banagher lying within the barony of Tirkeeran. The parish of Banagher in the barony of Keenaght remained intact. Within the database I have identified those townlands that were in one parish in 1831 and a different one by *c.* 1860. For example there were 17 townlands in the parish of Banagher (barony of Tirkeeran) in 1831. By *c.* 1860, eight of them were still in the parish of Banagher. The other nine townlands were in the new parish of Learmount (barony of Tirkeeran). In the database the name Banagher/Learmount identifies the nine townlands. There were also some townlands in the parishes of Aghadowey, Desertoghill and Errigal that are split between two parishes. These include the townland of Cullyramer (Aghadowey and Desertoghill) and the townlands of Mayboy, Shanlongford and Meencraig (Aghadowey and Errigal).

Column H provides the house number of each house within a townland or street. This house number is simply the number assigned by the enumerator. In general, I have found that the numbering of houses in each townland or street reflects the route taken by the enumerator as he moved from house to house along lanes and through fields in rural areas and along streets in towns.

Column J gives details of the number of families living in each house. There are 39,122 inhabited houses listed in this database. The official figure is 39,077. 37,423 of these houses were occupied by one family. The remaining 1,699 houses have two or more families in each house and I refer to these properties in the database as 'Shared Houses'. These houses require explanation and in order to filter them out in the Excel database I created **Column I**. This column does not contain data copied directly from the microfilm pages of the 1831 'Census' – any information in these columns has been created by me. For further notes on 'Shared Houses', the article on my website – 'An explanation of the term 'Shared Houses''.

Columns K to N provide the number of males and females in the family/families and the number of male and female servants living with each family/families. **Column O** gives the total number of persons living in each house as recorded on the microfilm pages. However, as I was creating the database I soon became aware of discrepancies between the 'official' total figures for households in Column O and the figures in columns K to N. In **Column P** I have used a formula to calculate a 'further' total that can be compared with the 'official' total in Column O.

Columns Q, R, S and T provide information on the religion of the members of each household – EC (Established Church) RC (Roman Catholic) PR (Presbyterian) and OPD (Other Protestant Dissenters) such as Covenanters, Baptists or Methodists, etc. No distinction is made between family members and servants in the columns on religion. However, usually, it is fairly easy to work out the religion of servants within a household. Note that there were no religion totals given in the microfilm pages for each household in a townland. Therefore I had to create **Column U**.

There are 55 entries in the database where no religion was given. I had to create a separate **Column V** that would identify these 55 entries. The 55 entries totalled 642 persons but only 19 families. 50 of the 55 entries were in the city of Derry/Londonderry. The gaol, asylum, infirmary, a military barracks and 14 boarding/lodging houses made up the greater part of figure of 642. Given the transient nature of the persons in these institutions and boarding houses, it is understandable that they were excluded from the later Religion count.

This later addition of the Religion data may have been partly responsible for a number of mistakes in the calculation the figure of 86 entries. So I have added a **Column W** which identifies these 86 entries with the code Ndt. I must admit that some of the mistakes could have been made by me when copying the numbers data from the microfilm pages.

Column X contains miscellaneous information and serves as a mechanism that identifies uninhabited houses, boarding/lodging houses, schools, churches and other public buildings. Sometimes families are found inhabiting some of these public buildings. There is also limited information on occupations. You will need to use Excel to 'Filter' out particular information in this column or field.

The following screenshot shows part of the data relating to the townland of Gorteade in the parish of Maghera. If you find it difficult to read the text simply read the exact same paper on my website.

Now you are ready to search the database. As I have said earlier, the Excel version provides greater flexibility.

However, for readers who have to use the PDF version, I have created a PDF2 file where the data are sorted by standardised surname, barony, parish and townland. Use PDF2 if you are simply looking for persons with a particular surname. With regard to the names of each head of household, I cannot guarantee that the surnames listed in the database are all correct. There are many variant spellings of certain surnames. To help overcome this problem I have used a system of standardised spelling (Column B) to group together variant spellings of a name, thereby making it easier to see patterns in the distribution of surnames.

I have also created a PDF1 file where the data are sorted by barony, parish and townland, and, the names of each head of household within each townland are sorted by house numbers – not alphabetically – as they were in the earlier databases. This PDF1 can give you an idea of where a family was living within a townland.

WORKING WITH 1831 'CENSUS RETURNS' AT TOWNLAND
AND STREET LEVEL

Since 1967/68 I have studied many localities within the county – probably around 20 townlands in rural areas and a number of streets in Derry/Londonderry, Coleraine, Limavady and Magherafelt. These locality studies have also generated associated studies of families. In order to highlight the important role that the 1831 'census returns' often play in a locality study or a family history study, I have selected the townland of Gorteade, Church Street in the town of Coleraine, and William Street in the city of Londonderry. These studies can be

Record No.	Surname [Standardised]	Surname as spelt in the Census Returns	Forename as spelt in the Census Returns	Barony	Parish 1831/c.1860	Townsland/Street [As Spelt in Document]	House No.	"Shared Houses"	No. of Families in House	No. of Males in Family	No. of Females in Family	No. of Male Servants	No. of Female Servants	Total Nos. in House in micro film pages.	Total Nos. in House SUM of Cols. K,L,M,N	EC	RC	PR	OPD	Total Religion SUM of Cols. Q,R,S,T.	No Religion	Numbers don't tally	Notes
24455	McGowan	McGowan	Sally	Loughinsholin	Maghera	Gorteade	1		1	5	3			8	8		8			8			
24456	Houston	Huston	David	Loughinsholin	Maghera	Gorteade	2		1	6	2			8	8			8		8			
24457	Kane	Kane	James	Loughinsholin	Maghera	Gorteade	3		1	3	5			8	8		8			8			
24458	Mallon	Mallon	Michael	Loughinsholin	Maghera	Gorteade	4		1	4	3			7	7		7			7			
24459	Lynch	Lynch	Bernard	Loughinsholin	Maghera	Gorteade	5	S.Hx	2	4	4			8	8		8			8			
24460	Lynn	Lynn	James	Loughinsholin	Maghera	Gorteade	6																Uninhabited.
24461	Lynn	Lynn	James	Loughinsholin	Maghera	Gorteade	7																Uninhabited.
24462	McCloy	McCloy	Alex.	Loughinsholin	Maghera	Gorteade	8		1	1	2			3	3		3			3			
24463	Henry	Henry	Rose	Loughinsholin	Maghera	Gorteade	9		1	1	4			5	5		5			5			
24464	Laverty	Laverty	James	Loughinsholin	Maghera	Gorteade	10																Uninhabited.
24465	Kane	Kane	Nedly	Loughinsholin	Maghera	Gorteade	11		1	3	5			8	8		8			8			
24466	McMaster	McMaster	George	Loughinsholin	Maghera	Gorteade	12		1	3	2			5	5		5			5			
24467	McMaster	McMaster	Peter	Loughinsholin	Maghera	Gorteade	13		1	1	2			3	3		3			3			
24468	McMaster	McMaster	Park.	Loughinsholin	Maghera	Gorteade	14		1	3	2			5	5		5			5			
24469	McMaster	McMaster	Sally	Loughinsholin	Maghera	Gorteade	15		1	1	4			5	5		5			5			
24470	Laverty	Laverty	John	Loughinsholin	Maghera	Gorteade	16		1	4	3			7	7		7			7			
24471	White	White	George	Loughinsholin	Maghera	Gorteade	17		1	1	4			5	5			5		5			
24472	Alexander	Alex.	William	Loughinsholin	Maghera	Gorteade	18		1	1	2			3	3			3		3			
24473	Kane	Kane	Archibald	Loughinsholin	Maghera	Gorteade	19		1	6	2			8	8		8			8			
24474	Stewart	Stuart	Archibald	Loughinsholin	Maghera	Gorteade	20		1	2	5			7	7				7	7			
24475	Nelly	Nelly	Joseph	Loughinsholin	Maghera	Gorteade	21		1	5	4			9	9			9		9			
24476	Cally	Cally	Daniel	Loughinsholin	Maghera	Gorteade	22		1	4	6			10	10		10			10			

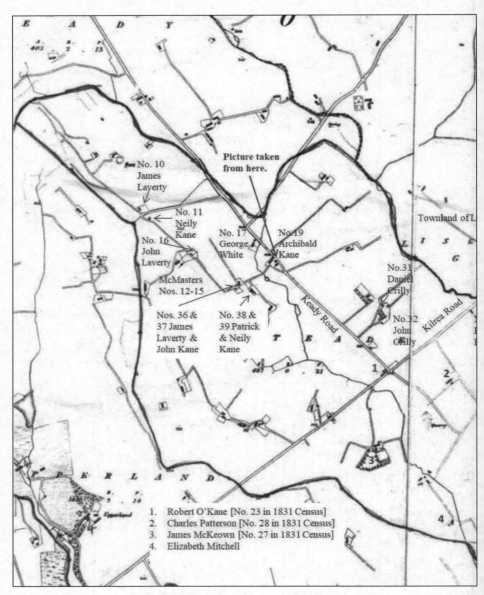

On the map:

E A D Y

No. 10
James
Laverty

Picture taken
from here.

No. 11
Neily
Kane

Townland of L

No. 16
John
Laverty

No. 17
George
White

No.19
Archibald
Kane

L I S G

McMasters
Nos. 12-15

No.31
Daniel
Crilly

Nos. 36 &
37 James
Laverty &
John Kane

No. 38 &
39 Patrick
& Neily
Kane

Kendy Road

No.32
John
Crilly

Kilrea Road

T E A D

1

2

3

4

E R L A N D

Upperland

1. Robert O'Kane [No. 23 in 1831 Census]
2. Charles Patterson [No. 28 in 1831 Census]
3. James McKeown [No. 27 in 1831 Census]
4. Elizabeth Mitchell

1st edition Ordnance Survey map of Gorteade, 1833

found on my website and only summary information on each locality is given here.

Gorteade

The townland of Gorteade straddles the main road from Maghera to Kilrea and was part of the civil parish of Maghera in the barony of Loughinsholin. Gorteade was the first ever townland that I studied in detail. This was back in the late 1960s/early 1970s. My companion during those early walks through the townland was the late Joe Doherty. Our task was to match the list of names in the 1831 'Census' with the list of names in the printed page of the Griffith's Valuation and then relate the numbering in the printed Griffith's page to the numbering of houses and plots of land on the 1859 Valuation Map and, ultimately, find each house and holding on the ground. The paper on my website titled 'Gorteade: Matching 1831 'Census' – 1828 Tithe – 1859 Griffith's Printed Valuation – and the 1859 Valuation Map' will take you through this process using databases and a look at the original sources, some of which are now available online. If you want more detail on some of the houses read the article on my website 'Houses in Gorteade 1831'.

Church Street, Coleraine

As its name implies, Church Street in Coleraine contains the parish church of St Patrick. The street runs eastwards from the Diamond towards Kingsgate Street which, as its name also implies, was the point where the King's Gate was located in the seventeenth century ramparts. The street is intersected by New Row and Park Street, formerly Rosemary Lane. Being part of the town of Coleraine, the street was located in the townland of Coleraine and Suburbs in the civil parish of Coleraine in the barony of North East Liberties. The records listed in this example will allow you to see the range of sources that you would need to consult in order to find out who was living in a street in a provincial market town during the period 1816 to c. 1860. The map of 1845 shows Church Street and the adjoining streets within the town. The 1831 'Census' is the only source that shows who was actually living in Church Street in that year. However, to find out,

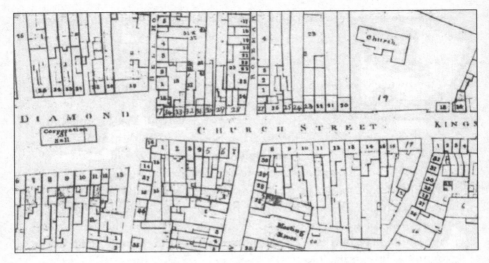

1834 Valuation map for Church Street, Coleraine

exactly, where families lived we need to match the census numbering to the valuation numbering. I have included the later 1859 Valuation because it can be useful in working out the exact location of some 1831 houses – as well as showing how much change took place in properties between the 1830s and *c.* 1860. See also Andrew Kane's excellent book *The Town Book of Coleraine*, published 2016 by Impact Printing, Coleraine & Ballycastle ((ISBN: 978-1-906689-68-1), which covers the entire tenements in the town leased from the Irish Society in 1816.

William Street in the City of Londonderry

William Street runs from the corner of Waterloo Street and Waterloo Place north-westwards towards St Eugene's Cathedral and is intersected by Rossville Street and Little James Street. Although the street lay outside the walls of the city, a distinction was made in nineteenth-century records between William Street (within), which lay within the city boundary in the townland of Londonderry, and William Street (without), which lay outside the city boundary in the townland of Edenballymore. Throughout most of the nineteenth century the city boundary in this part of the city was marked by Mary

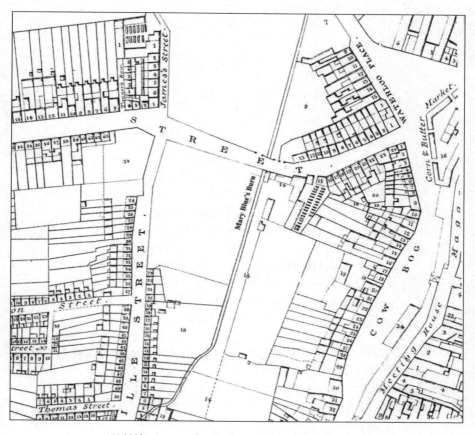

1834 Valuation map showing Lower end of William Street

Blue's Burn. The within, without division was dropped after the County Council Act of 1898. Comparing names and locations the 1830s is not as easy as it is in rural townlands. At the same time, sources such as Dawson's Voters' List of 1832 can be helpful. Also, there is not the kind of continuity in streets as there were in rural townlands.

A future for the past:
regeneration and compact living

ANGUS ANNAN

A breakthrough project in Belfast will see an iconic
Edwardian building converted to student residences.
The old College of Technology, that has been at the centre
of educational and industrial development of the city for
one hundred years, and lay empty for a decade, will now
be converted to address the growing requirement for
student residences.

The building was completed in 1907 and was known to generations of Belfast students and trainees as 'The Tech'. Like many other UK cities, Belfast has a growing population of students with two large universities and other tertiary education provisions driving the city student numbers to 40,000. The problem of student accommodation is not unique to Belfast with high student numbers in cities such as Leeds, student population 28,000, and Edinburgh, also at 29,000. Campus universities have the space to grow and to provide on-site accommodation but city universities have limited space for blocks of residences. The Belfast solution can be seen as a unique example of an alternative approach that may show the way for other cities.

At first sight the 'The Tech' will seem to have been an unlikely building for conversion. Built at the height of Edwardian confidence and splendour, it has large rooms with over four-metre high ceilings, corridors that could comfortably allow a military tank to pass and a magnificent Grand Central Hall with stained glass windows. The heating and ventilating system was advanced for its day with air ducts

The former College of Technology
© Mr Pany Goff

throughout the walls of the building, driven by a boiler house and a steam engine. All of this was operational until the closure of the building. The entrance foyer has classical columns with decorative plaster work and a grand staircase with wrought iron balustrading and as the structure is Grade B+ listed, all of these features have to be preserved. The Portland stone exterior elevations have been steam cleaned, needing only minimal repairs and pointing. The conversion also has the great merit of extending the operational life of the building in the education sector.

The Tech building must be typical of many in UK cities that have long outlived their original function and yet stand waiting for some lateral thinking and investment to take them to a new future. Some such city buildings in Glasgow and Aberdeen have found new life as grandiose restaurants and pubs but the Belfast example breaks new ground in addressing a growing problem of student living. Student life in the private rented sector is seen to be a difficult mix with ordinary family living. All the more so in the older terraced housing areas that still surround some universities where the student 24-hour lifestyle is causing long standing residents to move from the area, giving even more properties over to student lets.

Belfast was accorded city status in 1888 and the magnificent City Hall was opened in 1906. As industry grew in the city in the latter part of the nineteenth century with the population expanding to over 300,000 by 1901, Belfast was then the fastest growing city in the British Isles. The need for more technical education in the city was apparent. Such provision as existed then comprised the Working Men's Institutes, the Belfast Weaving School, the Technical School at Hastings Street and the Government School of Art. These all suffered from lack of space and underfunding. By 1889 the Belfast Chamber of Commerce was pressing for the establishment of a technical college to meet the expanding needs of a modern city. The Municipal Technical Institute of Belfast (MTIB) was set up in 1900 with the appointment of Francis C. Forth as the Principal and Director of Technical Instruction and the new building opened in 1907, constructed with the same stone as the City Hall. The previous disparate training offerings were all to be absorbed in the new institute. Initially evening classes were the main offering but as links were established with the engineering employers such as Harland and Wolff, Combe Barbour, Davidson's (Sirocco) and Workman Clark, provisions for day classes expanded. The college was to remain at the core of industrial training and the development of the city for close to one hundred years.

The choice of the site on College Square East was perhaps not altogether popular since the building would partially block the Georgian facade of the Royal Belfast Academical Institution ('Inst') and spoil the balance of the square. The fine Georgian-style houses on the north side included the Belfast Museum and the homes of some leading citizens. The governors of Inst had been in debt for some years and looked to the release of some ground as a solution, so a rental in perpetuity was agreed.

From the earliest years it was intended that higher technical education would be a feature of the operation and attempts were made to set up a collaborative arrangement with Queen's University so that technical students could progress to degrees. Eventually it became apparent that Queen's had no real interest in developing this link and the College decided to drop it. Another opportunity arose when the University of London allowed external students to sit for degree examinations. Very quickly Francis Forth arranged for the laboratories and workshops of the college to be recognised by the University of London and he was then able to announce progress to enable students to qualify for BSc degrees in Science and Engineering without leaving Belfast.

When the partition of Ireland came in 1921, it was industrial activity, and the productivity and the wealth that it created that stabilised the nascent state of Northern Ireland and assured the future. The college was central to this with training and materials testing facilities for the linen industry, mechanical engineering and ship building. Many of the great engineers of Northern Ireland took their early training at the college including Rupert Cameron (ship building), Chambers Brothers (motor racing) and Harry Ferguson (tractors). Thousands of students and apprentices were later to follow their example to such an extent that by the late 1950s the expansion was accommodated by holding many evening classes in the classrooms of secondary schools around the city. Day release classes were introduced in 1955 and the rapid expansion of these classes was covered by an annex created in the disused and rather grim Forth River Mills on the Falls Road. This accommodated all of the first year classes of the Ordinary National Certificates in mechanical and electrical engineering. It was hardly a stimulating environment, but it served as an interim measure for some years. A comment on this annex from a visiting American teacher on an exchange programme in 1959 and clearly suffering from culture shock: 'If the human mind set itself to the task, it could not conceive a place less conducive to learning than Forth River Mills'.

For all that, steady progress was made and the national certificate programmes made a huge contribution to technical education in the city, with the Higher National Certificate then taking five years of study and seen as the gold standard for many working class young men.

An important early step was the creation of the Trades Preparatory School, to focus on mathematics and technical subjects and to take boys forward from national school to enter apprentice training at sixteen. The school was later known as the Technical High School and entry was by an examination at the age of 12 plus. It was non-denominational and continued as an imbedded provision in the college until the late 1950s.

When the Tech conversion was completed in August 2016 it provided 292 en-suite study bedrooms in clusters with shared living rooms and kitchens plus 121 self-contained studios. There is 100 MB/s internet with free Wi-Fi throughout the building. The Grand Central Hall is to be the hub of the complex with common room facilities. It has been lightly conserved, retaining the stained glass windows with quotations from Shakespeare and other greats of the past. The library area, once the Chemistry Department, effectively a full upper floor above the central hall with exposed hammer beam roof trusses, has been retained and put to other uses in an innovative way. The building was originally constructed as a double doughnut with ground floor atriums and white glazed bricks lining the five-storey walls of the open courts. The atrium roofs have been removed to create open green courtyard spaces, brilliantly lit by daylight reflected from the glazed brick walls.

Apart from the challenges of converting a listed building, numerous practical problems had to be addressed. Ceiling heights were reduced, taking advantage of a match with the cross bars on the external windows and the high voids used as service ducts. Heating is distributed from a central gas boiler house and managed locally to each cluster or studio by a passive Heat Interface Unit (HIU), avoiding the need for individual gas boilers for heat and hot water. This approach improves heating efficiency with one large heat source running very efficiently, reducing CO_2 and saving on running costs, rather than multiple units running less efficiently. With Belfast downtown traffic running nearby, study bedrooms have been fitted up with acoustic double glazing and the wooden sash window counter weight columns have been specially treated to reduce the noise drum effect which would otherwise occur. Some modernisations from the past were reversed with replica doors constructed to match the surviving Edwardian wooden doors and stained glass panels back lit to advantage. Inescapably, the requirements of the Building Regulations and Disability Living had to be met and solutions negotiated with the Historic Environment Division.

The overall aim of the design was to produce premium quality student accommodation that will justify an appropriate rent level and contribute to the reputation of Belfast as an attractive city for higher education. The project was privately financed with an overall cost estimated at £16 million. Whist there is no internal retail provision it can well be imagined that regeneration in the form of cafes, sports and food supply shops will follow in the nearby streets.

The clear success of this conversion poses the question of whether this approach can be replicated in other cities where grand buildings from the past still stand empty, and perhaps loved only by a few, but in real need of a vision for a new future. It would be a shame if the listed status prevented change and served no real purpose other than to condemn the buildings to slow decay.

The Belfast Tech building will be known as the John Bell Building in honour of a well-known physicist who worked there.

The developer of the Belfast Old Tech was Watkin Jones/Lacuna. The regeneration project has been delivered under Design & Build procurement with Hamilton Architects working with O'Hare & McGovern Contractors.

SOURCES

Richard Hayward, *Belfast Through the Ages* (Dundalgan Press, 1952).
Bernard Crossland and John S. Moore, *Lives of the Great Engineers of Ulster* (Belfast Industrial Heritage Ltd, 2003).
Henry V. Bell, *Diligence and Skill: 100 years of Education at Belfast Institute* (Belfast Institute of Further & Higher Education, 2006).
Don McCloy, *Creating Belfast: Technical Education and the Formation of a Great Industrial City, 1801–1921* (The History Press, 2009).
The remark by the American exchange teacher was witnessed by the author.

Elementary education
in Victorian Belfast

DON McCLOY

Belfast was not entirely bereft of educational opportunity
in the early years of the nineteenth century. Indeed some
people were claiming that the growing town had by
then become an 'Athens of the North'.

Its better-off children had a range of educational opportunities: the
Academy, established in 1786, and the Academical Institution, in
1814, were the forerunners of the town's grammar schools – and,
indeed, of its universities. The early 1800s also saw various private
schools competing to enrol this class of children. For example, Robert
Telfair was offering lessons in writing, arithmetic, and book-keeping
from eight to nine in mornings and from four to six in afternoons in
his house in High Street.[1] An 1807 advertisement for 'Mr Acheson's
Commercial and Mathematical School' in Church Lane gives an idea
of the fees involved:[2] a quarter's teaching of English and Grammar cost
£1.2s.9d. Depending on your choice of economic model, that latter
sum would be worth between £700 and £1,400 in today's money.
There was a groundswell of opinion that these fees were far too high.
In 1792, a James Marten was complaining to the press about 'the
abuses and indolences of some of the Belfast schools'.[3] He alleged that
their main purpose was 'picking the pockets of parents'. Now, if
Marten, a master saddler, was finding the fees too high, what about
those poorer Belfast folk who were struggling to keep heads above
water?

Sunday schools provided a partial but nonetheless valuable response to the educational needs of poorer children. Henry Joy McCracken and his sister Mary Ann had launched such a school in the old Market House in 1786, but concerns about both the violation of the Sabbath and mixed education saw its demise after only a few years. A new Belfast Sunday School was opened in Ferguson's Entry in 1802; it was non-denominational. Thanks to the commitment of teachers and subscribers, the new school was able to move to much grander premises in Frederick Street in 1811. There, with attendances increasing, the new facilities allowed management to launch a day school as well as a Sunday school. In 1812 there were 695 pupils in the day school and a further 514 in the Sunday school.[4]

The Frederick Street day school adopted an educational methodology that had been developed by the Quaker Joseph Lancaster. Lancaster's scheme was economical and non-denominational. Its delivery was highly dependent upon senior pupils, or monitors as they were called. Before the school day commenced, the master would drill the monitors in their various tasks, and each would be expected to instruct, by rote, a group or 'draft' of pupils, usually eight in number.[5]

Lancaster's method used monitors to instruct 'drafts' of pupils

The growing popularity of this non-denominational Lancasterian School was a matter of concern in other parts of Belfast where religious and political views were not quite so liberal. The opening of a Presbyterian-dominated Sunday school in Brown Street in 1816 was one response to those concerns. Its curriculum focused initially on the reading of spelling books and the Bible, but the range of subjects was broadened considerably when a day school was added in 1821. There were no fewer than 600 boys and girls on the day school roll in 1825.[6]

The demand for Sunday schools in Belfast grew in step with population growth; there were 28 in the town and its environs by 1822. Created in 1821, the Belfast Sunday School Union embraced the large majority of these schools. By 1824 the Union could boast a membership of 28 Sunday schools, with some 300 teachers and 3,000 pupils.[7]

The Lancasterian Sunday School in Frederick Street was a notable absentee from the Sunday School Union's list of members. So too was St Patrick's School in Donegall Street. The Catholic hierarchy had decided to look after its own flock in its own way; so it set up its own Sunday school in St Patrick's Church in 1822. The new school was an immediate success with over 400 pupils attending its inaugural classes.[8] Like Brown Street and Frederick Street before, the Donegall Street Sunday school was soon complemented by a day school in a brand new building beside the church.

Gardiner Street area: Brown Street National School
PRONI Ref: LA/7/8/HF/3/22

NATIONAL SCHOOLS

The establishment of the Brown Street and St Patrick's schools provided further evidence of a growing gulf in the education of Protestant and Catholic children in Belfast. But the Whig government of the day was determined to achieve a truly non-denominational system of primary education in Ireland. After several unsuccessful attempts to do so, government decided in 1831 to place the matter in the hands of Commissioners for National Education in Ireland. This CNEI, as it was often called, would provide grant aid for the erection of new schools, for paying inspectors, providing gratuities to teachers, producing text books, and establishing and maintaining a model school in Dublin. Its first set of regulations was published in 1835.[9]

There was an initial intention to keep secular and religious education apart – with the latter taught outside school hours by the relevant clergy. But, the CNEI's insistence that pupils would only have access to the Bible at set times was to open a hornet's nest – especially in Presbyterian circles. In time, the various churches were voicing objections to the notion of a non-denominational system: they were concerned that the new arrangements were opening the door to proselytism.

Critics were rancorous in the extreme. When the national system was just getting underway in 1831, the Rev. Henry Cooke, champion of evangelical Presbyterianism, described it as 'the most cunning, the most daring, and the most specious attempt that has been made against Protestantism since the days when James II sent his ambassador to Rome to reconcile the nation to the Pope'.[10]

The CNEI struggled to placate the warring factions; it introduced its own series of religious books and instructed schools to make them available to all pupils at all times – not only at the times set aside for religious instruction. But, however tactfully composed, the content of these books still managed to offend religious sensitivities. In 1836 the Anglican bishop of Exeter described the CNEI's four-volume set of *Scripture Lessons* as 'a mutilation of the Holy Word'.[11] The Catholic hierarchy added fuel to the fire in 1837 when Archbishop MacHale asserted that 'to no authority on earth save the pope shall I submit the books from which the children of my diocese shall derive their religious instruction'.[12]

Thus, and not surprisingly, government hopes for a truly non-denominational system of primary education were dashed on theological rocks. By century's end some 62 per cent of the country's 9,000 national schools were attended by pupils of the one religious persuasion.

SECULAR MATTERS

The secular curriculum was not as. contentious as the sacred. The religious curriculum raised many passions, but the day-to-day secular curriculum with its relevance to the immediate needs of the town's children received much less attention and publicity. Designed initially for 6–12-year-olds, the original basic curriculum covered spelling, reading, writing, geography, geometry, arithmetic, agriculture or book-keeping for boys, and needlework for girls. Some schools introduced so-called Extra Branches – subjects like mensuration, drawing, music and algebra that were taught outside the usual school hours.

The CNEI insisted that rote learning would have a minimal role in curriculum delivery. Its Reading Books (later called Lesson Books), were an excellent innovation intended to broaden pupils' knowledge of the various subjects, including their practical uses. Book Five, the most advanced of the original set, included a substantial amount of scientific and technical material. A revised edition of 1846 included sections on mechanical properties of fluids, pneumatics, and the mechanical properties of air.

The words 'Book' and 'Class' tended to become synonymous in national schools. The particular book being studied indicated a pupil's stage of progression through his or her primary education. Pupils often needed more than a single year to master a particular book. Books one to three became the most common in schools, and the relatively small number of pupils who reached the fifth Book were usually around 12–14 years of age. In 1867 of some 700,000 national pupils, only around 50,000 were in their fourth or fifth books.[13]

Progression from one book to the next was granted when an inspector was satisfied that the pupil in question was ready for advancement. An inspector's most demanding task was the examination of every pupil in his schools. He heard every individual child read, inspected their writing, and tested their responses to questions on grammar, geography and arithmetic. On the whole, an inspector's job was an extremely demanding one. They reviewed the general state of a school, and looked to see if the practical rules for teachers were being observed – especially the primary rule of regularity and order – 'a time and a place for everything, and everything in its proper time and place'.

CURRICULAR EVOLUTION

Inspectors' reports were published annually, and taken together they exposed a gradual but continuing deterioration in pupil performance across the country. In 1869, for example, only 58% of national pupils passed the test on writing, and only 48% were able to demonstrate a satisfactory knowledge of geography. So Government decided in 1868 that the whole system needed a thorough review.

The ensuing Royal Commission reported in 1870.[14] Its ten-volume report, known as the Powis Report, concluded that pupil progress was less than satisfactory, that the competence of the teaching force had to improve, and that schoolhouse accommodation left a lot to be desired.

On curriculum, the Powis Report proposed new strict guidelines for teaching programmes and the related examinations. Compulsory subjects were to comprise the 3Rs for all classes; Grammar and Geography from third class upwards; Needlework for girls from first class upwards; and Agriculture for boys from fourth class and upwards. Powis also proposed a list of optional subjects that could be fitted in during or after school hours; they included Vocal Music, Drawing, Geometry and Algebra.

Perhaps the most significant outcome of the Powis Report was the introduction of a system of payment-by-results. A pupil's success in a particular examination at a particular level would bring a small financial reward to the teacher; eg 2s. 6d. for a pass in reading in third class. But payment-by-results had a stifling effect on curricular innovation: many pupils were crammed parrot-fashion to face annual inquisitions by inspectors, and teachers were tempted to pay most attention to the brightest and best attending of their pupils. Nevertheless, payment-by-results did, in fact, bring some overall improvements in pupil performance and in their attendance.

Despite the curriculum's several practical options like Handicraft, Cookery and Dairy Management, there was a groundswell of opinion that greater emphasis should be placed on practice. So another Royal Commission emerged in 1897; this one was asked to determine how far and in what form, manual and practical instruction should be included in the primary curriculum. The ensuing Belmore Report advocated a significant increase in the number of practical subjects: in addition to the 3Rs, pupils should have opportunities to study Practical Handwork, Drawing, Elementary Science, Cookery, Laundry Work, Needlework, Singing and Physical Exercise. This so-called Revised Curriculum would provide a better balance of the bookish and the practical.[15]

The Belmore Report sounded the death knell for payment-by-results. Inspectors no longer had the onerous task of examining every individual pupil. From then on, judgements about a school's effectiveness would be based on an inspector's observations of teachers at work and on oral examinations of representative groups of pupils.

DEVELOPMENTS IN BELFAST

In 1838, seven years after the inauguration of the national system, Belfast's primary school system was dominated by three schools – St Patrick's in Donegall Street, the Lancasterian School in Frederick Street, and Brown Street – although the last-mentioned did not join the national scheme until 1862.

But new schools were springing up across the town. In 1856, by which time the worst of the theological squabblings had subsided, the number of Belfast's national schools had grown to 40. Some, like the May Street School, were less than satisfactory, but many were more presentable and more effective. The Calendar Street schools, for example, were doing a good job. With 344 pupils in attendance the Catholic schools in Calendar Street had taken the lead in pupil numbers by 1856. Run by the Sisters of Mercy, the day school had an average attendance of 261, and the evening school 272. Inspectors' reports heaped praise on the Calendar Street School and its staff. Inspectors reported that: 'School-house consists of two commodious and convenient rooms, capable of accommodating about 250; rooms lighted with gas. Furniture good; a supply of prints, charts, tablets, etc; large globes; sets of maps, etc. Order and cleanliness of school and pupils excellent.'[16]

The number of Belfast's national schools increased in step with population growth: there were 71 across the town, with around 10,000 pupils in attendance when the Powis Commission started its review of the national system in 1868. The review showed that the Model

Schools on the Falls Road (see below) were well ahead in pupil numbers in 1868. Of the others, Brown Street and Barrack Street proved to be substantial institutions.

Continuing population growth put Belfast's national schools under considerable pressure – a pressure that intensified when the Attendance Act of 1892 required pupils to attend school until they were at least 14 years of age. The Act also prohibited the employment of any child who did not possess a leaving certificate of proficiency in the 3Rs.

These factors tended to increase the numbers attending the town's national schools. However, the schools' geographical distribution changed as Belfast grew. New and extended city-centre businesses forced a drift to the suburbs, which in those days were within easy walking distance from the city centre, for example, Ormeau, Balmoral, Malone, Ballymacarrett. New schools sprang up in the new suburbs. The migration to the suburbs reduced the numbers attending centrally-placed schools, so many of them had withered, closed or moved by 1870.

The size and shape of Belfast had changed considerably by 1905 when the population had risen to some 354,000. Of the 235 national schools at the time, 96 were under Presbyterian management, 53 Roman Catholic, 48 Church of Ireland, 20 Methodist, and 18 other persuasions.[17]

Belfast's primary schools fell into three major groupings; (a) ordinary national schools, (b) model national schools, and (c) half-time schools and agricultural and industrial schools where the emphasis lay on preparing young people for specific occupations. Each is described below.

ORDINARY NATIONAL SCHOOLS

The histories of Brown Street Schools and the St Patrick Schools in Donegall Street illustrate the range of opportunities available to the children in Belfast's ordinary national schools. They also give a feel for the problems faced by those who devoted themselves to the organisation and development of such institutions.

Brown Street

As mentioned earlier, the Brown Street Sunday and Day Schools had their origins as far back as 1812. The schools had set out to be non-denominational; but, with Presbyterianism the increasingly dominant creed amongst pupils and Management Committee, it was no surprise when the latter body backed the Presbyterian Synod's opposition to the Commissioners' restrictions on access to the Scriptures. The school's objectives underlined that opposition. In 1833 the aim was:

> to furnish such instruction in reading, writing, arithmetic and other branches of education as may prepare the pupils for usefulness in life – to train them up in habits of cleanliness and regularity – and to afford to all who choose it, a free and unrestricted access to the reading and study of the Holy Scriptures.[18]

Some 30 years were to pass before the Management Committee agreed to become a national school. However, affiliated or not to the CNEI, the Brown Street schools attracted respect and support from the citizens of Belfast. In 1852 the *Belfast Directory* described the school building as a 'commodious edifice' in which some 500 children of both sexes received a mercantile education. But subscriptions were falling, and that fact, plus a considerable relaxation in the CNEI's regulations concerning Bible reading, persuaded the school Management Committee to review its attitude to that organisation. It decided to seek the patronage of the CNEI in 1860.

The Brown Street schools continued to make important contributions to the education and welfare of Belfast's children throughout the last decades of the nineteenth century. However, enrolments in the day schools began to fall off as competing schools increased in number, and as local families moved out to the new suburbs and their new factories.

The new century brought little respite: in 1905 the average daily attendance in the Brown Street day schools had fallen to 229 – with nearly half of them infants.[19] However, a new development promised to bring increased numbers and increased funds to Brown Street. A neighbouring school – Campbell's Row National School – was also experiencing difficulties and it seemed that an amalgamation of the two schools would bring benefits to both. Under the control of the local Forth River Mill and the Falls Flax Company, Campbell's Row was largely concerned with half-time education – a system of primary education that was becoming increasingly popular in the town.

St Patrick's School, Donegall Street

Opened in 1829, St Patrick's Schoolhouse, Donegall Street, holds two records; it was the home of the first Roman Catholic school in Belfast, and, in 1833, the boys' and girls' schools became the town's first national schools. Four-square with pointed Gothic windows and Dutch gable, the schoolhouse still maintains an imposing presence beside St Patrick's Church.

The St Patrick's Schools sought and won grant aid from the CNEI in 1832. The application was signed by 15 Protestants and 18 Catholics. The building (at the present time listed and renovated) provided separate entrances to boys' and girls' schools. Both catered for substantial numbers of children, and both established evening departments.

But change was afoot. Dr Dorrian, Catholic bishop of Down and Connor, was concerned that Presbyterians were dominating the management of Belfast's national schools. Seeking more Catholic schools, he adopted an increasingly sympathetic attitude to the Christian Brothers who had opted out of the national system because it was inconsistent with the original aim of their society – namely, to give a sound Catholic education to pupils. Bishop Dorrian encouraged the Brothers to set up a school in Belfast, and he arranged for the national school in Divis Street to be converted for that purpose.

And so it was that the Christian Brothers opened their first school in Belfast in November 1866. Divis Street was soon attracting a large clientele, and, impressed by its success, the Bishop encouraged the Brothers to open another school in town. This time he sanctioned arrangements for them to take over the St Patrick's schoolhouse in Donegall Street. The Brothers set up an Industrial School for destitute children there in 1869; but it was a short-lived venture soon to be replaced by a more effective Industrial School in Milltown in 1873.

Back in Donegall Street the Brothers decided to concentrate on the development of a strong primary school.

That development saw the closure of the Donegall Street national schools; their pupils had to seek education elsewhere. Many boys went to the new Christian Brothers' School on the same site, but some moved to the new Industrial School at Milltown. Many girls transferred to other Catholic schools as well as to a new Industrial School run by the Sisters of Mercy on the Crumlin Road.

The Christian Brothers' School remained the sole occupant of the St Patrick's schoolhouse until 1887. However, by that time, the CNEI's restrictions on religious instruction had eased somewhat and the national system had become overtly denominational: so the climate was set fair for the re-establishment of national schools in the Donegall Street schoolhouse. From 1887 onwards the national and the Christian Brothers' Schools shared the building and both displayed their plaques above the twin entrance doors.

A third Christian Brothers' school followed in 1874. Built in Oxford Street and still standing, it was the gift of a Mrs McGill who saw the need for a school for the children of Catholic dock labourers and sailors. It housed St Malachy's Christian Schools.

Despite growing competition from the Brothers schools, the new Donegall Street national schools proved reasonably popular post-1888. Both schools, male and female, enrolled relatively large numbers of pupils, but attendances declined as other Catholic schools sprang up across the city.

MODEL NATIONAL SCHOOLS

The model schools were meant to be the jewels in the CNEI crown.[20] Each of the country's 25 school districts was to have its own District Model School. Ballymena and Newry, the first two in Ulster, opened their doors in 1849; the Belfast Model Schools followed in 1857. By 1867 Ulster had eight District Model Schools and a further six Minor Model Schools. (Minor Models played lesser roles in teacher training.)

At the opening of the Belfast Model in May 1857, the senior inspector defined a model school as one[21]

> established on such principles, organised on such plans, regulated by such a course of discipline, and conducted on such a method

of instruction as to be a model or pattern for teachers, school managers, and school committees to imitate … In addition, a model school is either attached to an institution for the training of young teachers, or is itself … a seminary for the same purpose.

The various district models had, in turn, to follow the example set by the Central Model School in Dublin's Marlborough Street.

Belfast's Model Schools were situated on a one-acre site at the bottom of the Falls Road. The building had two storeys and was square in plan with a small central quadrangle. In addition to boys', girls' and infants' schools, it housed an evening school for adults. Playgrounds to the rear and side provided separate recreation facilities for boys, girls and infants.

Each of the boys', girls' and infants schools at the Belfast Model had their own large schoolroom and associated classrooms. A schoolroom on the second floor was devoted, in the main, to adult evening classes; the building also contained a laboratory and apparatus for practical instruction. All schoolrooms had 'draft circles' placed at regular intervals on the floor around the room. These, marked by brass strips, were central to the Lancasterian teaching methods that were in vogue at the time. At intervals throughout the day, children of various classes would assemble at their draft circles where they would 'toe the line' whilst they listened to their teacher or monitor.

The Model School curriculum had a substantial practical flavour. At the School's formal opening in 1857, the Head Inspector remarked that: 'Exercises on the measurement of railway cuttings and embankments, of carpenters', bricklayers', masons', plumbers', painters' and glaziers' work, of ship's tonnage etc., will afford ample material for putting into practical operation the theoretical instruction in mathematical science.'

Inspectors carried out annual examinations, but the schools also arranged their own public examinations. These were grand occasions attended by parents and local dignitaries: after various musical entertainments, the children would sit on a temporary platform in the largest schoolroom where they would be quizzed by their teachers.

In addition to coping with some one thousand pupils every day, the Boys' and Girls' Models also prepared young people for careers in teaching. In those days of rampant gender discrimination, male trainees were called Pupil Teachers, and females Monitresses. Monitresses resided in private lodgings or in the homes of friends or relations, but the male Pupil Teachers had the privilege of living together with the Principal Teacher in property provided by the school authorities.

In their early years, the Belfast Models could claim to have been truly non-denominational – around one third of pupils were Catholic in 1858. However, the Catholic hierarchy's growing aversion to mixed education saw that percentage drop to a mere 5 per cent ten years later. The schools suffered a further setback when the Powis Commission of 1870 recommended their closure on the grounds that staff were enjoying preferential treatment, and pupils were dominated by children from the middle and upper classes. The Belfast Schools flourished nevertheless. They are still extant, although the original Falls Road buildings were burnt to the ground in 1920.

FOCUS ON INDUSTRY

National schools taught some practical subjects like handicraft and sewing but, other than training for the teaching profession, they made little attempt to prepare their pupils for particular careers. The large majority of schools set out to provide a general education that would help their pupils face up to the many and varied rigours and challenges of adult life. However, the CNEI devised other arrangements for providing some of their young charges with specific industrial training – half-time education, and agricultural and industrial schools.

Half-time education

Although criticised by many, the so-called half-time system gave many youngsters an introduction to the real world of industry and an opportunity to earn a wage whilst still of school age. The half-time system became popular in Belfast. But the system led to much abuse of child labour: the 1833 Factory Act obliged owners to ensure that children in their employ would attend school two hours a day for six days a week. Those regulations were stiffened in 1867 when employers were offered the choice of requiring children (a) to work for six and a half hours and attend school for three hours every weekday, or (b) to work for ten hours every weekday and attend school every other day.[23] The first arrangement placed an awful burden on children who often arrived at school tired and dishevelled. The alternate day scheme became the norm after 1874.

The mills and factories connected with the linen trade were by far the largest employers of Belfast's half-timers. Schools at Jennymount, Campbell's Row, and Beersbridge were the largest providers of half-time education in 1899. However, it became illegal after 1901 to employ children under 12 years of age. Numbers of half-timers fell thereafter.

Agricultural schools

Agricultural education became a significant component of the CNEI's portfolio in the nineteenth century; in a country heavily dependent upon agriculture Commissioners felt duty-bound to improve the standards of Irish agriculture. In 1838, the CNEI opened a model farm in Glasnevin to the north of Dublin. The complex straddled 52 acres, and included residential accommodation for trainee teachers. It set out to provide instruction in agriculture to pupils as well as preparing prospective teachers of the subject. Like other such schools, its agricultural produce was expected to make a useful contribution to running costs.

The year 1848 saw the appointment of an inspector briefed to oversee the development of agricultural education right across the country. Thereafter agricultural schools began to proliferate: they ranged from substantial and well-equipped farms to ordinary national schools with small farms and gardens attached.

There was an impressive development in Belfast. When the Falls Road site was purchased for the Belfast Model Schools, the CNEI also bought 109 acres of land at Balmoral. The ground was to be used for the establishment of a New Model Farm and a New Model Agricultural School. There was to be a close connection between the two model schools; the District Model supervised the literary instruction of the agricultural students, and its Headmaster and pupil teachers resided on the Balmoral campus.

But the Agricultural School was short-lived. The land at Balmoral was hard to work. With a mere four inches of topsoil and a subsoil of stiff clay, it proved well-nigh impossible to make the farm a viable enterprise. So the Model Farm and its Agricultural School closed in 1875 when it was converted into an Industrial School. The original buildings still survive on the site of today's Musgrave Park Hospital.

Agricultural education in national schools started on a downward spiral. Gardens and horticulture displaced farms and agriculture. Government concluded that agriculture needed the services of an education system at a level higher than primary, and that development was to be one of the major responsibilities of a new Department of Agriculture and Technical Instruction in 1901.

INDUSTRIAL SCHOOLS

Despite their name, Ireland's earliest industrial schools were more concerned with the alleviation of social problems than with improving the country's industrial capability.[24] They catered for pauper, vagrant, mendicant, orphaned and neglected children. In the first decades of the nineteenth century, the care of such children was left largely in the hands of religious orders and local philanthropists. Orphanages, both Catholic and Protestant, could be found in most parts of the country.

Those voluntary organisations were later complemented by new CNEI institutions. In 1846, the CNEI decided that it would offer some support to this worthy cause; so it launched a system of Industrial National Schools. Successful applicants for Industrial National School status received grants towards salaries and books. In addition to organised industrial instruction, all pupils had to receive at least two hours of literary instruction every week day. And suitably qualified instructors and rooms for practical work had to be available. The CNEI's annual report for 1854 heaped praise on the work of Belfast's Female Industrial National School in Frederick Street.

Whether voluntary or affiliated to the CNEI, the country's various Industrial Schools received a boost when the Industrial Schools (Ireland) Act was passed in 1868. From then on, instead of depending solely on philanthropic support or on CNEI grant, interested parties could apply for public grants towards the maintenance (but not the construction) of certified Industrial Schools. The boys and girls would have to receive a minimum of six hours of industrial education every weekday.

Following that legislation, St Patrick's School, Donegall Street, Belfast's first national school, broke yet another record when it launched the first Certified Industrial School for boys in the whole of Ireland in Milltown in 1869. The school catered initially for some 65 boys, and it had a small five-acre farm attached. As well as tending vegetable plots, the boys were taught boot-making, cabinet-making and tailoring.[25] The Milltown buildings were extended to accommodate 150 boys in 1878. Workshop products were sold on the open market and provided the boys with a small but steady income.

St Patrick's also opened a girls' Industrial School on the Crumlin Road on the same day – 27 August 1869 – as the opening of the boys' school at Milltown. Catering for 110 girls, it was managed by the Sisters of Mercy. Of the 56 new certified Industrial Schools created in 1880, 45 catered for Catholic pupils. The Sisters of Mercy and the Christian Brothers were the dominant providers.

Some of the town's disadvantaged Protestant boys received appropriate industrial training at the Balmoral Industrial School. First certified at Fox Lodge in 1884, the school later enjoyed the extensive premises of the former Ulster Model Farm at Balmoral. With over 400 boys on the books, the Balmoral Industrial School had become the largest Industrial School in Belfast by the end of the nineteenth century; and it was the only Industrial School for Protestant boys in the whole of the country. Its numbers practically quadrupled in 1899 when the training ship *Grampian* was abandoned and its inmates transferred to Balmoral. The *Grampian,* formerly called the *Gibraltar,* had been deposited in the mud flats of Belfast Lough in 1872 with the intention of preparing its young inmates for seafaring careers. However, the Belfast boys showed little enthusiasm for marine careers – in 1892 only seven of the 50 discharged that year went to sea.[26]

Belfast made a notable contribution to the development of certified Industrial Schools. The start of the twentieth century saw over one thousand boys and girls in the city's seven Industrial Schools. In addition to the St Patrick's Schools with their Catholic clientele, Hampton House in Balmoral Avenue and Shamrock Lodge at Ballysillan catered for Protestant girls. A 1901 survey placed Hampton

House and Shamrock Lodge top of the league of girls' Industrial Schools. Catholic boys and girls attended respectively Nazareth Lodge on the Ravenhill Road and the Sacred Heart at Whiteabbey. Unfortunately, the reputations of many of the country's Industrial Schools were destroyed in later years when extensive evidence of unacceptable treatment of the young inmates came to light.

CONCLUSION

The historical evidence points to troublesome but positive developments in primary education in Belfast throughout the nineteenth century. As the century progressed and as Belfast's industrial revolution gathered pace, the content of the school curriculum became more relevant to the needs of the time, and the organisation and funding of the system of primary education improved considerably.

NOTES

1   *Belfast News Letter*, 10 Aug. 1792.
2   Ibid., 18 May 1807.
3   *Northern Star*, 26 Dec. 1792.
4   Anon., 'Report of the Belfast Lancasterian Schools', *Belfast Monthly Magazine*, vol. VII, June 1812.
5   Anon. *The British System of Education; Being a Complete Epitome of the Improvements and Inventions practised by Joseph Lancaster, 1778–1838* (Washington, 1812).
6   *15th Report of the Committee of the Belfast Sunday and Brown Street Daily School Society* (Belfast, 1825).
7   *Belfast News Letter*, 12 Oct. 1824.
8   Ibid., 21 May 1824.
9   Donald H. Akenson, *The Irish Education Experiment: The National System of Education in the Nineteenth Century* (Routledge and Kegan Paul, 1970).
10 J.L. Porter, *The Life and Times of Henry Cooke* (London, 1871).
11 *Third Report of the Commissioners of National Education in Ireland* (Dublin, 1836).
12 *Dublin Evening Post*, 13 Feb. 1838.
13 *Royal Commission of Inquiry into Primary Education (Ireland)* (Dublin, 1870), p. 291.
14 *36th Annual Report Council for National Education in Ireland*, Appendix B (Dublin, 1869).

15   *Commission on Manual and Practical Instruction in Primary Schools Under the Board of National Education in Ireland: Final Report of the Commissioners* (Dublin, 1898).

16   *Twenty-Second Report of the Commissioners of National Education in Ireland*, Appendix E (Dublin, 1856).

17   *Appendix to the Seventy-Second Report of the Commissioners of National Education in Ireland* (Dublin, 1907).

18   82nd Annual Report of Brown Street Sunday and Daily School Society, 1894.

19   PRONI, ED/2/401, 6 Apr. 1905.

20   Robin Wylie, *Ulster Model Schools* (Ulster Architectural Heritage Society, 1997).

21   *Belfast News Letter*, 20 May 1857.

22   Op. cit.

23   Betty Messenger, *Picking up the Linen Threads: A Study in Industrial Folklore* (Blackstaff Press, 1982).

24   Christina J. Barnes, *Irish Industrial Schools 1868–1908: Origins and Development* (Irish Academic Press, 1989).

25   Barnes, op. cit.

26   Barnes, op. cit.

The Drennan-Duffin Archive:
a very Irish unionism

RICHARD HOLMES

One of the first publications of the new Public Record Office of Northern Ireland, founded in 1924, was *The Drennan Letters* (1931), edited by the Deputy Keeper Dr D.A. Chart. William Drennan, a founder of the United Irishmen in 1791, and of Belfast Academical Institution in 1810, acquitted in 1794 on a charge of sedition, was remembered by some as a literary man, part of an Ulster Enlightenment, and by others as a political radical, a Protestant nationalist.

The publication was the result of almost 40 years' work by Drennan's granddaughter, Maria Duffin, and her daughter Ruth Duffin, who edited, transcribed and annotated over 1,400 letters kept in a disordered box by Maria's father, Dr J.S. Drennan. This was only part of a lifetime's effort by Ruth and Maria to understand and memorialise their family history. Maria, an astonishing survivor from early Victorian Belfast, died aged 100 in 1954; Ruth, aged 92, in 1968. Ruth, originally a poet and novelist, in her latter years devoted her archival skill to compiling the records of her own lifetime, especially of her early life, the years of the Irish Home Rule crisis (she gave them to the Public Record Office).[1] Patricia Craig, in her recent memoir of her own complex Ulster family, suggests that Ruth in her role as Warden of the all-Protestant women's Riddel Hall at Queen's University may have betrayed her ancestor's legacy.[2] The allegation has often been made, but may be unfair. This article will tell the story of Ruth and the

Duffin family's efforts to preserve Drennan's memory, and how their concern with family history intersected with the politics and culture of their own time.

Ruth Duffin was born in 1877, eldest of nine children of Adam Duffin, a Belfast stockbroker, Liberal Unionist politician and later Northern Ireland Senator.[3] The Duffins had been early Ulster linen entrepreneurs and were Presbyterians (family money built Strand Church, Belfast and Cuningham Memorial in Cullybackey). The Drennans, William and his son, John Swanwick, were doctors. They belonged to the less orthodox Non-Subscribing Presbyterians; William's father Rev. Thomas Drennan, intimate friend of the Scottish and Irish Enlightenment writers, Francis Hutcheson and James Arbuckle, had been one of the first Non-Subscribing ministers. The Duffin children were brought up in their mother's church, as what Adam in the 1911 census called 'Unitarians'. The family were at the heart of Belfast's bourgeois elite. Rt Hon. Thomas Sinclair, wealthy shipowner, leader of the Liberal Unionists and architect of the Ulster Covenant of 1912, was an uncle (his daughter, Effie Sinclair Crichton, Ruth's closest friend, was a novelist whose work, according to reviewers, promised to do for Ulster what the Brontës had done for Yorkshire).[4] Their cousins included the Andrews family of Comber (also Drennan descendants), Thomas, another prominent Liberal Unionist and his sons J.M. Andrews, later Northern Ireland Prime Minister, and shipbuilder Thomas (one file of Duffin papers relates to the *Titanic* tragedy, in which Thomas, the ship's designer, himself perished).[5]

Ruth Duffin's first reference to the Drennan letters was in 1897, aged 19, when she noted in her diary that her mother had received a letter from a 'Mr Scott' asking about them. W.R. Scott, later Professor of Political Economy at Glasgow University, came from a family similar to the Duffins, Non-Subscribing Presbyterians and mill-owners from Omagh. Maria was pleased to help his research, eventually giving Glasgow University a collection of letters between William's father, Rev. Thomas Drennan, and Francis Hutcheson.[6] Scott's inquiry was the first sign of scholarly interest in the eighteenth-century Irish Enlightenment. He went on to publish a pioneering study of Arbuckle, the only biography of Hutcheson and, in his work on Adam Smith, to coin the phrase 'the Scottish Enlightenment' (he called Hutcheson its founder).[7] Later, the Drennan archive was the basis for an extensive range of historical research on the 'liberal' tradition in Protestant Ulster, in work by some of Ulster's best-known historians, notably A.T.Q. Stewart's *A Deeper Silence* and Ian McBride's 'William Drennan and the Dissenting Tradition'.[8] There was also, shortly after Scott's inquiry, a request from a different quarter, the nationalist William Drennan Centenary Club seeking a portrait of their hero for the centenary of the 1798 Rising. They received a polite rebuff from the Duffins: William 'had nothing whatever to do with rebellion'. Ruth wondered whether this would make them seem 'degenerate descendants'.[9]

Chart's edition of the Drennan letters was a selection only; a full edition in three volumes was funded by the Dublin government as part of their bicentennial commemoration of the 1798 Rebellion, and published by the Irish Manuscripts Commission under the chairmanship of the late Dr Brian Trainor. One of the committee, Martin Mansergh, saw this as supportive of the 1998 Belfast Agreement, saying that the Ulster Protestant Drennan should be remembered as 'the father of democracy in Ireland and of constitutional republicanism'.[10] The potential for controversial commemoration of Drennan was evident in 1891, in the first 'United Irish' centenaries, politically charged then by conflict over Gladstone's Home Rule proposals. In that year, a group of 'Parnellite Nationalists' paid tribute at William Drennan's grave, located in the Clifton House graveyard. Ruth's 83-year-old grandfather, Dr J.S. Drennan, wrote to the *Northern Whig* to dissociate himself, on the ground that 'my father had he been alive would have been a unionist'.[11] This prompted an angry response from one nationalist, Robert Johnston, father of the poet Ethna Carbery, who called Drennan 'a revolutionist of the most advanced type' and went on 'if the memory of the father suffers it will only suffer at the hands of the son'.[12] In March 1892, at a meeting of the Liberal Union club, Ruth's uncle Thomas Sinclair, as chairman, used the Drennans to illustrate what he called the change in Belfast Presbyterian sentiment from the 1790s.[13] He accepted that William Drennan was the author of the United Irish oath but insisted that he was 'never identified with the treasonable intentions of Wolfe Tone'. He repeated Dr J.S. Drennan's assertion that in the changed circumstances of the 1890s William would have been a unionist. In June of that year Sinclair was one of the organisers of the Ulster Unionist Convention, intended as the largest display of united unionist opposition to Home Rule, bringing together former political opponents, Liberal and Tory, Anglican and Presbyterian.[14] Old Dr Drennan produced a poem for the occasion, 'We Meet', which both asserted his Irish patriotism and his opposition to Home Rule.[15] Despite this family involvement in the Convention, there was some dissent from the insistent unity. The family church, the Non-Subscribing Presbyterians, were concerned that opposition to Home Rule was seen as 'the outcome of Orange intolerance and bigotry'. Fearing that the Convention was tending to threats of illegality, they voted not to send delegates (Dr J.S. Drennan was the oldest member present at the meeting but said nothing).[16] Adam Duffin, also a council member of the Liberal Unionists, struck his own mildly contrary note in the Convention planning. Ruth's diary recorded that 'Papa had insisted on placing 'Erin go Bragh' ('Ireland for ever') on the outside, though some people objected, why I don't know and can't imagine'.[17]

'Erin go Bragh' was also the motto of the Shamrock Club, an artistic society started by the teenage Ruth and her cousin Effie Sinclair in 1890 with the aim of promoting their native culture; Adam Duffin was the president. The Duffin family had a sense of national identity at odds with many at the 1892 Convention. One of the themes of the Convention was a claim to ethnic entitlement by 'Ulster Scots' as descendants of the seventeenth-century settlers. If the British government allowed Home Rule they would be betraying what Thomas Sinclair later called 'a sacred trust'.[18] The Duffins had no claim to Ulster-Scots identity (neither they nor the Drennans nor the Sinclairs could in fact trace seventeenth-century settler forebears). Ruth had been brought up to see herself as Irish and her family research partly aimed to establish a secure Irish ethnicity. Ruth and Effie were encouraged in their early artistic work by Adam's four unmarried sisters, the 'Duffin aunts' of Strandtown Lodge, Belfast.

At Strandtown, Ruth recalled, they would recite the 'Shan van Vocht' and 'the Wearin of the Green', for the benefit of their Duffin grandfather, 'a loyal old gentleman with a partiality for rebel songs'. Sometimes they would unfurl the green banner of the Irish Volunteers of 1789, and would feel ready to die for 'the Emerald Isle' (the phrase was in fact coined by Drennan in his poem 'When Erin First Rose').[19] Ruth shared her interest in family history with her aunts and this led to 'an ancestor hunt' to County Tyrone in search of ancient Duffins. In the village of Donemana, according to family myth, had lived a Charles Duffin, 'said to have fought for King James at the Boyne, and whose estates were confiscated ... for his rebellious principles'. They visited the ruined Donemana castle, Ruth recording that 'I hoped it was the ancestral seat ... but I'm sure it wasn't'. The best they found was an old vault in the name of 'Divin'.[20] Ruth's 1913 poetry collection *The Secret Hill* includes 'The Wild Geese', a nostalgic tribute to the exiled Jacobite gentry. She imagined their flight,

> Dead hopes behind us flinging,
> With only toil before ...

and later their return through Irish skies on their way to eternal rest, pausing over 'the land of their delight'.[21] This Irish identity was built partly on the family sense of William Drennan as an Irish patriot. This Irishness did not imply nationalist politics; the point of grandfather Drennan's poem 'We Meet' was that a true Irish patriot could believe in the union of 'Albion and Erin'.

The man most closely associated with Protestant nationalism in Edwardian Belfast was the eccentric solicitor F.J. Bigger, a friend and neighbour of the Duffin family.[22] He too had a close interest in Ulster genealogy, in the recovery of the history of the United Irishmen and in William Drennan (he knew the Biggers were Scots but he was a Celt by adoption). He was more warmly received than the William Drennan Centenary Club. Indeed, when Maria Duffin invited him to tea in 1896 to discuss his research, they agreed that they were relatives, through William Drennan's mother, a Miss Lennox from Derry.[23] When, in her twenties, Ruth decided to learn Irish, she turned to Bigger for help. He supplied a private teacher whom Ruth called 'a

Gaelic Leaguer'. She does not appear to have joined Bigger's Irish classes at Ardrigh, although she and her mother dined there, and were surprised by the portrait of his dead mother propped on a chair at the head of the table, with flowers in front.[24] On 30 April 1906, Ruth with all her extended family attended a ceilidh in the Ulster Hall organised by Bigger to celebrate the May festival of 'Beltaine'. That summer Bigger organised a major celebration of Gaelic culture in the Glens of Antrim village of Cushendall. Ruth attended with one of her 'Strandtown Aunts'. She wrote up her impressions in 'An Irish Feis', published in the Cheltenham Ladies College (her old school) magazine, carefully insisting that the organisers, the Gaelic League, were non-political.[25]

Through her twenties Ruth continued to work on editing and transcribing Drennan's letters alongside her own writing, her Irish lessons, a busy life of social engagement and charitable activity which she described as 'my Jekyll and Hyde life' and her tentative efforts, in default of marriage, to find a career. The letters, inherited in a state of total disorder, were not yet ready for publication. But Ruth missed no opportunity to talk about them to anyone who might be interested: in 1904 to her father's political colleague Sir Horace Plunkett; in 1907 to a Belfast clergyman, Canon Bristow, who showed her a miniature of a girl that Drennan was said to have loved, and led her to think about publishing the letters with portraits of all the main characters. In 1909 she met John Philpot Curran, descendant of William Drennan's lawyer, and showed him his ancestor's letter congratulating Drennan following his acquittal on sedition charges. The modern Curran she found 'a thoroughly delightful and irresponsible Irishman'. Ruth's own writing in these years included fiction, poetry and essays, and all had an Irish theme. She and Effie Sinclair met regularly, often at Strandtown Lodge, to read each other's work. Effie had more success with publishers, her first work published by Edward Arnold in London in 1908, and it seems that this may have persuaded Ruth to abandon fiction.[26] Her poems and essays however began to be published in journals. One notable outlet was the *New Ireland Review*, edited by the Jesuit Fr Thomas Finlay, which published her poems and an essay on 'Mr Shaw and Irish Character'.[27] Ruth had been introduced to Fr

Finlay by Sir Horace Plunkett. At the same time she was taking tentative steps towards employment, leading her, after work for the social reformer Hilda Martindale, to try what she called 'the Irish movement'. Again through Plunkett, she found a job working under George Russell ('AE') for the 'United Irishwomen', a satellite of Plunkett's aimed at involving women in the Co-operative Organisation.

Ruth's article on Shaw shows how she understood her 'Irish' identity in relation to contemporary Ulster unionism. Shaw claimed in the preface to *John Bull's Other Island* that, in contrast to common conception, the Irishman was rational, the Englishman sentimental. Ruth praised his play for showing the opposite. The real strength of Irish culture, she said, was in spirit and imagination. The Irish could not play at English pragmatism; what they offered the world was spirit and imagination. She discussed various Irish stereotypes, including the Belfast businessman:

> [he is] the most hardheaded and practical of men, second only to the Yankee in business capacity and push; a tireless worker with an inexhaustible fund of energy, and an eye in which the Hibernian twinkle had vanished in the effort to keep it fixed on the main chance; in fact, a man in whose busy life poetry and idealism were considered a mere waste of time.

This was close to the Ulsterman of Unionist propaganda, the epitome of reason and enterprise who, according to Uncle Thomas Sinclair, should not be forced into Home Rule with southerners who had neither. Ruth's article was a subtle rejection of the Sinclair ethos. It also relied on a nationalist reading of Irish history, in which Ireland had been prevented by colonial oppression from developing an independent economy. Ireland's future was as a retreat for the spiritually oppressed of industrial Europe. She concluded with a wish that the Irish would keep alive 'that higher factor of their nature which has survived so much adversity, and fulfil again her spiritual mission to the world'. Her cousin Effie, in her novel *The Blind Side of the Heart* (1915) took a rather different view. Her hero, Sandford, an English engineer building a reservoir in Ireland's west, falls in love with Eithne, a Protestant enthusiast for Celtic culture, whose portrayal may owe something to Ruth. She teaches him emotional enlightenment, the lesson Matthew Arnold had the 'Teuton' learn from the Celt. But he then abandons her for a sensible Edinburgh girl, preferring the 'warm and lamplit rooms' of the modern world to the wild 'visions' of Eithne.

In 1910 Ruth and her mother judged the work on Drennan sufficiently complete to make the first serious attempt to publish the letters, approaching Maunsel of Dublin, who were known as the leading publishers of the Irish Revival. The approach was unsuccessful. In 1911 F.J. Bigger brought out his own edition of one of Drennan's pamphlets, 'The Legislative Union: A Protest', calling on Drennan's memory as a rebuke to contemporary unionists, by then in a fury of resistance to the new Home Rule bill. In his preface he wrote 'Relatives and friends of the writer are still with us; let them not prove degenerate sons of a worthy sire'. There is no record of Duffin family involvement in this publication or response to it.

Ruth's contact with Maunsel probably came through her publications in *New Ireland Review*. In 1913 they published her poetry collection *The Secret Hill* (which also included work by her sisters, poems by Celia and drawings by Emma). The poems were reviewed in the *Irish Book Lover*, the journal of the Irish Literary Society. Bigger was closely associated with the Society, frequently writing in the journal, including a review of Effie's County Down novel *The Soundless Tide* and a note revealing her identity as daughter of Rt Hon. Thomas Sinclair. The review of *The Secret Hill* (which was anonymous) drew attention to the connection with Drennan, 'who first conferred on his country the title of The Emerald Isle'. In February 1914 Ruth was invited to speak to the Society on Drennan. Bigger does not appear to have been there but she was introduced by his close friend Dr J.S. Crone, who said that he took 'a grandfatherly interest', having known both J.S. Drennan and Charles Duffin, 'the leader of the old Liberal party in Belfast and champion of the people'. Ruth's talk made no attempt to evade Drennan's Irish patriotism or his radicalism, her talk including letters that showed Drennan as the originator of the United Irishmen in 1791. Love of Ireland, she said, was his ruling passion.

Apart from some help with footnotes from Isaac Ward, a noted local historian (soon after knocked down aged 83 by a pony and trap on North Street), little progress was made on the Drennan papers during the 14–18 war. The Duffin family were heavily engaged in the war. Four of Ruth's sisters volunteered as Voluntary Aid Detachment nurses (the war diaries of Emma Duffin were published in an edition by Trevor Parkhill in 2014). Her brother Terence Duffin was awarded the Military Cross in 1917 for gallantry in France. Maria Duffin's diary for this period goes little beyond a list of deaths and decorations. One exception was the sad entry in November 1918 recording Effie Sinclair's premature death (the fact that it was a suicide was not, however, mentioned).[28] There is an indication of the strength of family feeling about the war in a letter from 'Docie' (Theodosia), one of the 'Strandtown aunts', to F.J. Bigger. Regarding him as a friendly link with nationalist Ireland she thanked him for help already given and suggested that he might be able to ensure publication of some patriotic verse in 'the Nationalist press':

> one can make people welcome to their politics however differing from one's own but one cannot get over the disappointment that so many thousands of our countrymen are turning a deaf ear to the fight for righteousness and freedom in this worldwide struggle against military despotism …[29]

In 1921, in the midst of political drama over partition and civil war, the Duffins had a breakthrough with 'the old letters'. James Winder Good published a long article 'Two Ulster Patriots' in the Irish Jesuit journal, *Studies: A Quarterly Review*, which called for the letters' publication. Good, educated at Belfast 'Inst' (where Ruth attended for gym and extra-curricular activities, and where Adam was school secretary), had been one of the founders of the Edwardian Ulster Literary Theatre, of which Ruth and her family had been enthusiastic supporters. Good had been given access to the letters and praised the Duffins for their

> patient care sorting and arranging the mass of manuscript. It would not be easy to exaggerate the difficulties of the task. Drennan's correspondence, mainly with his sister, Mrs. McTier, runs to more than a thousand letters, ranging over a period which saw Grattan's Parliament, the struggle for reform culminating in the '98 rising, the passing of the union, and the years of reaction that followed the triumph of Pitt and Castlereagh. These letters were huddled together without sequence or coherence, and, since

many of them lacked either date or post-mark, the task of fitting them into chronological order was exceptionally difficult. Mrs. Duffin's industry and insight triumphed over all obstacles, and she has completed her labours as editor by appending to the letters a valuable series of biographical and explanatory notes. It is imperative that the correspondence should be published.

Good, a journalist, out of sympathy with unionist Ulster, had moved in 1916 from the Belfast *Northern Whig* to the Dublin *Freeman's Journal*. But, perhaps at the Duffins' request, he avoided any direct reference to contemporary politics. He drew a distinction between the romantic revolutionary Wolfe Tone and the more cautious Drennan, whose writing rather reflected 'the gossip of quiet folk in middle class parlours'. This might have looked like faint praise beside his injunction that the letters should be published, especially in a politically violent time. It did not produce offers and in 1924 approaches to both Oxford and Cambridge University presses provided further discouragement (the former said that publication would cost £1,100).

Publication came finally with the settling of borders and bureaucracy in the new divided Ireland. Dr D.A. Chart, who had been employed in Dublin Castle, elected to move to the north in 1922, shortly before the destruction of the records in the Four Courts.[30] One of his goals in the newly established Public Record Office of Northern Ireland was to track down privately held archives to replace what had been lost. His first publication, of the seventeenth-century Phillips survey of County Londonderry, was unlikely to be controversial. The Drennan letters, with their political potential, and connection to influential citizens, might be different. The publication was to be underwritten by the Department of Commerce but he suggested that the Duffins seek subscriptions from family and friends to offset the cost. The printed list of subscribers (itself an eighteenth-century fashion) provides a fascinating glimpse of the extended Duffin network in Ulster's liberal-leaning upper middle class and beyond. There were however some notable absences. Maria Duffin, by now a widow of 75, had contacted her relatives asking them to subscribe, and was distressed by the response of John Millar Andrews, the son of her cousin Thomas, brother of Thomas of the *Titanic*. He was at the time a Unionist minister of Labour (and later Prime Minister):

Johnnie evidently took fright at its being revealed that my
grandfather was a United Irishman. He came to make enquiries
from Edmund who told me. I wrote a letter stating the facts with
the result that not one of that family even replied ... Curious and
true- N of Ireland bigotry and narrowness. Poor Annie promised
one- no reply either from Eileen Andrews. I only hope JMA will
not interfere with the Record office ...[31]

In fact her fears were misplaced, and perhaps unfair (Andrews's father
had been quite happy in 1910 to supply Drennan material for the 'Inst'
centenary and to be known as his grandson).[32] Andrews in any case did
not interfere and in May 1930 the Minister of Commerce approved
funding for the project.

In Effie Sinclair's County Down novel, *The Soundless Tide*, her
protagonist Gillian Ward, wife of an Orange squire, dreads the Orange
march:

Oh dear, said Gillian, I had almost forgotten that tomorrow was
the Twelfth. It makes me hot again to think of it. What drumming
there will be, and the screaming of their wicked little fifes, and all
that crowd of enthusiastic men ... You never saw their dreadful
trampled field ... in the days when [my appearance] was expected
I had always a craven hope that the Twelfth would be wet, and
that I might stay at home.

That is very similar to Ruth Duffin's response to the Twelfth, as in
1910 when she insisted on going to work: 'Made my way into the
office through the procession and braying bands'. Liberal Unionists
like the Duffins and Sinclairs came from a political tradition that had
been defined by opposition to Orangemen and Tories. In the resistance
to Home Rule they found it necessary to unite with their former
opponents; hence the 1892 Convention. But even in that unity there
was scope for ambivalence. Adam Duffin's friend Sir Horace Plunkett,
an erstwhile Liberal Unionist MP, whom Ruth called 'a moderate
Home Ruler', told her he was sure her father had not signed the 1912
Covenant. In fact her father did sign but with an express reservation
that he might support a future measure of Home Rule if properly
passed into law (Ruth herself does not appear to have signed).[33]

Even in 1892 Adam had been concerned by Unionist threats to defy the law. Later he disapproved of what he saw as a growing 'ulsterization' and anti-Catholicism in Thomas Sinclair's opposition to Home Rule ('I want to impress on them not to harp on religious divisions').[34] The differences between Adam Duffin and Sinclair illustrate the scope for shades of opinion within unionism. They were present in the response of the 1890s to William Drennan. J.S. Drennan's protest at the visit of nationalists to his father's grave was supported by Dr. W.K. McMordie, brother of a Unionist Lord Mayor of Belfast, who insisted, however, that 'the men of '98 understood freedom, and asked for reforms merely to enable them to live as free men in their own country. We owe much of our present freedom to those who suffered in '98.'[35]

That was very far from the Conservative *Belfast News Letter*'s unequivocal condemnation: 'the United Irishmen never did and never could confer a benefit on the Irish people'.[36] It did not, however, go as far as the Ballymoney doctor James Nevin, representing a still more radical Presbyterian tradition, also writing to the *Northern Whig*. He said that the Parnellites should be given the same respect as the United Irishmen: 'I am a Protestant and I cannot believe that Nationalists would destroy my liberty'.[37]

William Drennan, according to his son and to Thomas Sinclair, was a conditional unionist: he said in 1817 that, as an Irishman, he could support union with Britain provided that all Irishmen were fully and fairly represented (he had in mind especially Catholic emancipation). The Duffin family could probably also be described as conditional unionists, supporting union provided it was compatible with their prized Irish identity, with a liberal outlook and in particular religious toleration. When it came to their ancestor's memory they were unwilling to assist convinced nationalists like Robert Johnston, or the related Centenary Club. F.J. Bigger and J.W. Good represented a strain of nationalist sympathy in Protestant Belfast, and both were determined to see William Drennan remembered and his papers published. The Duffins were willing to cooperate with them. The Duffins like the Drennans were closer to J.W. Good's description of 'quiet folk in middle class parlours' than to revolutionists, their papers of value, like their ancestor's, as a record of social life fully enjoyed as much as politics. But politics there were in both, and the enduring influence of Drennan on his descendants can best be summed up in Ruth's closing words on Drennan in her talk to the Irish Literary Society in 1914:

> He died on February 5th 1820 and by his directions his body was borne to the grave by six Protestants and six Roman Catholics, a wish which shows that to the end of his life he remained true to his principles of religious toleration and the union of Irishmen of all shades of opinion.

NOTES

1   The Duffin Papers (as yet not fully catalogued) are at PRONI, D2109 and include Ruth's personal diaries and letters (D2109/17/2–14 and 7–8).
2   Patricia Craig, *A Twisted Root: Ancestral Entanglements in Ireland* (Belfast: Blackstaff Press, 2012).
3   Obituary *Northern Whig*, 14 Mar. 1924.
4   Graham Greenlee, Gordon Lucy and William Roulston, *Thomas Sinclair: 'Ulster's most Prominent Citizen'* (Belfast: Ulster Historical Foundation and Ulster-Scots Agency, 2016); 'Effie' was the family nickname of Frances Elizabeth Sinclair; Obituary, *Belfast News Letter*, 3 Dec. 1918.
5   There is a contemporary biography paying tribute to Thomas's heroism, with preface by Horace Plunkett, Shan Bullock, *Thomas Andrews, Shipbuilder* (Dublin: Maunsel, 1912).
6   The letters dated 1736–46 are in Glasgow University Library, Special Collections, Ms Gen. 1018.
7   W.R. Scott, *Francis Hutcheson* (Cambridge, 1900); Obituary, *The Times*, 5 Apr. 1940.
8   Ian McBride, 'William Drennan and the Dissenting tradition', in *The United Irishmen, Republicanism, Radicalism and Rebellion*, D. Dickson, D. Keogh, K. Whelan (eds) (Dublin: The Lilliput Press, 1993), pp 49–62.
9   Diary of Ruth Duffin, 18 Dec. 1897, PRONI, D2109/17/4.
10 *Irish Times*, 3 Aug. 1998.
11 *Northern Whig*, 21 Oct. 1891.
12 *Northern Whig*, 23 Oct. 1891.
13 *Northern Whig*, 9 Mar. 1892.
14 Greenlee, *Thomas Sinclair*, p. 90.
15 *Poems and Sonnets* (London: Gilbert and Rivington, 1894).
16 *Northern Whig*, 31 May 1892.

17   Diary of Ruth Duffin, 12 June 1892, PRONI, D2109/17/3.

18   'The Ulster Scot is not in Ireland today upon the conditions of an ordinary immigrant', Thomas Sinclair, 'The Position of Ulster', in *Against Home Rule: the Case for the Union*, edited by S. Rosenbaum (London: F. Warne, 1912).

19   Correspondence of Charlotte, Ellen, Bessie Duffin, PRONI, D2109/4/3.

20   Diary of Ruth Duffin, 7 Aug. 1908, PRONI, D2109/17/12.

21   Ruth and Celia Duffin, *The Secret Hill* (Dublin: Maunsel, 1913).

22   Guy Beiner, 'Revisiting F.J. Bigger: a fin-de-siecle flourish of antiquarian folklore scholarship in Ulster', *Bealoideas* (2012); Eamon Phoenix, 'Francis Joseph Bigger: historian and Protestant nationalist' in *Feis na nGleann: A Century of Gaelic Culture in the Antrim Glens* (Belfast: Ulster Historical Foundation, 2005).

23   Letter Maria Duffin to F.J. Bigger, 14 Feb. 1896, F.J. Bigger papers, Belfast Central Library, MSS DU6–8.

24   Diary of Ruth Duffin, 28 July 1906, PRONI, D2109/17/10.

25   *Cheltenham Ladies College Magazine*, Autumn 1906.

26   E.F. Sinclair, *Peep-in-the-World* (London: Edward Arnold, 1908).

27   *New Ireland Review*, June 1909.

28   The only reference to suicide is in the death certificate, 25 Nov. 1918.

29   Letter Theodosia Duffin to F.J. Bigger, 20 Dec. 1916, F.J. Bigger papers, Belfast Central Library, MSS DU6–8.

30   Sean Magee, 'D.A. Chart 1878–1960: archivist, historian, social scientist', *History Ireland* (2003).

31   Maria Duffin diary, 30 Oct. 1929, PRONI, D2109/19/1.

32   *Belfast Telegraph*, 24 Nov. 1910.

33   Letter Ruth Duffin to Maria Duffin 15 Nov. 1912, PRONI, D2109/8/4; Patrick Buckland, *Irish Unionism*, vol. 2 (Belfast: HMSO: 1973), p. 225.

34   Adam Duffin to Ruth Duffin, 1 May 1912, PRONI, D2109/8/4.

35   *Northern Whig*, 22 Oct. 1891.

36   *Belfast News Letter*, 14 Oct. 1891.

37   *Northern Whig*, 23 Oct. 1891.

Irishmen exploring the Antarctic:
life aboard the icebreaker *Aurora Australis*

JAMES BARTLETT

Virtually the last stop before the continent of Antarctica,
Hobart in Tasmania has a long and rich maritime heritage.
Looking out across the city's bustling harbour, it is hard to
miss the emergency orange-coloured *Aurora Australis*,
which is the country's research vessel and icebreaker.
Moored here for six months of the year, it can be dwarfed
by the super-sized cruise ships that come through en route
to their guided tours further south, but its missions are
still vital – and harken back to over a century ago, when
explorers leaving here were setting off into the unknown.

Government vessels like the *Aurora Australis* are usually off-limits to
the public, but on my recent trip to Australia my wife and I were
lucky enough to secure a private tour – and were surprised to find that
two of the crew members had Irish roots. Born in Belfast, bosun (or
boatswain) Joe McMenemy is the senior deck crewman, responsible for
everything from the hull to rigging, anchors, cables, sails, and more.
He recalled how he first came to Australia in 1964, though his stay was
less than a year as his parents separated and he and his mother and two
sisters returned to Belfast, settling in Ballymurphy. When The Troubles
began in the late 1960s and early 1970s, the family emigrated for good,
taking the ship *Fairsky* on the long journey to Sydney, where they lived
with relatives in a suburb called Balmain.

Our guide for the extensive two-hour tour was ship's master Gerry
O'Doherty, who is in charge of vessel navigation. He told us some

interesting and amusing stories, and admitted that Argentina and New Zealand are in fact 'a tiny bit closer to Antarctica' than Hobart (depending on where you want to land). 'My dad Michael was from Donegal Town, and my mum Colleen was from Lifford, and I have relatives from Derry to Kerry', he said. 'Apart from two cousins here in Australia, all my family are there'. He explained that his father first came to Australia in the early 1950s with the RAF, who he had served with in the Second World War, and was then later seconded to the RAAF (Royal Australian Air Force).

Even so, it took a trip back to Ireland for Michael to meet his future wife. 'He was on leave when they met, and she came out to Australia to join him in 1957 and they got married. I came along a few years later', he laughed. Gerry explained further by email that the early 1970s was a 'tricky time' to be traipsing around Ireland for his Irish Catholic father who had roots in Donegal, but followed a career and working life with the RAF and RAAF.

'My dad was actually born in Dunoon when his Irish parents lived there for a time in the 1920s, so he was entitled to – and obliged to – a British citizenship as well as his Irish one, and there were some in his clan that didn't approve of his allegiance to "The Crown"', he noted.

'I think it was that very torment that made Australia an attractive place for him to call home; my mother much the same. At home in Australia though, they would often openly reject any Irishmen (and women) that wanted to bring The Troubles with them to Australia.'

Known affectionately as the 'Orange Roughie,' the *Aurora Australis* was built in Newcastle, New South Wales. 'That's where I was born', said Gerry proudly, adding that he and Joe were two of the eight crew (out of a total of 24) that remained on board while the ship was moored here during the heaviest winter months.

Both men have been at sea for decades. Joe has been 'working on all types of ships' since 1981, and on board the *Aurora Australis* for the last 12 years. Gerry has been there longer – close to 20 years – and while the ship once assisted in the offshore oil and gas industry, the focus now is fully on conservation and environmental matters, with the goal of monitoring climate change and keeping the Antarctic as pristine as possible. 'We're even locating and digging up decades-old old refuse dumps, and taking them away', said Gerry.

A multi-purpose research and resupply ship, the *AA* was launched in September 1989. It is 94.91 meters long and displaces 8,158 tons. The two engines – 12 and 16 cylinders – help the ship carry up to 116 passengers, and are nicknamed Jake and Elwood in tribute to *The Blues Brothers* film from 1980 that starred John Belushi and Dan Aykroyd. Fitted out with laboratories for biological, meteorological and oceanographic research, she can also facilitate up to three small helicopters, and at full capacity on a six-week voyage this also means that the huge ship's kitchen can get through 4,500 eggs, 1,000 kg of potatoes and 280 litres of ice cream.

The tricky – and dangerous – business of ice breaking is done in two ways: cracking large pieces and essentially bouncing them off each other like a game of pool, or with pure force – pushing as hard as the engines will allow. It can make for some very strange noises on board.

'It takes new crew members a while to get used to cracking, groaning, and screaming – it can seem like the hull is going to come apart', recalls Gerry.

Surprisingly, the image of the Antarctic as a windy and wild waste was not exactly true – at least when you are in the icebreaker. 'Everything is very quiet because of the ice. When it snows it gets even quieter, and the weight of snow, even though it looks soft, can make breaking really difficult'.

The desire to keep the Antarctic untouched is perhaps most obvious when you see pictures of dogs along the walls of the former bar. Though the ship has been 'dry' for years it is still called 'The Husky Bar', though the huskies themselves – once the very symbol of exploration – were banned from the Antarctic, just like all other animals.

Despite that lack of a bar there is clearly a great sense of humour on board, judging by some of the sea-related graffiti found in the workshops and research rooms. There is also an official-looking 'sign' that says: 'Quiet – Watchkeeper Asleep'.

As well as the bridge, cargo hold and other areas, Gerry showed us more homely parts of the ship including the sauna, gym, and library, whose wall of books contained many thrillers, but also, plenty about Antarctic exploration. 'It is hard to imagine now, in an age of GPS and computers, what it was like back then', said Gerry, 'and it's important to read the old books'.

In that heroic age of exploration, some Irishmen returned from their adventures as heroes. Kerryman Tom Crean took part in three major expeditions to Antarctica, including the tragic 1910–13 *Terra Nova* attempt on the South Pole that saw the death of Captain Scott – though Crean was awarded the Albert Medal for his earlier efforts on a long, solo walk to save a colleague. However, many of them were never seen again. County Down-born Francis Crozier was captain of the *HMS Terror* when it and the *HMS Erebus* successfully explored Antarctic region in 1843, though he was later to perish in the tragic search for the Northwest Passage at the top of the world in 1845. This disastrous venture – led by Sir John Franklin – was dramatised recently in television series 'The Terror', where Crozier was played by Jared Harris, and Franklin by Belfast-born actor Ciarán Hinds.

Moving back into the present day, Gerry told us that the *Aurora Australis* is at the end of its operational life-span of around 30 years, and that the crew's future is perhaps uncertain. A competition among Australian schoolchildren for the next icebreaker's name came up with *Nuyina* (which is the Tasmanian Aboriginal world for 'Southern Lights'), and this far larger vessel currently under construction in Romania at a cost of around $500m–$1 billion (AUD), though it will still be based in Hobart.

Gerry and Joe live happily with their respective families in different parts of New South Wales, but both express regret that they have not visited Ireland for years. 'I was only a young teenager when I visited there, so I didn't get to drink a lot of Guinness, only what I could get my hands on when the parents weren't looking', laughed Gerry. 'We spent a lot of time in the Lifford, Letterkenny and Donegal Town area. I loved the friendliness and warmth of the people (even if we were related). But most of all it was their great sense of humour that enamoured me to them'.

As for Joe, he admitted that he has not been back to Ireland since 1982, but he hopes to go back in 2019 'as it has been too long. I still have relatives over there and communicate with them on Facebook', (the notoriously temperamental onboard Wi-Fi notwithstanding).

Even so, while they both consider themselves 'Aussie through and through, we're still proud of our Irish heritage, and we still feel a bit of a "visitor" here', said Gerry.

Our heads spinning with information – and the sun slowly setting outside – we were about to climb down the long ladder back to terra firma when Gerry told us one more Irish-Australian connection: 'P & O, the company that owns the *Aurora Australis*, also owns and operates the *RV Celtic Explorer*, which is on charter to the Irish government and is off the south coast of Ireland right now'.

Update: A recent press release announced that the *Aurora Australis* 'will continue resupplying Australia's Antarctic stations through 2019/20, after which its replacement *Nuyina* is expected to be operational'. It was good news for Gerry and Joe, even though it might mean a delay on any travel plans, and just a little more time at the bottom of the world.

The history of Dublin Presbyterianism[1]

LINDE LUNNEY

The history of Presbyterianism in Dublin involves complex theology and politics and intriguing personalities, but is little understood in contemporary Ireland. In 2013 the Presbyterian Church in Ireland celebrated the 400th anniversary of the arrival in Ireland of the Scottish-born and -educated Edward Brice, acknowledged as the first Presbyterian minister to have a congregation in Ireland, at Ballycarry, County Antrim, from 1613. Thereafter for some time the Scottish church provided the first ministers for the rapidly increasing numbers of Scots settlers in Ulster in the last quarter of the seventeenth and first quarter of the eighteenth centuries, beginning the long association between Irish and Scottish Presbyterianism.[2]

However, looking at Presbyterian history from a Dublin viewpoint, one could somewhat peevishly point out that the 400th anniversary party could have taken place years earlier, if organisers had taken cognisance of other strands of Presbyterianism and of other parts of the island. The year 1994 would have been an equally suitable choice of a date, to celebrate the arrival in 1594 of the first identifiable Presbyterian minister in Ireland, though it should be acknowledged that this man did not serve a congregation as such in Ireland. The English puritan Walter Travers is one of the first, if not the very first, person in Ireland to have been ordained in the Presbyterian manner (possibly in 1578, in Antwerp), and became the most prominent Presbyterian in England. Probably to his own surprise, Travers was appointed first resident provost of Trinity College, Dublin in 1594.

131

The first fellows to be elected in Trinity, James Fullerton and James Hamilton, were Scots Presbyterians, and Humphrey Fenn, another of the early fellows, was an English Presbyterian.[3]

Though very soon there were congregations in Dublin influenced by the much more strongly-Calvinist theology of Scottish Presbyterianism, English Presbyterianism continued to influence dissenting congregations in Dublin. During the Cromwellian period in particular, the English brand of Presbyterianism was dominant for a time, and three congregations with a Presbyterian flavour were founded in Dublin by English Independents and English Presbyterians.[4] For most people, 'English Presbyterian' is almost an oxymoron; there are a few new offshoots of Presbyterianism in England today: the original denomination melded with the Congregationalists in 1972 to form the United Reformed Church.

Some of the Presbyterian congregations in Dublin gravitated towards the Scottish/northern form of Presbyterianism and eventually adhered to the Synod of Ulster. These split and re-formed and merged a few times (congregational history can be very confusing), but are represented today by Abbey congregation, whose roots go back to at least 1672. However, in the eighteenth century and possibly residually after that, the English brand of Presbyterianism persisted in some of the Dublin congregations and elsewhere in the south of Ireland. Those congregations met in the Presbytery of Munster, founded in 1696, which in 1809 joined the Presbytery of Dublin (founded soon after 1696) to form the Synod of Munster. Theologically there were significant differences between the Scots and the English modes of being Presbyterian. The English Presbyterian church after 1719 advocated a reliance on scripture alone, rather than on accepting any contemporary or man-made formulation of faith, whereas the northern and Scottish Presbyterians strongly supported the Westminster Confession of Faith and the use of the Larger and Shorter Catechisms derived from it.[5]

The split between the two theologies fanned the flames of what is known as the 'first subscription controversy' in Irish Presbyterianism in the early eighteenth century, when the denomination divided over whether or not signing up to the Westminster Confession or other doctrinal summary should be mandatory for ministers. Ministers influenced by a tendency towards non-subscription, not wishing to sign ('subscribe') a man-made formulation of doctrine, also increasingly distanced themselves from the view of salvation current in the Calvinism of the Scottish Presbyterian church. What was known as 'New Light' theology introduced a new tone and new vocabulary to Presbyterian discourse; highlighting the individual's own moral capacity and impulses and sincerity of belief as essential to salvation, and a relatively large proportion of the denomination turned away from the strictly Calvinist view that Christ's grace was sufficient for redemption. As the spread of the enlightenment and even of deism affected beliefs in all denominations, liberalism, incipient Arianism, moves towards Unitarianism, all influenced several congregations in Dublin, Cork and elsewhere in the southern half of the country, as well as more than a few in the northern parts, from the mid-eighteenth century on. At the same time, the mother church in Scotland was increasingly influenced by tendencies towards strict controls and to a dogmatism tied to the Westminster Confession.

In several towns like Clonmel and Cork and in Dublin itself there are or were churches called the 'Scots Church'. These congregations were not in general associated with a Scots founder or members, but the name was used to signify the congregation's orthodoxy on subscription and opposition to the New Light. Dublin's Scots Church retained that name until it merged with Ormond Quay congregation in 1938. However, the Scottishness which underlies culture and society in Ulster, and even more, the kind of Scottishness chosen as an identity by people in Ulster at various times in the past and in the present, has affected, *inter alia* of course, how one part of Irish Presbyterianism, that in the north, has viewed their own co-religionists in the Presbyterian Church in Ireland.

A defining moment in the evolution of the separation between north and south, which seems to have influenced Presbyterianism and also perhaps, politics, for generations to come, occurred when Rev. Henry Cooke, the autocrat of northern orthodoxy, attacked non-northern, non-Scottish Presbyterianism. Cooke (1788–1868) 'preached a popular blend of evangelical Protestantism and political conservatism' and is said to have reached a 'pinnacle of prestige and influence' in 1829, when he succeeded in bringing about the division of the Synod of Ulster to push out the Arians and non-subscribers into a separate synod.[6] Cooke's campaign against Arianism (which is one form of anti-trinitarian belief), went on throughout his life, and he seems to have particularly distrusted southern Presbyterianism.

When he was moderator of the Synod of Ulster in 1824–5, he claimed in his evidence to a parliamentary commission in London that the southern congregations were infected with Arianism and that this influence was so pernicious that Presbyterian congregations in the south were rapidly fading away numerically. The ensuing controversy, as southerners defended themselves, was bitter and very definitely unedifying. Several newspapers in September 1827 printed open letters from Cooke to two Dublin ministers. One of these Dublin men was James Armstrong who had befriended Cooke ten years earlier, when Cooke had been studying medicine in Dublin. Cooke wrote:

> Gentlemen, you wish to be called Presbyterians ... Alas! you form part of a degenerate Presbyterian church, part of which has fallen from its original purity into the depths of Arianism or Socinianism ... therefore do I disavow connexion with you. In the meantime may God give you space to repent.[7]

In another broadside in the Belfast press, 28 September the same year, he asked, 'Dear Mr A, what became of your prudence when you compelled me to this exposition of your present vanishing condition? Your congregations have withered like plants in a desert ...'.

Cooke alleged that one former meeting house of the Synod of Munster was in 1825 a blacksmith's shop, one a dog kennel and a third a cock pit. He jeered at them and their church organisation.

> You are a Synod. That's a big word! Now I offer you upon any ordinary Sabbath to produce as many hearers in the congregation of Killyleagh as you can produce on the same day in the whole synod of Munster. Give me one northern Presbytery and I shall form you a wilderness of synods of Munster.[8]

This is good tub-thumping oratory and was doubtless met with amused approval in the north. It is only fair to give a flavour of what Cooke's opponents had written in response to his earlier attacks. These were also published in the press, and the Dublin ministers gave (nearly) as good as they got. Armstrong described his former friend's theology as 'narrow, bigoted and exclusive', and he and his colleague Joseph Hutton wrote:

> We cannot express too emphatically our astonishment and regret that any minister could be found in the Synod of Ulster capable of wantonly and gratuitously hurting our feelings and abusing an opportunity afforded by the temporary office of moderator to convey unfavourable and erroneous impressions to the Legislature. We cannot conceive what motive could induce any minister to act in a manner so inconsistent with his sacred office and so prejudicial to the peace, the credit and the interest of the Presbyterian church in Ireland.[9]

One can indeed speculate about what were Cooke's motives for his attack on southern Presbyterianism. John Jamieson, the historian of the Royal Belfast Academical Institution, a Belfast school distrusted and attacked by Cooke (and at whose entrance, ironically, stands Cooke's landmark 'Black Man' statue), noted that 'once [Cooke] had gained supremacy in the synod [his activities] proved to be chiefly a cloak beneath which he sought to conceal his real objective, which was the destruction of political liberalism'.[10]

There is no doubt that Cooke's lasting and strong influence on Presbyterianism in Ulster gave his prejudices great weight in helping form attitudes, vestiges of which may survive into the present; and which may have coloured the northern Presbyterian outlook towards Dublin, and the south in general, during the latter half of the nineteenth century and afterwards. It is as if he is saying, 'If you can't even trust Presbyterians in Dublin, the south must indeed be a foreign and dangerous place'.

The nineteenth century was an age of imperialism, when the Scots of Scotland and also Ulster-Scots prided themselves on their multifaceted roles in extending empire and civilisation (via education, religion, hard work, etc.). The 'white man's burden' attitude of northern Presbyterians to the south of Ireland, which they would have regarded as being benighted by Catholicism, is well known, but has seldom been expressed so strongly as by Dr Dill of Cork in the 1839 General Assembly.

If you look to the north, your vision ranges over one unbroken scene of cultivation, studded with neat dwellings, having all the marks of comfort and contentment; if to the south, you behold extensive tracts of the most fertile soil waste and neglected, wretched cabins and more wretched inmates, remarkable for their barbarity, nakedness and filth.[11]

In response to the reported need for enlightenment, the northerners dispatched missionaries to work in southern areas, and not just to convert Catholics. Catholics of course resented this, as many local and national histories point out, but it is notable that some Presbyterians in the allegedly benighted areas seem not to have been too pleased at being treated as if they too needed to be converted; perhaps not too impressed to be so often on the receiving end of northern (Scots-type) Presbyterian superiority and even suprematism.

Cooke in the General Assembly rejoiced that some ministers of the Synod of Munster received the missionaries kindly, but criticised other ministers who had spurned northern intervention. In speeches to the General Synod about the lamentable state of affairs in districts which were under the care of the Synod of Munster, Cooke and his supporters spoke about the 'blasting breath of Unitarianism which had annihilated near half a hundred Presbyterian congregations' in the south of Ireland.[12] On that same occasion, the Rev. Dill from Cork quoted examples of how disastrously even actual Scots-born Scotsmen in those areas were falling away from original purity.

> I could tell you of a city in the south of Ireland from which a steamer plies every Lord's Day on pleasure trips, belonging to a Scotch company and every man of the crew, from the captain to the cabin boy is a Presbyterian. I could tell you moreover that such is the temptation thereby held out to desecrate the Sabbath that they are not only ruining thousands of Irishmen but that many young Scotchmen have fallen victim to seduction. I blush for the character of the Scottish nation. I grieve to think that a land which has ever stood forth as an example to the nations in Sabbath sanctification should have given birth to such degenerate sons. Surely things are bad enough in the south already.[13]

One of the Scottish-born Presbyterians, whose career in Dublin really should have caused concern to Cooke and the orthodox denomination, as they looked disapprovingly southwards, was Duncan Chisholm from Inverness, soldier, leather dealer, bankrupt, absconder. He turned up in Dublin calling himself George Mathews and became an elder in at least two Dublin Presbyterian congregations. Mathews seems to have had an apparently obsessive hatred of Arianism and especially of Unitarianism. In his campaign against Arianism Mathews joined several Dublin congregations in succession or concurrently, pretending to be himself a Unitarian, but with the intention, sometimes successful, of alienating the property of non-orthodox congregations. There were lawsuits and libel actions and parliamentary commissions of inquiry and a great deal of discussion in the General Assembly and in the newspapers.

The other aspects of Mathews's career were even less legitimate. He got a post as a clerk in Dublin Castle, with responsibility for paying out the *regium donum*, the state's yearly grants to Presbyterian ministers but, without any doubt, he played fast and loose with government money. According to *Chambers' Edinburgh Journal* of 1852, Mathews in 1839, 'by one stroke of his pen called into being three missionaries of his sect labouring in the south of Ireland', and apparently paid himself the stipends of the imaginary missionaries, about £500 a year. He set up a Presbyterian congregational library fund, costing £1,599, but which never funded any libraries; £100 of this was spent on a jaunt to London for himself and his wife. That was a considerable sum in 1840, and they must have had a very fine holiday. His other frauds were numerous and involved, benefiting his relatives as well as himself.[14]

Henry Cooke was formally the denominational agent, from 1845, for payment of *regium donum*; Mathews was the official making the actual payments. Surely Cooke knew about, and therefore presumably approved of, some of Mathew's questionable, even illegal, anti-Arian moves, but it is Cooke's failure to check Mathews's books or spot his fraud and financial wrongdoing that should, one would think, have caused questions to be asked about Cooke's lack of oversight, at least, or complicity at worst. However, amazingly, Cooke survived the scandal without censure or penalty; Mathews absconded again, leaving behind his wife and family.

Mercifully most of the Scots who flooded into Ireland from the middle of the nineteenth century through the first decade of the twentieth century were nothing like Mathews. Dublin was of course part of the United Kingdom within which Scots could follow job opportunities. The influence of so many Scots in Dublin at that time, working in brewing, distilling, banking, local government and insurance companies, among others, has not been much explored, and to an extent has been forgotten, but it must have been quite a significant feature of late Victorian and Edwardian Dublin.

In 1911 the census records that there were 4,008 people born in Scotland living in Dublin city and county, out of a Dublin population of about 400,000; so one in a hundred was a Scot, and over 1,200 of these were heads of households, so Scots influence on families that they established in Dublin must have been quite considerable. For comparison, and again perhaps this is a significant indication of northern attitudes, there were only 1,958 people who had been born in County Antrim living in Dublin in 1911 and only 2,200 born in County Down. In other words, rather surprisingly, there were nearly as many Scots as Ulster-Scots in the city.[15]

Jameson's whiskey was founded by Scots; large shops like Arnotts, Weir's jewellers and what was once a well-known grocery business in the city, Findlaters, all were Scots founded. Scottish engineers worked on Dún Laoghaire harbour. Scots in Dublin established a Burns club, a St Andrew's Society and St Andrew's College, and were influential in several Presbyterian congregations, for instance in St Andrew's in Blackrock. There was even a missionary effort in Dublin by the United Presbyterian Church of Scotland, which aimed to provide a familiar form of worship for exiled Scots. In 1860 the UPS received a donation of £1,000 (which was a lot of money then) for the specific purpose of establishing a mission for the Dublin Scots and from 1863 a Scots Church met in the Pillar Room of the Rotunda Hospital. A formal church was established in 1866, and this is now represented in the congregation of Clontarf and Scots.[16]

The congregation of Christ Church at Rathgar was founded in 1865, partly by wealthy Scots living in the southern suburbs. They selected a

Scots architect to design the church; one of three the same man designed for Presbyterian congregations in Dublin, which is why Christ Church Rathgar looks very like the church in Dún Laoghaire, and both look like Findlaters Church on Parnell Square. Scottishness of course was remarkably popular throughout the United Kingdom in Victorian times, partly because of Queen Victoria's fondness for all things Scottish, and the Scots certainly collectively had quite a presence in Dublin culture and social life; there is a considerable quantity of interesting newspaper reports about the Dublin Scots and their activities.

Perhaps the increased numbers of Scottish adherents in the south may have influenced the Synod of Munster's 1854 decision to seek union with the northern General Assembly of the Presbyterian Church in Ireland, though the pressures of the economic conditions after the Famine, as well as the desire to foster political as well as religious unity, must also have been significant. However, even after the two church organisations united, the two parts of Presbyterianism, north and south, continued to have widely different experiences; Dublin, for instance, was almost untouched, at least directly, by the extremely significant Ulster Revival of 1859, which arguably lastingly reshaped northern Protestantism as a whole.

It seems to me there are grounds for wondering how much of Cooke's distrust of southern Presbyterianism persisted in northern Presbyterianism even years after Cooke's heyday. As an example, in 1911, for instance, the Synod of Dublin suggested to the General Assembly that there should be a new Directory for the Public Worship of God; for 12 years, Rev. J.C. Johnston from Union Chapel, Dublin, and his committee worked on it, but in the end the Assembly refused to publish it, or support it, and Johnston noted that appalling difficulties had been placed in the way of the Dublin initiative.[17] It would be interesting to know how many moderators of the General Assembly have been born in what is now the Republic of Ireland?

When Ireland became independent of the United Kingdom, everything changed for Scots here. Although as late as 1929, the St Andrew's Day dinner of the Dublin Scottish Benevolent Society in Clery's restaurant was told that 'some fine day you will be running the Free State' and they drank a toast to 'the land we live in', Ireland was no longer part of the system within which Scots could move with freedom; at other Scots dinners, speakers complained that their children would have to learn Irish compulsorily, something that they much resented.[18]

Between 1911 and 1926, Presbyterian numbers living in the Irish Free State fell by 35.5 per cent male and 29.5 per cent female, from 13,084 in Leinster in 1911 to 8,589 in 1926.[19] There were also 2,495 people in Ireland describing themselves as Church of Scotland in 1911; that option was not available to the 1926 respondents. Only a small number of those Presbyterians who left Ireland, relatively speaking, would have been Scottish-born, but certainly Scots departed Dublin along with Dublin-born Protestants of all complexions, radically changing the social and religious scene in Dublin, and leaving Dublin to become a much more homogeneously Irish-born and Catholic city than it had been before independence.

Ten years ago, when I first started to think about the historical differences between northern and southern Presbyterianism, there was nothing to suggest that there would be any contemporary relevance in presenting a glimpse into this forgotten history. History, as it always does, moves on; the years since partition did indeed push the two jurisdictions further apart, but then from the middle of the twentieth century, the two nations' involvement in Europe and the end of the Troubles seemed to have increased mutual understanding and contact. However, recent events and changes in society here in Ireland may once again be highlighting some of the old differences between the two parts of the island. But in the present topsy-turvy world, Irish people who now live and work in London may have to consider leaving their lives there, post-Brexit, as the Scots left Dublin after 1921, and even more strikingly, the official Presbyterian denomination in Ireland has distanced itself from the Church of Scotland, which northerners would once have regarded as the mother church, and some southern Presbyterians are contemplating aligning themselves with that Scottish denomination, now more liberal theologically than the Irish version, in protest at a vote taken in this year's Irish General Assembly, on matters which will affect people in same-sex relationships.

Strange times indeed, and only time will tell how things turn out.

NOTES

1   This historical sketch was originally presented in the Dublin Festival of
      History, September 2018, and the large audience in the Royal Irish Academy
      encouraged hopes that it would stimulate interest in the topic.

2   Articles by Andrew R. Holmes, especially 'Presbyterian religion,
      historiography, and Ulster Scots identity', *The Historical Journal*, 52:3 (2009),
      pp 615–40, and his book *The Shaping of Ulster Presbyterian Belief and Practice
      1770–1840* (OUP, 2006), works by Finlay Holmes, especially his histories of
      the Presbyterian church in Ireland, and Alexander S. Cromie, *Controversy
      Among Southern Presbyterians* (privately published, 2000), have all been useful
      sources for this paper, and can provide much more information and
      background on these complex historical and theological topics.

3   Francis J. Bremer and Tom Webster (eds), 'Irish Puritanism', *Puritans and
      Puritanism in Europe and America*, Vol. 1 (ABC Clio, 2006).

4   Steven C. Smyrl, *Dictionary of Dublin Dissent: Dublin's Protestant Dissenting
      Meeting Houses, 1660–1920* (A. & A. Farmar, 2009), p. 17.

5   The Westminster Confession of Faith, first established in the late 1640s by
      meetings of theologians and clergy in Westminster Abbey, was originally
      intended to bring about uniformity in British Protestantism. It is an
      exposition of Protestant belief, mainly derived from Calvinist teaching, and
      heavily influenced by the Puritan and Covenanter theology of the day. It lays
      out doctrines common to most forms of Christianity, but particularly stresses
      the supremacy of Scripture and the insufficiency of faith for the individual's
      salvation. The Westminster Confession supported the Scottish preference for
      Presbyterian structures of church governance which were then unfamiliar in
      the rest of the British Isles, and was strongly sabbatarian, opposed to state
      influence on religion, and very anti-Catholic. It has historically formed the
      basis of the belief and doctrine of many nonconformist denominations,
      especially Presbyterianism, worldwide.

6   Finlay Holmes, 'Henry Cooke (1788–1868)', in James McGuire and James
      Quinn (eds), *Dictionary of Irish Biography* (CUP, 2009).

7   *Belfast News Letter*, 11 Sep. 1827.

8   Ibid.

9   *Southern Reporter and Cork Commercial Chronicle*, 23 Aug. 1827.

10   R.F.G. Holmes, 'Controversy and Schism in the Synod of Ulster in the 1820s',
      in J.L.M. Haire, *Challenge and Conflict: Essays in Irish Presbyterian History and
      Doctrine* (Belfast, 1981), p. 40.

11   *Belfast News Letter*, 2 July 1839.

12   Ibid.

13   Ibid.

14   *Chambers' Edinburgh Journal*, 16 (1852), p. 93; Smyrl, *Dublin Dissent*, p. 40.

15   Census of Ireland 1911, online at www.census.nationalarchives.ie.

16   'The Scots Church 1864–2003', on the website of Clontarf and Scots church
      at www.clontarfchurch.ie/the-scots-church-1864-2003 (accessed 9 Dec. 2018).

17   Robert S. Tosh, 'Presbyterian worship through the ages', *Bulletin of the
      Presbyterian Historical Society of Ireland*, 28 (2001–03), pp 9–10.

18   Sir Walter Nugent, reported in 'Haggis and speeches', *Sunday Independent*, 1 Dec. 1929.
19   www.cso.ie/en/census/censusvolumes1926to1991/historicalreports/census1926 reports.

From Bangor to New Orleans:
the peregrinations of James Hull,
a United Irishman in the United States[1]

The United States of America was a political refuge for
many thousands of people from Ireland in the period
before and after the 1798 Rebellion. A sizeable proportion
of them were Presbyterians from Ulster, within which
Presbyterian ministers formed a small, though significant,
element.

Some of these men went on to have successful ministerial careers in
America, such as Rev. John Glendy, formerly of Maghera, County
Londonderry, who was admired by Thomas Jefferson and who was
offered (though he declined) the chaplaincy of both the US House of
Representatives and the US Senate. Others virtually disappear from
view. The careers of very few of the Presbyterian probationers (i.e. men
who had been licensed to preach, but not yet ordained) who found
sanctuary in the United States have been traced with any success.[2]
However, with regard to James Hull, who grew up in Bangor, County
Down, it is possible to explore his life in America in comparative detail.

FAMILY BACKGROUND AND INVOLVEMENT IN THE 1798
REBELLION

James Hull was a son of the manse. His father, Rev. James Hull senior,
was from Limavady, County Londonderry, and in 1749 he was
ordained minister of the Presbyterian congregation in Cookstown,
County Tyrone. Fourteen years later he was installed as minister of

Bangor, County Down. Hull senior served as moderator of the Synod of Ulster in 1769. His sermon to the Synod in 1770 was subsequently published in Belfast as: *Religion Founded upon Knowledge, and Productive of Forbearance, Moderation, and Peace. A Sermon Preached before a General Synod, of Protestant Dissenting Ministers; at their Annual Meeting in Dungannon, June 26th, 1770, and published at their request.*[3] As was generally the case for Presbyterian ministers at this time, Hull supplemented his ministerial income earnings through farming and the letting of land. He had a holding at Rathgill in Bangor parish, which he advertised for letting in July 1770. The land comprised two farms, each of around 20 acres, on one of which was a newly-constructed house.[4] By the spring of 1781 Hull was in considerable financial difficulty and was forced to dispose of his lands to cover his debts.[5] Latterly his home was at Ballyvarnon in Bangor parish.

In 1791 Hull senior clashed with a fellow minister, Rev. James Simpson of Newtownards – who was later to become a United Irish exile in the United States – over doctrinal matters. According to the Bangor minister, the accusation was 'that I blindfolded and deceived my hearers by preaching doctrines contrary to my conscience to please them.' In addition, Simpson, a strict Calvinist, had claimed that Hull denied the divinity of Christ and the atonement. Upon investigation it was found that Hull was not guilty of the former, though he did have, according to one witness, a rather unorthodox view of the latter.[6] Rev. James Hull continued to minister in Bangor until his retirement in 1793.[7] He died on 30 March 1794. According to a short notice in the *Belfast News Letter*,

> In his family, he was indulgent and tender-hearted. As a Preacher, he was collected, rational and manly, and in his hours of social intercourse, while he supported the ministerial character with dignity, he exhibited the dispositions of a Christian and the manners of a gentleman.[8]

Hull senior's wife was later described as a woman 'distinguished not only for her intellect, but her patriotism and was an intimate friend of Lord Castlereagh'.[9]

According to the inscription that was placed on his tomb in New Orleans, James Hull junior was born in Belfast on 15 May 1776.[10] He may have received some of his education at the recently established Belfast Academy for a pupil at that establishment named James Hull was awarded a premium for his Greek and Latin examination results in 1791.[11] We do know that Hull junior matriculated at Glasgow University in 1792.[12] After completing his university studies, he is said to have 'travelled extensively under circumstances highly favourable to intellectual improvement'.[13] Following in his father's footsteps, he began to prepare for the Presbyterian ministry and in 1796 was licensed by the Bangor Presbytery. By this time he may already have become associated with the United Irishmen. As far as his actual involvement in the rebellion is concerned, we know that he was closely associated with David Bailie Warden, probably being the 'Mr H' who accompanied Warden on a reconnaissance expedition to Newtownards on 7 June 1798, the same day as the first insurgent uprising at Antrim and five days before the crucial Battle of Ballynahinch. Soon afterwards he rallied faltering support for the United Irishmen in Bangor.[14]

Among the depositions made before Rev. James Cleland, a County Down magistrate, there is the following statement: 'Saw Revd. James Hull at Bangor ... saying he was going for the cannon ...'.[15] This suggests a certain belligerence on the part of the young probationer and Hull's prominence is further indicated by the fact that he was included among those for whom a reward of 50 guineas was offered.[16] In the event, Hull escaped to America. At the meeting of the Synod of Ulster of June 1799 the Bangor Presbytery reported that Hull, along with John Miles and David Bailie Warden, 'having been charged with being concerned in the insurrection of June 1798 & not having stood their trials, but as they understand having sailed for America, are not to be considered as probationers under their care.'[17]

AUGUSTA, GEORGIA

On arriving in America, Hull headed for Augusta, Georgia, where, as Katharine Brown has noted, there was 'a close-knit Ulster community'; furthermore, it became the location of a 'significant colony of United Irishmen and their sympathizers'.[18] Already resident in Georgia was Hull's brother, George Irwin Hull, who had married Sarah Williams in Savannah in 1795, and was a federal marshal in both Savannah and

Augusta; he died in October 1800 in Augusta, leaving one son, Thomas H. Hull. Other members of the family to settle in Augusta included James Hull's mother Jane or Jean who died in 1820; his sister Jane who died 1817; his brother Dr Hugh Montgomery Hull[19] who subsequently moved to New Orleans and died there in 1805; and another sister who married Dr Benjamin Harris of Augusta.[20]

Possibly James Hull had ambitions to become a Presbyterian minister in America but, if so, these were dealt a blow by the fact that his former presbytery in Ireland refused to grant certificates of probation to him and the other probationers under its care. The General Assembly of the American Presbyterian Church had issued a ruling in 1798 that only ordained ministers with appropriate credentials would be admitted and then only after a year's probation.[21] Nonetheless, not long after arriving in Augusta, Hull – who in America was usually referred to as James F. Hull, the middle initial standing apparently for Foster[22] – began to preach and conduct marriages. The first marriage ceremony he is known to have performed was that of a Dr Burke and Miss Elbert on 5 May 1799. A week later it was announced in the *Augusta Chronicle* that he would be conducting the service in St Paul's Church on the following Sunday.[23] His preaching was acceptable to the local populace with good attendances at his services, and in July 1799 he was invited to continue his ministry in Augusta for a six-month period. It was hoped that those who were in agreement with this would offer him reasonable financial support. In January 1800 he was invited to remain in Augusta for the whole of that year.

In the summer of 1801 Hull made plans to visit the new capital, Washington, and pay his respects to the President, Thomas Jefferson. He secured three letters of introduction. One was from George Walton, a signatory of the Declaration of Independence and a former governor and senator for Georgia. In introducing Hull, Walton wrote that he was 'the established and principal Clergyman of this City', adding that his 'talents and virtues have acquired and secured the esteem and respect of the Citizens here; as his personal decorum and deportment will, no doubt, do every where.' A second letter was secured from Senator Abraham Baldwin which noted that Hull was a native of Ireland and the son of a Presbyterian clergyman, and that he had come to America to escape 'political persecution'; Baldwin considered Hull to be 'a Gentleman of good education, of good morals and a good Republican'. The final letter was written by Congressman John Milledge who stated that that Hull's 'talents, and correctness of Character' made him 'amiable' to the inhabitants of Augusta. Hull passed on all three letters to Jefferson on 25 September 1801.[24]

At some point in the following year Hull seems to have given up full time preaching to pursue a career as a lawyer. He was still performing marriages in May 1802, though by December of that year, when he married Magdalane Agatha O'Keefe ('an Irish lady of great beauty and elegance'),[25] he was James F. Hull Esq., not Reverend. His reasons for this change of direction are not clear. He studied law under John E. Anderson of Augusta, from whom he received his certificate to practise as an attorney. His legal practice in Georgia was not as successful as he had hoped and he moved to Henley, Cambridge (now Ninety Six), South Carolina, where he was naturalised on 30 October 1805; those supporting his application included John Cormick, himself a United Irish exile in Augusta.[26] His application for admission to the Bar in South Carolina was supported by Thomas P. Carnes of Columbia (Anderson having died shortly after issuing the relevant certificate to Hull) who stated on 29 November 1805 that he had known Hull for at least five years and believed him to be a 'person of strictly moral & upright character & deportment'.[27] Some information on Hull's legal career has come to light. For example, on 27 November 1806 he was one of three men to receive a power of attorney from Eliza Cormick in Dublin to act for her in the matter of her divorce from John Cormick, Hull's friend and fellow United Irish émigré.[28]

ST LOUIS, LOUISIANA TERRITORY

At some point prior to 1812, Hull moved to St Louis, Missouri (then part of Louisiana Territory), which had an expanding Irish population. A number of the town's residents had been involved in radical and seditious activities in Ireland in the 1790s, among them Joseph Charless from County Westmeath, the founder, in 1808, of the *Missouri Gazette*.[29] Hull continued his legal career in St Louis and when a vacancy for a judgeship arose in early 1812 he sought support from various quarters for his candidacy. Among those to whom he turned was an old friend, Colonel Hammond, who personally delivered a letter to the mayor of Washington, Robert Brent, on or before 30 January. In passing on this recommendation to President James Madison, Brent admitted that he had no personal knowledge of Hull though he was said to be a 'a man of probity and Talents acting as attorney at Law ... and altho a decided Republican in principal has never joined in the violence of party spirit.'[30] Further petitions on Hull's behalf arrived in the following weeks. One submitted by two inhabitants of Louisiana Territory, John Rice Jones and Clement B. Penrose, argued that it would 'give general satisfaction to the inhabitants, both French and Americans.'[31] It seems that Hull was not successful in securing this appointment. He was, however, active in public affairs in St Louis and indicators of this include his delivery of the oration at the Fourth of July celebrations in 1812 and a week later his acting as secretary at the town meeting held in response to the outbreak of war with Great Britain.[32] In October of that year he announced that he would be standing for the General Assembly, though it does not appear that he was elected.[33]

NEW ORLEANS

In 1814, seeking new opportunities and perhaps even in response to frustrated political ambitions in St Louis, Hull moved to New Orleans. According to one historian, many United Irish exiles 'looked to New Orleans as an attractive refuge' and a significant Irish community developed there in the early nineteenth century; the first St Patrick's Day celebration was held in 1809.[34] In New Orleans Hull was to become the city's Episcopal minister, though the precise circumstances that led to this are not altogether clear. One source states that he came to New Orleans to take charge of a church, officiating first of all as a Presbyterian minister before, at the request of the church members, taking orders in the Episcopal Church.[35] Another account relates that when Hull arrived in New Orleans he was unsure whether to practice law or preach. However, what helped him make up his mind to pursue the latter was finding the bar 'abundantly and ably supplied', while the Protestant ministry was represented by someone 'of no high pretensions'.[36] Whichever may have been the case, the Episcopalians in

New Orleans, presumably aware of his past career as a minister, invited Hull to preach to them soon after his arrival in the city.

At this time the Episcopal Church in New Orleans was without a minister of its own, the previous rector, Rev. Philander Chase, having resigned in 1811. When Hull arrived in the city the religious services were being taken by a Methodist preacher, William Winans. In order to accommodate Hull, Winans was asked to vacate the pulpit. However, upon hearing what he felt were 'obliquities in the Christian and Ministerial character' (Winans described Hull as 'a boon companion at wine, and an adroit Whist-player'), he refused to do so, causing some consternation. In order to defuse the situation, Winans proposed that he would preach at 10 o'clock in the morning allowing Hull to follow him at 11 o'clock, a suggestion that was accepted. On the day in question, 11 June 1814, Hull arrived to take the service in a 'ruffled shirt and black gloves'.[37]

Hull's preaching proved popular with many of the Episcopalians in New Orleans and he was invited to be their minister once Winans's contract with them had expired on 1 January 1815. He was regarded by some as 'a Scholar and an eloquent Orator', though Winans dismissed his supporters as the 'fashionable and gay elements' of the congregation.[38] It is also possible to detect some local political tensions contributing to the choice of Hull as minister. Hull's main supporter was the leading Jeffersonian Republican in New Orleans, A.L. Duncan, while Winans was accused of being a tool of the Federalist Edward Livingston, later to become Secretary of State during Jackson's first term as president. Hull's background and politics would certainly have made him popular with the Jeffersonians in New Orleans. At the same time, Winans claimed that he himself was 'an enthusiastic Jeffersonian'.[39]

A mere week after Hull began to officiate full time in New Orleans the famous battle was fought on 8 January 1815.[40] An anecdote of Hull's contribution to the American cause has been preserved:

> Of the two protestant ministers in New Orleans, a Mr Hull is particularly distinguished. He is by birth an Irishman, and is said to have made himself remarkable during the troubles of his native country; at all events he is looked upon as a clever man, and

possessed of much sound sense. He payed a visit to General Jackson, who accosted him on entering, thus: 'I don't presume you will go with us to fight the enemy?' 'Why not, General, if you will take me along with you?' 'How could you help us dear black coat?' 'Why you know I have had some rencontres with the red coats, and perhaps I could be of some use to you.' 'Well, I am going to take a ride to the lines, you may come along with me; have you a horse? 'No Sir.' 'Bill,' cried the General, 'get Beelzebub saddled for the parson!' And with judgment and discretion, which did equal honour to his understanding and to his republican sense, he availed himself of the counsels of the rector, which, as I was assured by several respectable people, proved to be neither superfluous nor unserviceable.[41]

Hull ministered in New Orleans for over a year before indicating to the congregation that, having carefully considered the claims of the Episcopal Church, he would like to be ordained. Accordingly, a committee of the vestry met with him and offered him the position of rector.[42] In order to prepare himself for ordination, Hull travelled to New York to pursue further study and was received into holy orders there in October 1816.[43] A month before this he had made a return visit to Augusta to preach.[44] During this period the first Episcopal Church building in New Orleans was constructed. It took the form of a small brick edifice in the shape of an octagon and was in the Gothic style. It was called Christ Church and was the forerunner of the present Christ Church cathedral.[45]

MINISTRY IN NEW ORLEANS

Hull remained in New Orleans until his death in 1833. There was a wide divergence of opinion on the performance of his clerical duties. William Winans, the man he had supplanted in New Orleans, was scathing in his criticism of Hull's ministry and preaching:

> The ministry of Mr Hull was a great evil. … Pity that he was unfortunate as to preach a Religion he did not experimentally and practically understand to a people who emphatically needed Religious instruction, as the people of New Orleans then most unquestionably did. … His ministry would have been just as it was, had he substituted Socrates for Jesus Christ, and Plato for St Paul.[46]

Winans further charged Hull with being a notorious drunkard, and of frequently being under the influence of opium or brandy, or both, even during 'seasons of official ministration'. He firmly believed that New Orleans would have been no worse off in having no religious services than those provided by the Irishman. Winans, of course, had his own issues with Hull. A more sympathetic verdict on Hull's time in New Orleans relates that the congregation 'greatly prospered' under their rector with the results 'largely of a spiritual character'.[47] Another view of the Episcopal clergyman is provided by the distinguished British architect Benjamin Henry Latrobe who spent his final years in New Orleans where he died in 1820. Latrobe gave the following assessment of Hull's preaching style:

> He is a man of good talents & of an exemplary character. His sermons are plain & useful discourses, well composed, never rising to energetic eloquence and never sinking below mediocrity of argument or style. His delivery has only one fault, without which it would be really excellent: he drops his voice at the close of every period to the lowest tone of its compass.[48]

Hull is credited with improving relations between the Episcopal Church and other denominations in New Orleans.[49] He gave permission for members of the Presbyterian congregation in New Orleans to worship in Christ Church until they had a building of their own, while he contributed $300 towards the construction of the first Presbyterian meeting house.[50] He was close friends with the eloquent and much respected Presbyterian minister in New Orleans, Rev. Sylvester Larned, officiating at his funeral in 1820.[51] In 1825, he attempted to establish a seaman's mission in New Orleans.[52] Hull was also responsible for establishing a successful school for young ladies in New Orleans, which was continued by his daughter Sarah.[53] In 1825, a rectory was begun next to Christ Church with Hull himself contributing just under $1,300 of the $8,500 cost.[54]

There is only limited evidence that Hull kept in touch with other United Irish exiles in America. We do know that on 26 August 1820 Hull wrote to William Sampson in New York to offer his condolences on the death of Sampson's only son, John Philpot Curran Sampson.[55] Sampson junior had died of a fever after only a few days' illness aged only 25. He had moved to Louisiana in 1818, where he had been admitted to the Bar and had been appointed deputy to the Attorney-General. However, he had resigned from this position to become a newspaper editor, thinking that he could have had a positive influence on public affairs through the press. At the same time, when Hull wrote to William Sampson he did so as one 'whom you may recognise as having been introduced to your family four years ago', indicating that there had been no long-standing relationship between the two. Hull knew the Porter brothers, sons of Rev. James Porter, who had been executed in 1798 for alleged complicity in the rebellion, regaling them with stories of their father, whom he would have known in Ireland.[56]

FINAL YEARS AND DEATH

Towards the end of his life Hull began to suffer increasingly from ill-health. In the hope that it would benefit his condition Hull spent the summer of 1829 at White Sulphur Springs, Virginia.[57] On 10 January 1830 Christ Church was consecrated by the visiting bishop of Connecticut, Dr Brownell. A week later the bishop administered confirmation in the church for the first time. Brownell left New Orleans with the impression that the Episcopal Church in the city was in a thriving condition. However, while it was said of Hull that 'he worked with all his zeal until he could no longer work', it is also apparent that his health and consequent inability to fulfil all his ministerial responsibilities was affecting the general well-being of his congregation, giving the vestry serious cause for concern.[58] Eventually, in February 1832, an assistant minister, Rev. Ulysses M. Wheeler, was appointed.[59] In late 1832 there was an attempt to have Hull removed, leading to a major row with the vestrymen. Hull refused to go, claiming that he was protected by Canon law.[60] However, the vestry declared the rectorship of Christ Church vacant, though a stipend of $1,200 was allowed to Hull for the rest of his life.[61]

Hull died of tuberculosis on 6 June 1833. In his last weeks this 'lingering consumption' had left him confined to his house. At the time of his death, New Orleans had just experienced an outbreak of cholera, though Rev. Theodore Clapp, the local Presbyterian minister, recorded that Hull had never 'left the city in sickly seasons but fearlessly continued at his post however great and alarming the mortality around him.'[62] He was buried in the Girod Street Cemetery that he himself had played his part in creating in 1822. Prior to this, Protestants in New Orleans had used a section in St Louis's Cemetery. In the early 1820s additional burial space was needed and on 10 August 1822 the city council authorised the mayor to sell to the Christ Church congregation, represented by Hull and the vestrymen, a tract of land for a cemetery.[63]

In 1957, after years of neglect, the cemetery was deconsecrated. By this time Hull's once fine tomb was a crumbling ruin.[64] Hull's remains were among those that were removed to a special crypt in the Hope Mausoleum in Christ Church Cathedral.[65] He was survived by his wife Magdalane and daughter Sarah. The fate of another daughter, Rosetta Lincoln, is unknown. She had been born on 10 November 1823 and baptised in Trinity Church, Natchez, Mississippi, on 6 May 1826.[66] Magdalane Hull died on 5 December 1844 aged 54.[67] Sarah Hull died some time after the Civil War.[68]

NOTES

1   This essay derives from the author's chapter on Hull in Peter Gilmore, Trevor Parkhill and William Roulston, *Exiles of '98: Ulster Presbyterians and the United States* (Belfast, 2018), pp 99–108. I would like to reiterate my thanks to Erick Montgomery of Historic Augusta for sharing information on Hull.

2   In his excellent study of political exiles in America Michael Durey was forced to admit that, with the exception of the well-known David Bailie Warden, he had not been able to trace the fates of any of those Presbyterian licentiates (excluding Covenanters) who had emigrated as a result of their involvement in the United Irishmen and/or 1798 Rebellion (Michael Durey, *Transatlantic Radicals and the Early American Republic* (Lawrence, KS, 1997), p. 189).

3   The style of this sermon has been described by the nineteenth-century Presbyterian minister and historian Thomas Witherow as 'clear and manly', but the doctrine 'does not rise above a cold morality. It is New Light divinity throughout': Thomas Witherow, *Historical and Literary Memorials of Presbyterianism in Ireland (1731–1800)* (London and Belfast, 1880), p. 327.

4   *Belfast News Letter*, 17 July 1770.

5   *Belfast News Letter*, 24–7 Apr. 1781.

6   Andrew R. Holmes, *The Shaping of Ulster Presbyterian Belief and Practice, 1770–1840* (Oxford, 2006), p. 150.

7   *Fasti of the Irish Presbyterian Church*, p. 148.

8   *Belfast News Letter*, 1–4 Apr. 1794.

9   W.B. Sprague, *Annals of the American Pulpit*, vol. 4 (New York, 1858), p. 561.

10   The statement that Belfast was his place of birth may refer in general terms to the area in which he was born (Belfast is around 12 miles from Bangor), though it is possible that his mother did give birth to him while in that town.

11   *Belfast News Letter*, 24–8 June 1791.

12   W. Innes Addison, *The Matriculation Albums of the University of Glasgow from 1728 to 1858* (Glasgow, 1913), p. 166.

13   Sprague, *Annals of the American Pulpit*, vol. 4, p. 561.

14   Kenneth Robinson, *North Down and Ards in 1798* (Bangor, 1998), pp 55, 58.

15   PRONI, D714/3/29.

16   *Belfast News Letter*, 20 July 1798.

17   *Records of the General Synod of Ulster from 1691 to 1820*, vol. 3 (Belfast, 1898), p. 216.

18   Katharine Brown, 'United Irishmen in the American South' in David A. Wilson and Mark G. Spencer (eds), *Ulster Presbyterians in the Atlantic World: Religion, Politics and Identity* (Dublin, 2006), p. 96.

19   Educated at Apothecaries Hall, Dublin, he was the first apothecary of the Belfast Dispensary, 1792–5 (R.S.J. Clarke, *A Directory of Ulster Doctors (who qualified before 1901)*, vol. 1 (Belfast, 2013), p. 479; R.W.M. Strain, *Belfast and its Charitable Society* (Oxford, 1961), pp 154, 156).

20   Information provided by Erick Montgomery.

21   Durey, *Transatlantic Radicals*, p. 189.

22   There is no evidence for this middle name in any Irish source, though this is not unusual with Irish immigrants to America. However, it is not clear where the middle name of Foster came from.

23   *Augusta Chronicle*, 12 May 1799 (reference supplied by Erick Montgomery).

24   'To Thomas Jefferson from George Walton, 25 June 1801,' Founders Online, National Archives (http://founders.archives.gov/documents/Jefferson/01-34-02-0355, ver. 2013-06-26). Source: *The Papers of Thomas Jefferson*, vol. 34, 1 May–31 July 1801, Barbara B. Oberg (ed.) (Princeton, 2007), p. 455.

25   Sprague, *Annals of the American Pulpit*, vol. 4, p. 561; Magdalane was a native of Dublin.

26   *Ancestoring*, III, p. 9 (reference supplied by Erick Montgomery); Durey, *Transatlantic Radicals*, pp 129, 159.

27   Statement of Thomas P. Carnes, South Caroliniana Library, Columbia, SC (reference supplied by Erick Montgomery).

28   Egan Family Collection, Northwestern State University of Louisiana (http://library.nsula.edu/egan-family).

29   *Dictionary of Missouri Biography*, Lawrence O. Christensen, William E. Foley, Gary Kremer, Kenneth H. Winn (eds) (Columbia and London, 1999), pp 162–3; Michael C. O'Laughlin, *Missouri Irish: The Original History of the Irish in Missouri* (Kansas City, 2007), pp 37–8; William Barnaby Faherty, *The St Louis Irish: An Unmatched Celtic Community* (St Louis, 2001), pp 1–16.

30   'To James Madison from Robert Brent, 30 January 1812 (Abstract),' Founders Online, National Archives (http://founders.archives.gov/documents/Madison/03-04-02-0170, ver. 2013-06-26). Source: *The Papers of James Madison*, Presidential Series, vol. 4, 5 Nov.

1811–19 July 1812 and supplement 5 Mar. 1809–19 Oct. 1811, J. C. A. Stagg, Jeanne Kerr Cross, Jewel L. Spangler, Ellen J. Barber, Martha J. King, Anne Mandeville Colony and Susan Holbrook Perdue (eds) (Charlottesville, 1999), p. 157.

31   C.E. Carter (ed.), *The Territorial Papers of the United States. Volume XIV. The Territory of Louisiana-Missouri 1806–1814* (Washington, DC, 1949), pp 530–31.

32   F.L. Billon, *Annals of St Louis in its Territorial Days, from 1804 to 1821* (St Louis, 1888), pp 37–8, 71. He is referred to as 'James T. Hull' with reference to the Fourth of July celebrations, though this is probably an error (found elsewhere in relation to his middle initial); at the town meeting he is referred to as James F. Hull.

33   *Missouri Gazette*, 31 Oct. 1812.

34   Earl. F. Niehaus, *The Irish in New Orleans* (Baton Rouge, 1965), pp 3–12; rather surprisingly, the author makes no reference to Hull in this volume.

35   Sprague, *Annals of the American Pulpit*, vol. 4, p. 561.

36   Ray Holder, 'Methodist beginnings in New Orleans, 1813–1814' in Charles E. Nolan (ed.), *Religion in Louisiana* (Lafayette, 2004), p. 241.

37   'Dr James F. Hull, Rector of Christ Church Cathedral, of New Orleans' in *Hull Family Association Journal* (Spring, 2000), p. 6.

38   *Louisiana: A Guide to the State* (Baton Rouge, 1941), p. 130.

39   Holder, 'Methodist beginnings in New Orleans', p. 242.

40   An account of the battle by Hull appeared in the press: *Missouri Gazette*, 25 Feb. 1815.

41   Charles Sealsfield, *The United States of North America as They are* (London, 1828), pp 81–2.

42   H.C. Duncan, *The Diocese of Louisiana, Some of its History, 1838–1888; Also Some of the History of its Parishes and Missions, 1805–1888* (New Orleans, 1888), p. 52.

43   *Journals of the Convention of the Protestant Episcopal Church in the Diocese of New York Episcopal Church. Diocese of New York* (1844), p. 338.

44   Information provided by Erick Montgomery.

45   Mary Louise Christovich, Roulhac Toledano, *New Orleans Architecture: Volume II: The American Sector* (Gretna, LA, 1998), p. 21.

46   Holder, 'Methodist beginnings in New Orleans', p. 248, quoting from 'Autobiography of William Winans', an unpublished manuscript in Millsaps-Wilson Library, Millsaps College, Jackson, Mississippi.

47   Duncan, *The Diocese of Louisiana*, p. 53.

48   Benjamin Henry Latrobe, *Impressions Respecting New Orleans: Diary & Sketches, 1818–1820* (1951), p. 98.

49   Dictionary of Louisiana Biography (http://www.lahistory.org/site25.php), referencing Timothy F. Reilly, 'Religious Leaders and Social Criticism in New Orleans, 1800–1861' (PhD dissertation, University of Missouri at Columbia, 1972).

50   John Smith Kendall, *History of New Orleans* (New Orleans, 1922), vol. 2, p. 710.

51 Ralph Randolph Gurley, *Life and Eloquence of the Rev. Sylvester Larned; First Pastor of the First Presbyterian Church in New Orleans* (New York, 1844), p. 98.

52 Glenn Robins, *The Bishop of the Old South: The Ministry And Civil War Legacy of Leonidas Polk* (Mercer University Press, 2006), p. 66.

53 Duncan, *The Diocese of Louisiana*, p. 53. Hull's daughter Sarah Sinclair Hull may have been given her middle name in honour of Rev. William Sinclair, a Presbyterian minister in Newtownards, County Down, who was also forced into exile in America for his alleged involvement in the 1798 Rebellion. The two men would certainly have known each other in Ireland.

54 'Dr James F. Hull, Rector of Christ Church Cathedral, of New Orleans', p. 6.

55 A transcript of this letter is included in William Henry Curran, *The Life of the Right Honourable John Philpot Curran* (New York, 1820), pp xxix–xxx.

56 PRONI, D3579/2: referred to as Rev. James Hall [sic].

57 'Dr James F. Hull, Rector of Christ Church Cathedral, of New Orleans', p. 6.

58 Duncan, *The Diocese of Louisiana*, p. 53–4.

59 Ibid., p. 54.

60 Dictionary of Louisiana Biography (http://www.lahistory.org/site25.php), referencing Timothy F. Reilly, 'Religious Leaders and Social Criticism in New Orleans, 1800–1861' (PhD dissertation, University of Missouri at Columbia, 1972).

61 *Jewell's Crescent City, Illustrated* (New Orleans, 1873), not paginated.

62 Theodore Clapp, *Autobiographical Sketches and Recollections: During a Thirty-five Years Residence in New Orleans* (New Orleans, 1858), p. 232.

63 Leonard Victor Huber, Peggy McDowell, *New Orleans Architecture: Vol. III: The Cemeteries* (Gretna, LA, 1996), p. 18.

64 Leonard Victor Huber, Guy F. Bernard, *To Glorious Immortality: The Rise and Fall of the Girod Street Cemetery, New Orleans' First Protestant Cemetery, 1822–1957* (New Orleans, 1961), p. 37. The cemetery is now the site of the New Orleans Superdome (Christopher M. Duncan, 'Benjamin Morgan Palmer: southern Presbyterian divine' (PhD dissertation, Auburn University, 2008), p. 86).

65 See Eric J. Brock, *New Orleans Cemeteries* (1999), p. 109 for a photograph of the plaque to those ministers re-interred in Christ Church, including Hull.

66 http://genealogytrails.com/miss/adams/christenings-natches.html.

67 *History of the Yellow Fever in New Orleans, During the Summer of 1853 …* (Philadelphia, 1854), p. 67.

68 'Dr James F. Hull, Rector of Christ Church Cathedral, of New Orleans', p. 6.

Great Famine histories
and Irish historiography

L.A. CLARKSON

MARGUÉRITE CORPORAAL
Relocated Memories:
The Great Famine in Irish and Diaspora Fiction, 1846–1870
Syracuse University Press, 2017
pp 320   ISBN: 978-0-8156-3513-0   pb $34.95

PATRICK FITZGERALD & ANTHONY RUSSELL (EDS)
John Mitchel, Ulster and the Great Irish Famine
Irish Academic Press, Dublin, 2017
pp 224   ISBN: 978-1-9110-2475-0   pb   €22.99

BRYAN MacMAHON
The Great Famine in Tralee and North Kerry
Mercier Press, Cork, 2017
pp 384   ISBN: 978-1-7811-7467-8   hb   €31.50

ENDA DELANEY AND BREANDÁN MAC SUIBHNE (EDS)
Ireland's Great Famine and Popular Politics
Routledge, New York and London, 2016
pp 240   ISBN: 978-0-4158-3630-2   hb   £92

CHRISTINE KINEALY, JASON KING, GERARD MORAN (EDS)
Children and the Great Hunger in Ireland
Quinnipiac University Press & Cork University Press, 2018
pp 328   ISBN: 978-0-9904-6869-1   pb   €25

The flow of Great Famine publications continues unabated. The historian Sir John Clapham once described the British Industrial Revolution as 'a thrice-squeezed orange'. On this measure the Irish

Great Famine is heading towards thrice-times-thrice – and thrice more again. The five books reviewed here add to an ever-growing harvest of publications from a variety of authors. According to the editors of *Ireland's Great Famine and Popular Politics,* since the 1990s 'historians have not been overly interested in the Great Famine', and have left the field to scholars from other disciplines. I am not convinced historians have given up the fight, but the present volumes show that Great Famine has become a fertile area for literary critics, librarians, educationalists, folklorists, archivists, museum curators and even taxi drivers.

Relocated Memories is a prime example. Marguérite Corporaal is Professor in English Literature at Radboud University, Nijmegen. Her book has been warmly praised by literary theorists, one of them claiming that, it 'is one of the most important contributions to Famine studies in recent years.' She has made a detailed study of 62 fictional works and 24 'other texts' relating to the Great Famine published between 1846 and 1870, some in Ireland, some in Britain, and some in North America, which demonstrate 'that the uncritical identification of the Great Famine with silence is problematic in many respects and needs to reassessed'.

The kernel of her thesis is that memories of the Great Famine changed over place and across time. Famine fiction written in Ireland or in Britain 'imagines a temporal transmission of memory, often drawing analogies between the Great Famine and other events from colonial history that generate a palimpsestic heterochrony of Irish time'. Famine fiction written in North America, on the other hand, 'tend[s] to imagine the relocation of Famine memories primarily across space – as legacies that can travel with emigrants to their new homelands, for example – but also as painful pasts that can be pushed back to the safe boundaries of homeland territories, thereby creating the possibilities to reimagine utopian New Irelands in the new settlements of the American West.' It may be because I am not a literary theorist that I pall when I read that famine fiction bears 'witness to a liminality of remembrance'; or that 'the experience of famine is displaced diegetically and temporally as well as spatially'. There is a great deal more of this kind of language that may discourage readers from struggling through Professor Corporaal's survey of neglected sources.

The collection edited by Fitzgerald and Russell was originally presented in 2015 at the annual Great Famine Commemoration held for the first time in Northern Ireland, the symbolism of which, the editors instruct their readers in school-masterly fashion, 'should not be lost on any of us'. The individual essays do not hang well together. All relate to the Great Famine, but only two concern John Mitchel; and four are not about Ulster at all.

The book opens with an essay by Christine Kinealy on 'the women of Belfast and the Great Famine' that investigates the efforts of middle-class and mostly Protestant ladies to raise money to assist their suffering sisters (and their families) in other parts of Ireland. It fits well with her recent book on the role of private charity in alleviating the hardship caused by the Famine.

This is followed by a characteristically perceptive piece from Cormac Ó Gráda on 'the demography of the Famine in Ulster' that modifies the assertion, made several times in the volume, that Ulster suffered as severely as the rest of the country during the crisis. Using data drawn from the censuses of 1841 and 1851, together with measures of excess mortality calculated by Mokyr (1985), Ó Gráda shows that population losses across the province varied greatly from place to place; and they were more the result of emigration than of excess mortality and missing births, contrary to the experience in other provinces.

Jason King moves west, to Limerick, from where, in 1847, 5,000 residents of Curragh Chase migrated to Upper Canada in a project sponsored by a local landowner, Stephen de Vere. What is unusual about this scheme is that the landlord decided to go with his tenants to establish a New Jerusalem. Alas, de Vere's dream did not work out. There were many deaths from fever on the journey out, the arrival at Grosse Isle was chaotic and the journey north daunting. De Vere's once loyal tenants did not prosper and he became increasingly alarmed by the republican spirit developing among many of them. Disillusioned, he returned to Ireland where he became an MP for Limerick and agitated for better conditions on the emigrant ships.

Of the two essays on John Mitchel only one directly concerns the man. An elegant paper by James Quinn explores Mitchel's views on landlord-tenant relationships in Ireland before and during the Famine, and his thoughts on American slavery in the Ante-Bellum South. Mitchel is the hero of Irish nationalists who frequently repeat his vitriolic condemnation of British policy. What Mitchel lacked in logic he more than made up by the power of his pen. His admirers have more difficulty with his defence of American slavery. Mitchel believed American slaves were treated by their owners better than Irish landlords treated their tenants, a proposition that is probably wrong but is at least debatable. He also argued that Africans were born to be enslaved by white men, an opinion that even many of his contemporaries found unacceptable and which today would leave him condemned as a racist.

Mitchel was brought up in Newry, which is Anthony Russell's cue for examining the impact of the Great Famine on the hinterland of the town although, as he points out, Mitchel's views on the Famine were formed by his experiences in the west of Ireland. The Newry hinterland is defined as six baronies in south Armagh and south County Down. Russell employs evidence from the Poor Commission of 1833–4, the Devon Commission, the censuses of 1841 and 1851, and records of the Newry workhouse to arrive at the not very surprising conclusion that the poorest districts suffered the greatest losses of population.

An essay by Cathal Póirtéir explores the value of folklore in understanding the Great Famine. It also touches on the issues of memory discussed by Corporaal, although without the jargon. And, not quite finally, there is a paper by Ciarán Reilly on remittances from America to family members still living in Ireland during the Great Famine, which shows just how important these sums were in alleviating suffering. The book concludes with what the editors describe as 'Japanese rapid-fire presentation style, *pecha kucha*'. These are six fragments by a medley of authors under the collective title of 'Different Writers, Different Perspectives'.

The Great Famine in Tralee and North Kerry is the work of a local historian who knows every hedgerow, townland and parish in his region. This has led him to assume that his readers are similarly well informed, but I for one would have appreciated a map to guide me around the byways of Tralee and north Kerry. The study is firmly grounded in local sources such as newspapers and the correspondence of local poor law officials, civil engineers, justices, priests, rectors, local gentry and businessmen. These sources provide him with the striking titles of the ten chapters that take us from 1845, a year marked by the 'dark and withered appearance' of the crops, to the more cheerful 'Times are mending' that blossomed in 1852. Both years get a chapter apiece, as do 1848 ('Graves call to you for vengeance'), 1849 ('The poor are sinking'), 1850 ('An unprecedented and unexpected influx of pauperism'), and 1851 ('Take Fortune's tide the world is wide'). However, 1846 and 1847 are divided into six-monthly periods labelled chronologically, 'Soft words no more'; 'On the very verge of famine'; 'A chill feeling of despair'; and 'What under Heaven are the people to do?'

The titles catch the changing moods of the time but the chapters themselves are burdened by repetitive detail. The author only rarely raises his eyes to consider wider issues. There are the occasional obligatory condemnations of Charles Trevelyan, British relief policies, and absentee landlords, but there are no angry charges of genocide. The picture that emerges is of a community overwhelmed by a catastrophe beyond its ability to cope. It was a disaster that afflicted primarily the bottom segment of society, a segment described in a local newspaper as 'the once stalwart tillers of the soil' (p. 323). The reporter commented that these stalwarts were absent from the annual races held on Ballyeagh Strand in September 1852, wiped out by death or emigration, but he noted cheerfully that the stands erected for the '*beau monde*' and the '*bourgeoisie*' were once again well populated by the better-off enjoying themselves.

Ireland's Great Famine and Popular Politics is unconcerned by the minutiae of suffering. Its starting point is Michael Davitt's assertion, often repeated, that the starving peasantry were remarkably passive, failing to 'assert even the animal's right of existence.' Not so, according to the editors who claim the focus of their volume 'is popular politics broadly defined, that is, non-élite action ('combined and otherwise'), the ideas that animated it, and the state and social groups towards which it was directed' (p. 5).

Two contributors, John Cunningham writing on food riots and attempts to block the export of grain from Ireland throughout 1846, and Mac Suibhne's account of the spread of the Molly Maguires and similar forms of rural protest into west Donegal during the 1850s, show conclusively that the peasantry was far from passive. Other contributors, though, have difficulty in keeping to the brief. David Jones's account of the graziers who bought much of the encumbered land after the Famine, is an admirably clear account of the complexities of Irish land tenure, but has little to say about popular protest.

And what of the lavishly footnoted 'Walking Backward to Heaven?: Edmond Ronayne's Pilgrimage in Famine Ireland and Gilded Age America' by Kerby Miller *et al*? Ronayne was born into an Irish-speaking community in south-east County Cork in 1832. He learned English at the age of nine and became a protégé of the local Catholic priest. In 1850–51 he was converted by Protestant missionaries working for the Irish Society and began teaching in their schools. In 1856 Ronayne, now with a wife and two sons, headed for Canada, disillusioned by both Catholicism and Protestantism. In Quebec he became a proselytising teacher among the city's Irish Catholics. He joined the Orange Order but soon transferred his allegiance to the Masons. In 1865 Ronayne moved to Chicago, then a boom city after the Civil War, to try his luck. He fell on hard times and turned to the Masons for help, even though he had renounced them before leaving Quebec. He caught fever and was nursed back to health by Catholic nuns. He then earned a living by peddling goods including picture-postcards of Fenian leaders. Eventually he prospered and set himself up as a teacher and began investing in property. He re-joined the Masonic Order and became active in their relief activities after the Chicago fire. He was then converted by the evangelists Sankey and Moody, abandoned the Masons (again) and thereafter 'relied totally on the Scriptures and his new relationship with Jesus.' Miller speculates that Ronayne might have been a Fenian before he left Ireland. Perhaps he was; or perhaps not. All we really can be certain of is that Ronayne was a mixed-up Irish emigrant.

David Miller's essay on 'Soup and Providence: Varieties of Protestantism and the Great Famine', struggles with definitions. 'Popular politics', he points out, is a term used to describe the actions of people 'without special rank or position in society' (p. 59). Yet the Protestant clergy of the Church of Ireland were part of the establishment, more likely to curb popular politics than to encourage it. In a closely argued essay Miller suggests that the Famine's political impact came mainly after the event by changing Irish politics from largely Anglicans versus non-Anglicans in 1798, to Protestant versus Catholics in 1886. Whether this was popular politics or high politics is a matter of debate.

The remaining two essays engage more closely with the theme of popular politics. Melissa Fegan provides a thoughtful account of how contemporary writers, most of them socially distant from the poor, tried to understand the horrors of the Famine. And Ciarán Reilly's essay on the work of land agents is set around John Ross Mahon, the agent for Major Denis Mahon who cleared 1,000 families from his Strokestown estate in 1847 and was assassinated for his trouble by members of a local secret society, allegedly with the connivance of the parish priest.

The contributors to *Children and the Great Hunger in Ireland* manage, most of them, to keep to the subject. This collection of thirteen essays is the latest publication from Ireland's Great Hunger Institute at Quinnipiac University. Three excellent essays by Christine Kinealy, Gerard Moran and Simon Gallaher concentrate on the fate of children in workhouses during and after the Famine; and Jonny Gerber, a 'biological anthropologist', in a novel paper examines the bones of more than 500 children excavated from the mass burial ground attached to the Kilkenny workhouse. Many of them show lesions caused by scurvy, as well as evidence of untreated wounds and infections, and signs of stunted growth resulting from malnutrition.

Three writers consider the treatment of Irish orphans abandoned at Grosse Isle and in New Brunswick. Mark McGowan challenges a widespread belief that orphans were adopted by French-Canadian families and integrated into their own families. There was no adoption in the legal sense at the time and few orphans were treated as family members. Most were used as domestic or agricultural labourers and many did not stay long with the host families. Koral La Vorgna tells of a failed attempt to establish a school for orphans in New Brunswick. And Jason King has a poignant tale of the efforts of one seven-year-old orphan who did make good (he became a priest) who 30 years later vainly searched for a younger sister who had been left behind in Ireland. The final four essays are grouped under the heading

'Representing Trauma' and speculate how the memories of the Great Famine have become embedded into children's literature, historical narratives, childhood recollections, and survive in half-remembered Irish words and phrases used in everyday conversation.

The volumes under review show that the squeezing of the orange has not yet reached exhaustion point, although diminishing returns may have set in. The continuing fascination with the Great Famine over the last four decades raises wider questions about the direction of Irish historiography. Some of the recent offerings are of questionable quality. Of greater concern is that the focus on the Great Famine strengthens a common belief that Ireland is exceptional. For example, a contributor to *Children and the Great Hunger* writes that the Irish 'are remembered in the historical record as victims – as a people of terrible genocide or Famine'. Is this all the 'historical record' has to say about Ireland; and is it true?

The belief in exceptionalism extends beyond the Great Famine. When assessing the economic performance of Ireland since 1922 the Irish-born Oxford economist Kevin O'Rourke has written recently, 'when I was a young boy in primary school, we were taught that post-independence Ireland was poor but uniquely virtuous. Today, we are taught that it was poor and uniquely wicked. Both positions are misguided: we were never as different as people have made out.'[1] As for the Great Famine, it was, says O'Rourke, 'genuinely unusual – the last mass subsistence crisis in peacetime Western Europe with the exception of the Finnish famine of the 1860s'. But the emigration rates it triggered were exceeded by those of Italy and matched by Norway; and the forces that drove people from Ireland – high fertility and rural poverty – were the same everywhere.

The image of Ireland as a famine-tortured land is at best myopic. I began teaching Irish history in the 1970s, concentrating on economic and social developments since the sixteenth century. As a newcomer to the subject I was struck by the enormous transformation of Ireland from a small, impoverished, society in the sixteenth century into the modern, democratic, nation we see today. It was a transformation achieved without an abundant endowment of natural resources and without the acquisition of a great empire. For most of the time the country was tied economically and politically to Britain and society was blighted by religious discord. And during the 1840s Ireland suffered a late and devastating famine.

Notwithstanding such disadvantages Ireland today stands high among the modern democracies. It is to be welcomed that what one contributor to *Children and the Great Hunger* calls 'The Great Silence' on the Great Famine has been shattered. But cries of anguish, blame and victimhood should not drown out a more optimistic story. The emergence of modern Ireland, too, is part of the historical record.

1   K.H. O'Rourke, 'Independent Ireland in Comparative Perspective', *Irish Economic and Social History*, vol. 4 (2017), p. 19.

REVIEW ARTICLE

Documenting the transatlantic Covenanting strain

EULL DUNLOP

GEOFFREY ALLEN (COMPILER)
The Covenanters in Ireland, A History of the Congregations
Cameron Press (c/o Covenanter Book Centre, www.covenanterbooks.com), 2010
pp 464   ISBN: 978-1-9054-5504-1   hb   £15

GEOFFREY ALLEN (ED)
Covenanters in Ireland, Introducing the Reformed Presbyterian Church
Cameron Press (c/o Covenanter Book Centre, www.covenanterbooks.com), 2012
pp 86   ISBN: 978-1-9054-5505-8   pb   £4.99

ADAM LOUGHRIDGE
The Covenanters in Ireland
Cameron Press, 1984 (with reprints)
pp 150   ISBN: 978-0-9513-1400-5   pb   £4.99

165

'Nearly all Americans of Presbyterian ancestry think that they are descended from the Covenanters' runs the somewhat tongue-in-cheek comment of a gently chiding, Belfast-based, genealogist with special insight into denominational histories. Readers of *Familia* dedicated to discussion of the variegated culture of 'the Scotch-Irish people' will therefore readily appreciate the importance, on either side of the Atlantic, of this substantial, well-illustrated volume, whose contents arguably exceed its straightforward title. As will be shown, this solid compendium printed on heavy art paper will introduce readers to a tradition whose byways are not necessarily known beyond limited circles.

COMPANIONS

To avoid confusion let us first mention two companion publications from the same publisher.

1 A slim, well-illustrated, very manageable booklet edited by Geoffrey Allen, *Covenanters in Ireland, Introducing the Reformed Presbyterian Church* (2012), with accompanying CD-ROM, offers a whistle-stop tour 'from the Scottish Reformation to the signing of the National Covenant of 1638 and Solemn League and Covenant of 1643, to "The Killing Times" of 1684–1688, and through the Williamite Revolution to the twenty-first century'. Putting matters briefly, those who have long aspired to see recognised Christ's kingship over the Nation, the ideal of the so-called Second Reformation in Scotland, readily recall the crucible of persecution and suffering and insist that they remain spiritually and morally vigilant in this day and generation.

2 A more intensive, more demanding, study is the late Professor Adam Loughridge's *The Covenanters in Ireland* (1984, with reprints). The fruit of a postgraduate thesis, that item of general coverage now finds its localised complement in the volume under review which, perhaps open to titular confusion with Loughridge's work, presents in one volume diverse material which had been under collection since the 1940s. Partially disclosed in Loughridge's articles, 'Where we worship', in the denomination's periodical, *The Covenanter Witness* from 1975 to 1977, information on all past and present congregations is now more readily available to a wider readership.

PRESBYTERIES

Following contextual material which might more logically have been *pre*ceded by the Notes and Acknowledgements and which with typographical boldness leaves no doubt about the identity of those considered heroes of the Covenanting faith in Scotland and then Ireland, we have entries for individual congregations of the Irish Synod's four presbyteries. Noticeably based in the nine-county province of Ulster, their 40 or so congregations are often rural, set predictably in areas of deep Scottish influence and sometimes taking their names from the unique Irish land division that is the townland. This volume takes a reader, living in County Antrim near Kellswater meeting-house (the 'Capital of Covenanting' in Loughridge's memorable phrase) in the townland of Carnaughts, but intent on exploring provincial ground, on a fascinating tour. How much more so for the far distant reader deeply curious about families who once worshipped in a place still invoked in inherited lore?

From Cullybackey to Drimbolg to Ballyclabber and the long defunct Ringrash, among other locations, in the Northern Presbytery; from Ballyclare to Dromara to Bailiesmills and 'formally disorganised' Ballymacashon in the Eastern; from Ballenon to Creevagh to Loughbrickland and Rathfriland in the Southern, and from Bready to Milford to Stranorlar to the long dissolved Gortlee in the West, we have potted histories of congregations and ministries. One notes a constant, even formulaic, emphasis on pastoral fidelity in what appear to be steady rather than spectacular situations. But, human nature being what it is (and we are working within a framework of sin and salvation), such approbation cannot quite be universal. A case of deposition from a rural ministry is recorded in very few words, as is the dissolution of an urban congregation after unspecified 'difficulties' requiring investigation by the relevant presbytery. There appears to be no detail about a minister, sometime based in England, who reportedly developed eccentric episcopal interests utterly antithetical to Presbyterian ecclesiology.

DIVISION

At this point, while positively recognising the denomination's over-arching commitment to its concept of doctrinal and ecclesiological purity, we note in the ebb and flow of local circumstances some examples of congregations moving in or out of the Reformed Presbyterian camp. There were congregations constituted in local circumstances by secessions from other denominations, as other originally Covenanting congregations eventually joined the General Assembly of the Presbyterian Church in Ireland. Two examples in the latter category were Eskylane and Loughmourne, congregations of a 60-year secession (1842–1902) from the Synod which is also represented by a handsome red-brick building in Belfast's Botanic Avenue. Now 'sadly' occupied by a night-club, it was obviously once a place of Protestant worship. Last used for that purpose by a congregation of the Evangelical Presbyterian Church (originally the Irish Evangelical Church, arguably a remote reflection (1927) of theological differences emerging in early twentieth-century Princeton), the meeting-house speaks to historians of the short-lived Eastern Reformed Synod. As explained, the context of division in the Irish Synod in 1840, like that in the American Church in 1833 and in the Scottish Church in 1863, was the enduring question, that of Covenanting attitudes to civil government. Entirely logically, the closing pages of the compendium whose purpose is quintessentially proclamatory are devoted to re-affirmation of Reformed Presbyterianism's 'Distinctive Principles', which set the personal and societal bar very high indeed.

CLANS

Despite the inbuilt capacity for division of churches deriving from the Reformation, old Covenanting families in Ulster will not be offended by others' standard observation that they are 'clannish'. Admittedly there have been examples of marrying-out liturgically (compare, in the broadest sense, Jewish 'assimilation') from a church tenaciously committed to exclusive psalmody, as also of marrying-in, but one is still much struck by interconnections when browsing through the very valuable *Fasti* of Reformed Presbyterian ministers who served on both sides of the Atlantic. As these lists distinguish between those who ministered in the main Irish Synod and those who temporarily tabernacled within the Eastern Reformed camp, as well as those who served in the small Reformed Presbyterian Church of Scotland, so there is a very valuable roll-call of Irish-born ministers who served in the Reformed Presbyterian Church of North America. A head-note helpfully provides the reader with a simple but essential guide to four stages of division which lie behind that continuing denomination of some 75 congregations, now based largely in north-eastern Kansas, Central Indiana and Western Pennsylvania. This reviewer with lifelong involvement in education would be particularly interested to learn more of the ethos and constituency of their Geneva College, Beaver Falls, and Reformed Presbyterian Theological Seminary, Pittsburgh.

MIGRATION

In addition to the cases of William Martin (1729–1806) and William Gibson (1753–1838), first and second ministers of Kellswater, we select a few other examples suggestive of ministerial migration. Born in the parish of Ahoghill, County Antrim, and suspected of revolutionary instincts at home, John Black (1768–1849) supposedly became the first Covenanting minister settled west of the Alleghenies. Like Armour McFarland (1808–94) of County Tyrone, and Ohio, in typifying the Ulster-Scots trend in nomenclature by having a surname as a forename, Boyd McCullough (born at Rathfriland, County Down, 1825) was installed by the nicely-named Lakes Presbytery. Manifesting the tendency for internal movement which might speak of smaller rather than larger charges, he ministered variously in Michigan, Minnesota, Wisconsin and Pennsylvania. Born at Moylarg, near Cullybackey, County Antrim, and followed to America by a namesake (1790–1872) from the same townland, Samuel Brown Wylie (1773–1852) was a teacher who had been suspected of United Irish tendencies at home. He was 'the first Covenanter minister ordained [1800] in America'; who travelled widely, up to Vermont and, in opposition to slavery, down through the South; and who occupied academic positions in Pennsylvania. The American *Fasti* valuably document the wide diffusion (with the entry for the far-travelled Robert Andrew Blair (1876–1960) of Aghadowey, Ohio, China, Kansas and Slippery Rock,

Pennsylvania, being duplicated) of migrant ministers with Ulster names and ancestry and sometimes record details of descendants, the building-bricks of the diaspora. Historic connections have, of course, often been maintained across the Atlantic and there has been co-operation in various missionary ventures. Reformed Presbyterianism in Canada and Australia also derives from Irish roots.

REFORMED PRESBYTERIANISM IN IRELAND

In Ireland today, in its numerically modest way, Reformed Presbyterianism claims to be in generally good heart. While it has long had its dynasties, sometimes strengthened by inter-marriage between long-established families, lately its constituency and indeed ministerial roll have also been extended by the incoming of those who, dissatisfied with more liberal trends elsewhere, have sought a more conservative theological home. Given earlier comment about the Covenanters being concentrated in the north-east, we note the sober, measured descriptions of past ventures (as in Dublin and Cork) which were not sustained, as well as the expressions of hope for new outreach in northern locations. With more educational opportunity than ever available to those in the pews (and the Covenanters, if salt and light, have not been the least-socially privileged in society), the denomination's historic commitment to an educated ministry – typical of the churches of the Reformation preoccupied with the central authoritative text of Scripture – is maintained by a small theological college. For logistical reasons, but arguably with some interactive practical benefit, its academically well-qualified staff combine teaching with their pastoral charges. And, as the volume under discussion proves, there has lately been a new concentration on Covenanting history and, more acutely, theological heritage.

DESIGN FEATURES

Finally, some further comment on visual aspects of a work which is encased in appropriately Presbyterian blue boards designed by Mark Thompson of County Down, long an enthusiastic student of Ulster's Scottish heritage. As happily acknowledged at the outset, this volume (which, like *Covenanters in Ireland*, might have benefited from much greater editorial care and consistency) is replete with illustrations, some of them very rare indeed. Readers in, say, Quinter, Kansas, may be enabled in some measure to imagine where an Ulster ancestor once worshipped in the plain Reformed style. For some with optical difficulties, the widely-spaced type might usefully have been sized up and for this reviewer at least there was what he reluctantly calls a running distraction. The Covenanting banner, 'For Christ's Crown and Covenant', is an all-important, succinct statement of the denominational vision, whose importance one would not wish to diminish. However, the banner's reproduction in black miniature at the foot of each page doggedly diverts the eye. Its use as a header, aligned left and right, might have been more comfortable, with page-numbers then being discreetly re-located as a central footer.

Stepping back from minutiae, however, one heartily commends a not quite perfect but thoroughly welcome joint achievement by the Church History and the Bookshop and Publications Committees of the Reformed Presbyterian Church in Ireland. Postage costs notwithstanding, copies of this Covenanting encyclopaedia are bound to have crossed the Atlantic and to have travelled up country. Further migration in a story of many migrations, ideological as well as physical! All-in-all a valuable work of reference.

REVIEW ARTICLE

And still they come:
the Easter Rising and beyond …

RICHARD McMINN

BRIAN HUGHES (ED.)
Eoin MacNéill: Memoir of a Revolutionary Scholar
Irish Manuscripts Commission, 2016
pp 160   ISBN: 978-1-906865-61-0   hb   €25

DAITHÍ Ó CORRÁIN, JAMES McGUIRE, W.J. McCORMACK,
CONOR MULVAGH, JOHN McCAFFERTY
Analecta Hibernica, No. 47
Irish Manuscripts Commission, 2016
pp 250   ISBN: 978-1-906865-60-3   pb   €30

CIARA BOYLAN, SARAH-ANNE BUCKLEY, PAT DOLAN (EDS)
Family Histories of the Irish Revolution
Open Air/Four Courts Press, 2017
pp 240   ISBN: 978-1-84682-682-5   pb   €22.45

SÍOBRA AIKEN, FEARGHAL MAC BHLOSCAIDH, LIAM Ó DUIBHIR,
DIARMUID Ó TUAMA (EDS)
*The Men Will Talk to Me: Ernie O'Malley's
Interviews with the Northern Divisions*
Merrion Press, 2018
pp 300   ISBN: 978-1-78537-164-6   pb   €19.99

CONOR McNAMARA
*War and Revolution in the West of Ireland
Galway, 1913–22*
Irish Academic Press, 2018
pp 220   ISBN: 978-1-78537-160-8   pb   €16.99

TOM BOYLAN, NICHOLAS CANNY, MARY HARRIS (EDS)
*Ireland, 1916–2016: The Promise and Challenge of National
Sovereignty*
Open Air/Four Courts Press, 2018
pp 168   ISBN: 978-1-84682-681-8   hb   €29.95

It was F.X. Martin's article, 'Eoin MacNéill on the 1916 Rising', in *Irish Historical Studies*, xii (1960–61), which first highlighted in full detail the moral reservations expressed by the 'revolutionary scholar' about the proposed Rising, from whose planning he had been deliberately excluded by Connolly and Pearse. These reservations, which he had committed to paper in a 1917 memorandum, lay behind his decision to issue, as President of the Irish Volunteers, the famous, or infamous, countermanding order of Easter Sunday. This event was to dog him for the remainder of his career and despite his subsequent internment by the British, rendered him a traitor to some on the republican wing of nationalism. MacNéill had a long and interesting career as both a politician and serious scholar. Michael Tierney's 1980 memoir, *Eoin MacNéill: Scholar and Man of Action, 1867–1945,* drew the attention of historians and the general public to the full complexity of that career. However, MacNéill himself in 1932 had begun to dictate a personal account of his life and in particular his own perspective on 'the historical events in which he had taken part'. While incomplete, fragmentary and in need of editorial revision, it is a version of this document (now in the UCD Archives) which the Irish Manuscripts Commission has made available in this handsome volume, edited and introduced by Brian Hughes of the University of Exeter. While the output of new publications on '1916 and all that' shows little sign as yet of reducing, all those interested in early twentieth-century Irish history will welcome having easy access to this important historical source document. Indeed, as Hughes points out, 'given the circumstances of its creation [dictated over a long period of time to two different journalists without recourse to notes or other sources], it often feels more like the record of a conversation with MacNéill than a work of autobiography'. Inevitably, there is a degree of repetition and 'many of its themes and topics are underdeveloped'. It is very much history in the raw, but none the worse for that.

The 200-plus original typescript pages include coverage of MacNéill's early life in Glenarm, County Antrim, which the editor in his introduction somewhat misleadingly describes as 'a small Catholic enclave', whereas MacNéill himself stresses that 'there were three Protestant denominations in the place' and 'the local people of different religions got on remarkably well together' – which indeed would be my own experience as an east Antrim native. MacNéill also provides quite a detailed account of his role in the foundation and work of the Gaelic League, of which he became Vice-President in 1903 and President in 1916. He gives his personal perspective on the foundation of the Irish Volunteers in November 1913 and on the build-up to the Easter Rising, including the much discussed countermanding order (reproduced on the dust jacket, where it is cleverly superimposed by designer Wendy Dunbar on a family group photograph showing MacNéill with his cherished pipe clenched in his mouth).

The memoir also ranges over MacNéill's time as a member and minister in the first Dáil, notably as Minister of Education in the first Irish Free State government and as that government's representative (and to an extent scapegoat) on the ill-fated Boundary Commission in 1924. He provides a moving account of the shooting and subsequent death a few hours later of his fellow Minister, Kevin O'Higgins in 1927, events to which by accident he personally was a witness. Thereafter, the document rather peters out, even though MacNéill resumed his impressive academic career, including his UCD professorship in early Irish history, until his death from cancer in 1945 at the age of 78. This return to the safety of *academe* followed his failure to win a seat in the June 1927 general election when he had again stood as a Cumann na nGaedhael candidate. Interestingly, it was in this academic phase of his career that MacNéill played a vital role in the foundation of the Irish Manuscripts Commission, which he chaired from 1929 to his death in 1945. Given his contribution to its genesis and consolidation, it is fitting that the Commission should be the publisher of the MacNéill memoir.

Indeed, as Hughes notes: 'For MacNéill, the [Irish] language and culture were key and indisputable elements of national identity and always more important than political or state power' (although on mature reflection he believed the Gaelic League 'should have kept entirely clear of politics' and blamed himself for failing to have prevented this (p. 45)). Thus, it is a pity that the memoir omits a detailed treatment of his academic life and achievements, which were many, other than his work with the Gaelic League and a brief reference to some of his early writing on Irish history. There are other major gaps, most notably very limited coverage of the Irish Civil War (1922–3). MacNéill astonishingly suggests that the Parnell split over the O'Shea divorce case in 1890 was 'deeper and sharper and more widespread than anything we experienced afterwards even at the height of the civil war in '22'. This is especially the case when one recalls that his own family divided on the issue of the Treaty and that his son Brian was shot and killed by Free State troops at Benbulben in September 1922 in controversial circumstances. But perhaps, as Hughes suggests, the whole episode of the Civil War was too painful to face, for a man who couldn't even bring himself to visit the cross at Benbulben that marked his son Brian's death and who had been a minister in a government which had presided over the execution of former comrades.

However, the reader does gain much valuable insight into MacNéill's political career, including his belief that Edward Carson was the key to any understanding of early twentieth-century Irish history: 'Carson, nominally the leader of Ulster Orangeism, actually the agent of London politicians, transformed the whole situation in Ireland and opened the way for the overthrow of the English regime' (p. 47). Despite his Glenarm upbringing in a mixed community, MacNéill seems to have underestimated Protestant attachment to the unionist cause, blaming this solely on cynical British sectarian manipulation (see, for example, p. 119 where he argues that without it, 'we should soon have a united Ireland'). The MacNéill memoir, however, is at its most valuable in providing a key insider's account of both the Easter Rising and the Boundary Commission debacle, even if its author is at pains to offer a defence of his own controversial role in both events and to dismiss reports by third parties of conversations at which they had not been physically present.

As Brian Hughes emphasises in his short introduction, MacNéill 'was no pacifist' but 'had very clear ideas about the conditions that would justify armed action by the Volunteers'. He was strongly opposed to military action without a significant chance of success. Without that, to fight was 'morally wrong'. Those who led a doomed rebellion in order to make a statement would 'incur the guilt not only of that action itself but of all its direct consequences'. For MacNéill, to kill in such circumstances would equate to 'murder'.

As for MacNéill's role as the Irish Free State's representative to the Boundary Commission, created under Article 12 of the Anglo-Irish Treaty to settle the precise delineation of the Northern Ireland border, MacNéill describes it in his memoir as 'the most disagreeable duty I had ever undertaken for to my mind it was nothing short of an outrage on Ireland'. Leaked reports, that the Commission would recommend little change, led MacNéill to conclude that his position had become untenable and he resigned both his seat on the Commission and his ministerial post. MacNéill in the memoir is keen to stress his doubts from the outset about Article 12 and to condemn those who expected the Commission to make major boundary changes, given its remit and membership. However, as Hughes argues, while MacNéill was 'in many respects, a scapegoat for the Free State government … his own inactivity did nothing to help matters'.

The Irish Manuscripts Commission's forty-seventh annual report outlining its work during the calendar year of 2015 (published as usual in the year following) contained, as has become a regular practice, a selection of unpublished historical documents of significance. Given the publication date, it was hardly surprising that the four substantial documents chosen on this occasion related directly or indirectly to the Easter Rising. The Commission's high editorial standards have been well maintained throughout the volume, with an introductory essay by the editor(s) of each of the documents, along with a series of comprehensive and informative footnotes. There are no illustrations, which given the target readership, is not a surprise. However, most readers would have benefited from the inclusion of a detailed street map of 1916 Dublin, given the constant references by the autobiographical authors of three of the four accounts reproduced here to the geography and layout of the city's streets and roads, not to mention its public buildings. Fr Murphy, for example, describes his frequent journeyings during Easter week 1916 in minute detail, leaving this reader at least a little confused at times!

Daithí Ó Corráin of DCU presents us with a fascinating memoir by Jeremiah Joseph O'Connell, better known as 'J.J.' or 'Ginger' O'Connell, on account of his red hair and moustache, of his role and experiences as a senior member of the Irish Volunteers in 1914–16, along with a brief reflection on the reorganisation of the organisation in 1917. Frustratingly, there is no first-hand account by O'Connell of the Rising itself and only a short analysis of the significance of its consequences, notably the internment together of groups of Volunteers in prison camps. 'The man who was released from Frongoch at Xmas

1916 was a professional soldier – quite another man from the enthusiastic nationalist who turned out in Easter week' (p. 102).

O'Connell has tended to feature only briefly in many accounts of the Irish revolution, apart from his brief starring role as a kidnapped prisoner in the Four Courts in June 1922. Given his popularity with the newly-created National Army, as a prisoner of the Republicans besieged in the building, he provided a valuable *casus belli* and managed to emerge unscathed from the smoking ruins. Professor Charles Townshend (*Political Violence in Ireland*, 1983, p. 289) has described O'Connell as 'the nearest thing to a military expert that the Volunteers possessed'. This memoir demonstrates that Townshend's judgement was accurate, although O'Connell's actual professional military experience was limited to his service in the 69th (New York Irish) Regiment of the US Army in 1912–14. However, O'Connell was a keen student of military history and almost seems to have consciously promoted his claimed expertise through public lectures, articles in the columns of the *Irish Volunteer* newspaper and his energetic criss-crossing of the whole country (in part by bicycle) to promote training and better organisation, working closely with Eoin MacNéill and Bulmer Hobson, in the years from 1914 to 1916.

Despite not being a member of the IRB and notwithstanding his role in conveying Eoin MacNéill's countermand order on Easter Sunday, 'he held a string of posts at headquarters level in the Irish Volunteers, IRA and National Army between 1915 and 1924'. From 1925 until his early death in 1944, he seems to have been shunted downwards in rank to a series of lesser posts, for example, as the OC Army School of Equitation and then Director of the Military Archives in the 1930s. Indeed, the writing of the partial memoir sometime between 1934 and 1936, the editor suggests, may have been part of a campaign against the failure to recognise, for pension purposes, his military service prior to April 1917.

Whatever its motivation, the memoir is 'a very accurate document', which 'gives a unique insight to the challenges of rebuilding the Volunteers after the split in September 1914'. O'Connell's incessant travels gave him a unique knowledge of the organisation, its popularity or otherwise, and its state of training across the whole island. As the editor notes, its value is enhanced, because its timespan (September 1914 to March 1916) is 'not well illuminated in the witness statements collected by the Bureau of Military History'. Ably supported by Bulmer Hobson, O'Connell was an organisation and training man *par excellence*. As O'Connell himself put it, 'the fact is both Pearse and MacDonagh (Plunkett also) believed that the art of war could be studied in books without any trouble being taken to fit the book theories to material facts, or to human nature' (p. 59). Pearse may have believed that the Volunteers must become 'a real army, not a stage army', but it was O'Connell, acutely aware in particular of the gulf in military standard between the Dublin Brigade and the rest of the country, who did the work to try and bring this about. However, despite O'Connell's 'underappreciated pragmatism, organisational capacity and military knowledge', there was only so much that one man in a railway carriage or on a bicycle could achieve, as this extremely detailed insight into the military preparations of the Volunteers during a crucial period makes clear.

Mrs Marion Kelleher's round-robin letter to family members in the immediate aftermath of the Rising in Dublin (edited by James McGuire of UCD and the IMC's Chairman in 2015) provides a more limited, eye-witness perspective on the events of Easter week itself. As the editor acknowledges, the letter of some 5,500 words written over the mornings of 10–11 May, 'does not add to knowledge or understanding of the military events and high politics of the 1916 Rising – it is, rather, a vivid account from the side lines of the impact of armed hostilities on domestic life in a prosperous inner-city suburb' [Leeson Park]. Isabel Marion Kelleher was the daughter of a prominent Londonderry businessman and Presbyterian, active in unionist politics, Sir John Johnston (1843–1919). Marion was the first woman to enter TCD but rather than taking a degree, opted for marriage to one of Trinity's leading academics, the mathematician, Stephen Kelleher, a Roman Catholic and supporter of Home Rule. Thus, 'she brought an unusual perspective to events'.

Henry Hanna's 'A Citizen's Diary', edited by W.J. McCormack, provides its readers with a somewhat wider account of the events, although again from a perspective of hostility, like Marion Kelleher, towards those involved in the Rising. Hanna, a Belfast-born

Presbyterian from a middle-class family, was an established practising barrister in 1916 and later to become a High Court judge under the Free State government. In 1916 he was living at 54 Lansdowne Road in south Dublin. Thus, as McCormack suggests, although not unique, Hanna's narrative 'provides a valuable perspective on the domestic disruption the rebellion caused the unionist population in those parts of the city that experienced, or were close to, the fighting'. Indeed, both Kelleher and Hanna report, for example, the difficulties in obtaining even basic supplies such as bread (although this was somewhat eased by having servants to dispatch on search missions). But the most valuable aspect of the Hanna diary stems from the fact that its author was a member of the often derided Volunteer Training Corps (VTC) – the sometimes mocked 'Gorgeous Wrecks'. As such, he participated in uniform on Easter Monday 1916 in a morning training exercise at Ticknock in the Dublin mountains and was one of the 'mature' part-timers who came under heavy fire from Irish Volunteers as they attempted to return to base at Beggar's Bush Barracks, suffering multiple casualties. The inclusion by Hanna of a useful sketch map of the Barracks and surrounding streets further enhances the account and underscores my earlier comment about the volume's overall lack of map illustrations. As McCormack notes, 'the role of the VTC has been neglected by historians of the Easter insurrection', so the Hanna diary helps to fill the gap. For McCormack, responsibility for the attack on this elderly 'Dad's Army' unit, has to be placed at the door of Plunkett, often praised for his tactical skill in defending the nearby Mount Street Bridge. We owe the preservation of the diary in the TCD archives to the inclusion of a typed copy amongst the papers of the playwright Denis Johnston (1901–84), whose family also lived on Lansdowne Road.

The archives of the Capuchin Order hold 42 typescript pages of an account of the experiences of one of its members, Fr Columbus Murphy, dated 29 July 1916 (so not a diary in the strict sense) during the Easter Rising. It is, however, written in diary format. Conor Mulvagh and John McCafferty of UCD provide a balanced and informed introduction to what is an important primary source, given Murphy's almost ubiquitous presence at many of the key events and locations. Indeed, his ability to move around the city centre, equipped with military permits, clearly aided by his priestly role and unscathed throughout, was quite remarkable. His account complements those of fellow clerics, Fr Augustine Hayden and Fr Aloysius Travers, but the editors conclude that that of Fr Columbus is more comprehensive and accurate, especially since it was not originally intended for publication. Thus, for example, he is willing to draw attention to witnessing the first child casualty of the Rising (baby Séan Foster), an interesting anticipation of the wider net eventually cast by Joe Duffy's best-selling 2015 book, *Children of the Rising*.

Certainly, Fr Columbus was often in the right place at the right time. This was a week that saw him 'tend to the wounded, try to deal with the growing number of dead and, ultimately, play a central role in the negotiations for surrender'. Following the cessation of hostilities, the focus of Fr Columbus' work changed; 'prioritising prison visitations, he concentrated on the welfare of female combatants [including Constance Markievicz], before moving on to tend to the spiritual needs on [sic] the first batches of condemned rebel leaders'. Thus, as a piece of first-hand testimony, the account is of great value.

However, as the editors correctly point out, 'the partialities of the author are revealed in the text'. Instances of public drunkenness all pertain to British soldiers in contrast to the sobriety of the rebels, who resist the temptations of the abundant wine cellars of the Four Courts. Irishmen in British uniforms, of all classes, behave with kindness. Fr Columbus, the editors point out, is also anxious to play down the 'manifest enmity which existed between rival sections of Dublin's citizenry'. Thus, his narrative 'can be seen as part of a wider nationalist project of building national unity out of a mythologised retelling of the story of Easter 1916'. Although he begins in quite neutral tones, by the later stages of the document, 'the volunteers' become 'the boys', with General Maxwell 'playing the Nero part' in the burning of Dublin, while 'the Republican flag …' is 'proudly and brazenly afloat' above the General Post Office, as Fr Columbus gazes down from his grandstand location on the top floor of Jervis Street Hospital. However, he also wryly acknowledges (p. 177) 'that the fifteen acres of the Phoenix Park would scarcely be large enough to hold all those who, in confidence, claim to have fought in the General Post Office; where the garrison was scarcely three hundred all told'.

Readers of this journal in particular will empathise with the warning issued by Professor Gearóid Ó Tuathaigh in his eloquent and succinct introductory chapter in *Family Histories of the Irish Revolution*, reviewing the shifts in the historiography of the revolution of 1913–23 during the century since the revolutionary events themselves. Having outlined the major growth in the study and writing of family history in recent decades and its role as 'an enabling framework', he reminds readers of this collection of essays that 'engagement with the revolutionary decade through the lens of family history presents its own challenges – there are hazards as well as rewards'. He then sets out both issues with his usual clarity in several paragraphs that all practitioners of family history would do well to read. Indeed, the whole chapter should be on the reading list of students of modern Irish history.

But as Ó Tuathaigh reminds us, despite the traps lying in wait for the historically unwary, 'there are regions of the past that only memory knows'. So to take one example at random from the diverse range of family history essays which are contained in this volume, the study of the Shaw family of County Westmeath by Olga Cox Cameron and John Cox sheds fascinating light on the career of Patrick Walter Shaw (1874–1940), a wealthy Catholic Mullingar businessman and politician, with an 'ostentatious lifestyle', the owner of 23 horses, whose family home, Belsize, was a 'haven of middle class comfort', with food and wine lavishly dispensed by the genial host who 'liked to wear diamonds' and boasted of owning both the first car and the first radio in Mullingar. Initially, a Redmondite county councillor in favour of British army recruitment and hostile to the Easter Rising about which he wrote a personal letter of apology to the King, but always a pragmatist, he later aligned first with Sinn Féin in 1921 and subsequently with Cumann na nGaedheal, as a TD for Longford-Westmeath 1923–32. The authors report the story that during a Dáil election campaign, a hostile slogan was painted on walls around Mullingar: 'Where was Shaw in 1916?'. This didn't trouble Patrick Shaw greatly, as he simply paid someone to paint below: 'Fairyhouse! Where else?'. Such are the invaluable nuggets that memory, in the context of family history, can yield.

The volume has a short Foreword from no less than the President of Ireland, Michael D. Higgins, who succinctly states its *raison d'être*. 'The staff community of NUI Galway have embarked on a project of ethical remembering of the founding events of our state and its context.' Or as the joint editors put it in their introductory chapter: 'This volume presents a selection of stories from current and retired staff … on how their ancestors participated in the Irish revolution'. They also stress that 'the volume has been written from a history of family and a life course perspective'. They then explain that 'life course refers to a multi-disciplinary approach to better understanding the elements and dynamics of an individual's life journey and how this is influenced by socio-economic, political and cultural contexts'.

So, in a sense, this is not 'pure history' as such and comes with some sociological theory and scaffolding. Indeed, while some of the contributors have a background in the discipline of history, the majority have a different academic pedigree. However, as noted above, the 15 core essays (arranged under three distinct themes – 'Women and Gender', '1916–21' and 'The Irish Revolution and Beyond') still have much to offer the historian. Inevitably, some are concerned with more significant historical figures than others and some are less informative, either because of the limitations of surviving source material, or the *omerta* observed by some of the now deceased participants in the War of Independence and the Civil War of 1922–3. The editors, in making a selection from what was probably an even larger number of potential essays, have tried to ensure some balance by including Redmondite (Patrick Shaw and Tom Kettle), socialist (Martin Savage and Peadar O'Donnell) and RIC (Head Constable John Dillon and Sergeant Michael Long) perspectives. Apart from Chris McNairney's account of the career of his grandfather, 'Dan McCann: IRA Artificer and a "Dangerous Man"', there is relatively little discussion of the Northern Ireland perspective, especially from a unionist point of view. However, Antony Wheatley's account of the life of his great uncle Major John (Jack) Morrogh does give readers an insight into the dilemmas (ultimately leading to permanent exile from Crosshaven, County Cork after 1921) faced by an Irish career military officer from a wealthy Catholic background, albeit one who had been involved in the attack on the GPO in 1916 and who subsequently featured in a frequently reproduced group photograph of British army officers with the captured Sinn Féin flag from the top of the building. This photograph is one of a number of black and white illustrations integrated into the text of some, but not all, of the chapters.

'Women and Gender' as a theme is represented by Micheline Sheehy Skeffington's essay on her well-known grandparents Hanna and Francis Sheehy Skeffington, while Niamh Reilly's important essay on the IPP politician and MP Tom Kettle (who was killed in action in a British uniform at the Somme in 1916) reveals him to be a progressive and social-democratic thinker and certainly on the gender issue far in advance of his leader John Redmond. Pat and Michael Dolan's account of the life of their aunt Eilish Dolan reveals her to have followed an extremely varied political and religious path for a child of anti-Treaty, Catholic, Dublin parents, including an interlude as the wife of a Methodist minister in Donacloney, County Down and as a Deaconess at Belfast's Grosvenor Hall! A reversion, via the Church of England, to Catholicism, subsequent to a second marriage, followed in due course, along with a late career as a novelist and playwright. Anne and Colm Byrne's grandmother, Molly Bastible, was a more conventional Gaelic League activist, school teacher in Scoil Mhuire (Dublin), Abbey Theatre actress and member of Cumann na mBan – clearly one of Roy Foster's 'vivid faces'.

The second section of the book '1916–1921', apart from the Major Jack Morrogh story mentioned above, consists of a number of essays on lower or middle-ranking republican rebels and combatants – Richard Healy, Martin Savage, Pat Fallon and Bernard Brady (Barney 'the Miller') by their descendants. The major themes which emerge here relate to class, internal migration and the self-imposed vow of silence taken by Civil War combatants.

The third section, which deals with 'The Irish Revolution and Beyond', contains the stories of Paddy Maher, executed by the Crown in all probability in error for alleged participation in a 1919 raid to free IRA prisoners from a train at Knocklong railway station; the Belfast perspective as seen by IRA activist Dan McCann (born in the Markets area and an internee for a considerable time on the prison ship *Argenta*); Peadar O'Donnell's lifelong struggle on behalf of revolutionary socialism as well as his successful writing career; and

Michael Canavan's IRA service in County Galway and subsequent imprisonment for his role on the anti-Treaty side in the Civil War – an essay somewhat short on details because of the limited archival evidence and the lack of 'a strong inter-generationally shared narrative'. The essay on Michael Lang and John Dillon, as noted previously, provides a useful RIC perspective, while that on the Shaw family of Mullingar reveals examples, as the authors put it, of *'Cantans intra et extra Chorum'*. On the one hand there is Patrick Shaw, the wealthy, 'gambling and womanizing' TD for Longford-Westmeath, ever careful to trim his political sails to the prevailing wind, while on the other hand there is the austere, ascetic figure of his son, Francis (Frank) Shaw, SJ, Celtic scholar, orthodox Catholic, Redmondite and Fine Gael in his political views – very much *'intra Chorum'*, racked by tuberculosis throughout his life and ultimately as a result, addicted to painkillers and weighing only seven stone.

However, the fiftieth anniversary of the Easter Rising in 1966, with its accompanying celebrations, led Frank Shaw to 'sing' very much outside the choir, with his strongly worded and for that period deeply controversial, revisionist paper on the Rising and its leaders. Shaw's 'The Canon of Irish History' was initially rejected by the Jesuit journal *Studies*, which only published it in 1972 to assert copyright after his death two years earlier. As Patrick Maume has recently observed in the same journal, Frank Shaw's political and religious convictions overlapped into his scholarly preoccupations. We therefore should not be surprised that he was willing to light the blue touch paper that was to set off the explosion of controversy over revisionism in modern Irish history. For some Fr Shaw was one of the 'evil godfathers' of revisionism, for others he was a courageous historical pioneer, willing to sing *'extra Chorum'*. In the absence of much in the way of published biographical sources for the Shaws, *père et fils*, Olga Cox Cameron and John Cox are to be commended for their courage and willingness to reflect on their grandfather and uncle, 'warts and all', in the context of the one hundredth anniversary of the Easter Rising.

In his masterly review of the historiography of 'The Irish Revolutionary Decade, 1913–23: Voices, Narratives and Contexts' in *Family Histories of the Irish Revolution*, referred to above, Gearóid Ó Tuathaigh noted that: 'Early first-hand accounts of the revolutionary events … came mainly from writers who themselves had been involved or had personal acquaintance with the acts and organisations that had made the revolution'. He cited Ernie O'Malley's 'acclaimed' *On Another Man's Wound* (1936) as a good example.

Ó Tuathaigh also referred to the official Bureau of Military History (BMH) project from 1947 onwards to collect evidence from surviving participants and the parallel, unofficial, one-man recording process undertaken by O'Malley:

> conducting interviews and taking detailed notes (initially for his own information) from veterans of the War of Independence and the Civil War, many of whom would have been reluctant or unwilling to participate in any collective project under the direction of, or sanctioned by, the government: the material from these informants would not be published until much later.

In one of his footnotes Ó Tuathaigh notes two such publications, both of which were edited by Cormac K.H. O'Malley – the Kerry interviews (2012) and the Galway interviews (2013). Other recent volumes cover Clare and west Cork. The new Merrion Press volume *The Men Will Talk to Me* now adds the Northern Divisions interviews (effectively the bulk of the six NI counties, plus Donegal, most of Monaghan, and parts of Cavan and Louth) to the pool of published material, although it should be noted that O'Malley conducted no fieldwork in Northern Ireland, preferring to undertake interviews in other locations, such as Dublin, so the coverage may have been a little limited by this situation. Indeed, O'Malley himself had only a limited on-the-ground knowledge of the north.

A useful map in *The Men Will Talk to Me* indicates the geographical boundaries of the five Northern IRA Divisions, which do not of course equate to the normal county boundaries. It also needs to be remembered that, as Eve Morrison has calculated, almost 80 per cent of veterans interviewed by O'Malley had been active in Munster and Leinster. It is therefore hardly surprising that this volume contains interviews with just 14 individuals, although there are a number of key figures among them, including Peadar O'Donnell (1st Northern Division), Dr Patrick McCartan (2nd Northern Division), Seamus Woods and Roger McCorley (3rd Northern Division) and Frank Aiken

(4th Northern Division). The 5th Northern Division (Cavan/Monaghan) is not represented. Three 1st Northern Division interviews relating to the south Donegal area were not discovered in time to be included in this volume, as O'Malley had chosen to include them in his notebooks with his Sligo interviews. The vast majority of O'Malley's total of 122 'combatant' interviews are today in the UCD Archives, although a few ended up with the O'Malley papers in New York University (Archive of Irish America).

While clearly they are a vital and unique source, especially for the anti-Treaty perspective on the Civil War since the majority of the interviewees were anti-Treatyites (ten out of the 14 in this volume), it is important to recognise the difficulties for researchers posed by what Eve Morrison has described as 'O'Malley's notoriously illegible handwriting' and the virtual impossibility of constructing 'an accurate overall assessment of his aims and methodology'. Nor did he interview any female activists. Researchers will therefore welcome the appearance of this volume of carefully edited source material, supplemented by exhaustive endnotes, short biographical sketches of both interviewees and of individuals referenced in the endnotes, a preface by Cormac K.H. O'Malley (whose relationship to Ernie O'Malley is not made clear), a detailed 'chronology of the War of Independence and Civil War in the North', two sets of black and white plates plus photographs of each interviewee integrated into the text, and an extremely valuable essay by Eve Morrison, based on her doctoral research on the O'Malley notebooks, outlining the methodology and chronology of the interviews. This I was puzzled to find tucked away at the end of the volume. In my view, it deserved to be inserted after the Preface, given its importance for the reader.

Certainly, one would have to concur with the publisher's claim that the interviews in the volume are 'startlingly direct' and important as source materials for such events as 'the mobilisation of the Dundalk Irish Volunteers for the 1916 Rising, the events of Bloody Sunday (1920), the Belfast Pogroms, and the planning of … escapes from the Curragh and Kilkenny Gaol'. However, this is essentially a volume of primary sources, which supplements the BMH witness statements (only four of the 14 interviewees represented here participated in that government-sponsored initiative). Indeed, two extensive interviews (with John McCoy and Thomas McShea) have not been included because they largely replicate both men's BMH statements, along with two short ancillary interviews by O'Malley with Joseph and John Sheeran of Ballyshannon. For the general reader therefore, this volume may not have the same appeal as it will to the researcher or student, given that it does not have structured narrative threads but is rather a much more fragmented collection of raw evidence, some of it very chilling in nature, for example, as the veterans recall, in a matter-of-fact manner, their role in assassinations of RIC officers and Auxiliaries in locations such as central Belfast, or in the case of Inspector Oswald Swanzy coming from his church in Lisburn (p. 89).

One of the general editors, Fearghal Mac Bhloscaidh, does, however, provide a 20-page general introduction to the content of the interviews, highlighting significant issues and some of the interviewees' comments about them. He wears his political heart on his sleeve, writing from a clearly stated, anti-partitionist, pro-republican perspective. He is keen to reject Alan Parkinson's 2004 view that the term 'pogrom' has been misapplied to the inter-communal disturbances in Belfast in this period. For Mac Bhloscaidh, partition was not inevitable. 'Ulster unionists based their hegemony on a heady mix of incendiary rhetoric, brutal mob violence, police death squads and financial inducements to loyalty through employment in the yards, factories and Specials'. He argues that 'the sectarian impulse did not emanate from republicans', that northern republicanism has been 'largely airbrushed' from history, and that northern republicans during the Truce period and prior to the Civil War had been abandoned by Collins, Mulcahy and O'Duffy. Indeed, he describes Collins as 'oscillating between tragic hero, villain and fool' ... 'from the republican perspective the evidence points to Collins as Iago rather than Othello' ... 'GHQ had effectively hung the northern IRA out to dry' by failing to support a general uprising, or even seriously challenging partition. This, he argues, is borne out by the interviews. 'Fortunately for those who desire a non-sectarian future based on republican concepts of freedom and equality, in Ireland still the dead walk around'.

Somewhat by contrast, Cormac K.H. O'Malley warns readers that

> the editors of this volume have relied on the integrity of O'Malley's general knowledge of the facts of this period and his ability to question and ascertain the 'truth', but clearly the details related here to O'Malley reflect only the perceptions of the individual informants rather than the absolute historical truth.

Equally, Ó Tuathaigh more generally has cautioned that 'accounts by witnesses were recorded between thirty and forty years after the events described' … 'how life had "turned out" for Ireland and for the narrator was the canvas against which even the sharpest memory or the most scrupulous recollection shaped its narrative of earlier events'.

In reviewing Terence Dooley's excellent study of the *Irish Revolution, 1912–23: Monaghan* in *Familia*, no. 33 (2017), the first of a projected series of county studies from the Four Courts Press, I noted the value and importance of approaching this controversial period of Irish history from a localised perspective. Clearly, the editorial team at Irish Academic Press is of a similar view and indeed would now appear to have got ahead of the game with the publication of McNamara's study of Galway, based upon his doctoral thesis. This too is a very soundly researched and balanced account of a tricky subject, although unlike Dooley, McNamara largely leaves the controversial Civil War period alone, choosing the year 1922 as his end point rather than 1923. While he does provide relevant statistical tables, appendices on the casualties of violence in the county and the membership of the three Galway IRA flying columns in 1921, comprehensive endnotes and a bibliography, there are only two photographs (reproduced on the front and rear covers) and more seriously no maps. Indeed, I found this last omission a little frustrating, given the constant geographical references in the text, which appeared to assume knowledge of places which many readers outside the county (myself included) would not possess.

As McNamara rightly acknowledges in his introductory chapter, a county-based approach to analysing the realities of the period 1913–22 is not new. David Fitzpatrick's pioneering 1978 study, *Politics and Irish Life 1913–1921*, an examination of war and revolution in County Clare, signposted the road which others such as Peter Hart (Cork), Michael Farry (Sligo), Marie Coleman (Longford) and John

O'Callaghan (Limerick) have followed, while Joost Augusteijn has ranged over a number of counties in his important analysis of the motivation of IRA volunteers and how they moved into violent activism after 1916. Even in the case of Galway, as McNamara honestly and fully acknowledges, Fergus Campbell had much to say more than a decade ago about both the intriguing subject of Liam Mellows and the attempt at a 1916 rising in Galway and also about the wider question of the extent to which the extensive and continuing land agitation and associated rural violence in the county from 1891 to 1921, with its widespread cattle and sheep driving and firing of guns into houses, etc., interacted with the War of Independence.

McNamara provides us in this book with a salutary reminder of just how violent the rural areas of Galway continued to be as a result of unresolved issues arising from the 1903 and 1909 Land Acts in a county where rural poverty changed little as a result of land re-distribution, with the large graziers the chief beneficiaries. 'The suspension of land distribution during the War heightened the sense of disappointment and desperation among small farmers, just as steadily rising prices increased the profits of middling farmers'. The temporary suspension of emigration during the First World War (as in other counties) added fuel to the flames. 'The road for the bullock and the land for the people' seemed to many to be the only way forward. So 'Counties Galway and Clare were exceptional in the opening decades of the twentieth century for the degree of violence over land'. With the hard-pressed RIC trying to hold the ring, the bishop of Galway, Dr Thomas O'Dea, in a letter to mass-goers in one parish, condemned the perpetrators as 'outlaws worse than the blacks of darkest Africa'! Meanwhile, in a garrison city or town such as Galway or Ballinasloe, a different, more peaceful Redmondite world existed and indeed this was true of the east of the county more generally.

McNamara reminds us that these political 'fault lines', which also included generational tension between 'an older, more respectable generation of nationalists and an impatient generation of young revolutionaries', were often hidden before 1916 by 'the unchallenged hegemony' of the IPP. 'A sectarian rift' in some areas between the small Protestant community and the Catholic majority was a further complication, as was the return of ex-servicemen after 1918. Thus, McNamara understandably is of the view that a 'uniformity of experience of political upheaval across diverse regions cannot be assumed in a society where an intensely local sense of identity saw national events interpreted through distinctly local prisms of identity and allegiance'.

McNamara also investigates, in the Galway context, how 'pivotal developments' associated with the outbreak of war in 1914 revived the physical force tradition in politics, 'ultimately destroying the IPP' ... 'a victim of its support for the British war effort'. Like other western rural regions, despite the identification of Galway city with the famous Connaught Rangers and the urgings of the leading members of the local nationalist elite such as Máirtín Mór McDonogh and Stephen Gwynn MP, backed by the four local newspapers, recruitment to the British armed forces was weak, even from the outset of the conflict. Indeed, as McNamara points out, Connacht provided the lowest number of recruits of all four provinces.

The situation in Galway was of course fairly unique outside Dublin in the case of the Easter Rising and this may have created additional new political tensions. The county was one of the few places outside the capital where there was a significant mobilisation of Irish Volunteers during Easter Week 1916 under the leadership of the 'enigmatic' Liam Mellows. McNamara feels that 'the national aspect of the 1916 Rising has been neglected to the detriment of a full appreciation of the aims of the Rebellion's planners'. McNamara argues that events in Galway illustrate 'the potential for popular mobilisation that existed outside the capital', critically dependent of course on the successful landing and distribution by rail of a substantial shipment of German arms. Thus, 'the traditional orthodoxy that the confusion caused by Eoin MacNéill's countermand order prevented a nationwide uprising from erupting, should be treated with caution'.

However, McNamara's own detailed account of events highlights both the naïve and inexperienced behaviour of the Volunteers, whose support was limited to certain rural areas and the opposition they faced from the National Volunteers and the supporters of the IPP in urban areas, including Galway city, 'who cheered on the navy and RIC, and who gathered to throw mud at republican prisoners'. In any case the

'Galway Rebellion was doomed once the *Aud* failed to land her cargo of rifles and ammunition off the Kerry coast'. However, the three hundred men deported from the county in the aftermath of these events would learn their revolutionary trade as graduates of Frongoch and other 'universities' of subversion. The older IPP generation of leaders was no match for them, while Sinn Féin's 1918 land tillage campaigns proved extremely popular and the conscription crisis of April/May 1918, compounded by the so-called 'German plot' arrests that followed, ensured the defeat of the 'auld stock' of Irish politics across the county in the 1918 general election.

McNamara analyses the War of Independence in three detailed chapters and concludes that the pattern of IRA activities is similar to that discerned by a number of historians in other parts of Ireland, i.e. regional variations within counties as well as between different parts of the country. In the case of Galway, 'the Volunteers in the north of the county, along with those in the western districts of Connemara, carried out the bulk of attacks on the Crown forces while the towns, and parts of the east of the county, remained relatively unaffected by violence'. These attacks, mainly on police elements rather than military, were sporadic and carried out by a relatively small force of active Volunteers concentrated in distinct areas where they could rely on sympathy and support. Indeed, as the conflict escalated, 'the pool of active Volunteers became smaller as the intensity of state reprisals grew more ferocious and the nature of republican violence became more lethal'. McNamara notes that the Volunteers killed eight people between January 1920 and the Truce in July 1921.

'No noteworthy attacks were attempted, in the larger towns of Galway, Loughrea, Ballinasloe or Tuam', which McNamara argues reflects the failure of the Volunteers 'to garner significant support in Galway's towns'. However, he echoes Brian Hughes, in stressing that 'killing should not be employed as a yardstick of the success or failure of the republican campaign'. Lower level activities such as the establishment of republican courts, acts of theft and arson from the Crown forces and the boycotting of the military and especially the police were more widespread. Mobilisation in specific areas often reflected inspirational local leadership. But at the height of the conflict, civilian life in many districts continued largely as normal, military and police still socialised in local pubs and hotels and even the Galway Races and the March Fairs in Tuam were unaffected, with large crowds reported.

Despite these contrasts, McNamara argues that in terms of violence perpetrated by Crown forces in the rural areas of Galway, the county was at the upper end of the scale, with 26 deaths between October 1920 and May 1921, of whom only 11 were active republicans. Of these, 25 were in the east of the county and included a priest, a pregnant woman, a serving RIC constable and a retired army officer. Seven IRA volunteers were 'shot while trying to escape'. McNamara feels that while this violence undoubtedly in the short term weakened and hampered, through fear, the IRA campaign, it 'outweighed the threat the Volunteers represented' and in the longer term, given its 'reckless' nature, alienated popular opinion, as Joost Augusteijn pointed out in *The Irish Revolution 1913–23* (2002).

As for the controversy between historians over whether Crown forces' reprisals were largely the result of immoral behaviour by some of those on the ground (Charles Townshend), or were the result of a policy of assassination sanctioned at senior government level (Borgonovo and Doherty), McNamara hedges his bets somewhat. 'The Crown forces were considerably more violent in Galway than elsewhere in Connacht but just why there were so many reprisals in the county is unclear' (p. 158).

No book dealing with the War of Independence dare ignore the other major historiographical controversy originally ignited by the late Peter Hart in 2003 with the publication by Oxford University Press of his *The IRA at War, 1916–23*. A study of events and statistics relating to west Cork had led Hart to conclude, as early as 1998, that sectarianism directed against the Protestant minority community was 'embedded in the vocabulary and syntax of revolution'. More generally, Hart argued that a campaign of ethnic cleansing took place in many parts of the country. East Galway and 'the dreary steeples of Ballinasloe', he cited as one of his examples. 'As revolutionary violence spiralled upwards, more and more of its victims were civilians and more and more of them were Protestant' (Hart, 2003). Other historians, such as Brian Hanley for example in 2008, have taken a different view, arguing that terms such as 'genocide' and 'ethnic cleansing', 'should be banished from serious discussion on the matter'.

McNamara takes a measured approach to this potentially tricky issue. For him the Hart thesis in the case of Galway is 'highly problematic' and far too simplistic. While he accepts that the Protestant experience of revolution in Galway 'was undoubtedly negative' and that there was a relatively high level of Protestant emigration in these years, the latter was part of a long-term trend predating the rise of militant republicanism. As for the negativity issue, sectarian hostility against Protestants in some areas was very much linked to the unresolved land issues and to social and economic resentment against the exclusion of Catholics from employment in many big houses, landed estates and urban businesses (especially at senior levels). 'Revolutionary upheaval provided the opportunity especially with the collapse of the RIC and the later Civil War to settle "old scores"'. So class antagonism, sectarian resentment and opportunistic criminality fused together. As for IRA activity, he notes that the three alleged civilian 'informers' shot dead in the county were all Catholics. But he also notes an escalation of violence during the Civil War period against ex-RIC men and examines the Ballinasloe evidence of hostility towards Protestants from 1918 onwards, in part as a response to the violence against Catholics in Belfast. Thus, McNamara concludes that 'it was certainly a frightening time to be a Protestant in parts of the countryside but these attacks should not be exaggerated and claims of ethnic cleansing are unsustainable'. The debate will no doubt continue, as the actual centenary of such events approaches.

While at times this book's style and use of language reflects its origins as a doctoral thesis, it is nonetheless an excellent and evidence-based account which gives the reader a real insight into the regional variations, even within a single county area never mind the whole island, of the revolutionary period from 1913 to 1922. Nor is it a dull read. Many fascinating by-ways are explored. For example, we are reminded on pp 146–7 that the notorious Nazi radio propagandist, William Joyce ('Lord Haw Haw'), may have been in an earlier existence an informer for the Crown forces in Galway city, with a possible involvement in the reprisal execution of a Catholic priest. Thereafter, he joined the 4th Worcester Regiment and departed with it to England, where much later he was to be hanged as a Nazi collaborator in Wandsworth Prison in 1946. Equally, who knew that the single biggest loss of life in the west of Ireland during this period was the death of nine Irish-speaking fishermen, blown to pieces by a mine (allegedly German according to the authorities, but McNamara thinks possibly British) they were in the process of retrieving from the sea as salvage near Inverin on the southern shores of Connemara on 15 June 1917, one of several such incidents but by far the most serious?

Finally, in an interesting echo of the post-Civil War situation in Monaghan explored in Terence Dooley's 2017 book, referred to earlier, it turned out that the 'auld stock' of Redmondites in Galway, seemingly consigned to political oblivion by Sinn Féin in 1918, had remarkable powers of survival. As elsewhere, Galway city's most prominent wealthy Redmondite businessman, Máirtín Mór McDonogh, an implacable opponent of the 1916 Rising, was elected to Dáil Éireann in 1927 and again in 1933. His friends and former IPP Westminster MPs, William Duffy and James Cosgrave, made similar electoral comebacks in the 1920s. It would seem that, as in County Monaghan, there was life in the 'auld stock' yet! These realities once again beg that much-debated question – just how 'revolutionary' was the Irish revolution?

One way of attempting to answer the question as to the 'revolutionary' nature, or otherwise, of the so-called Irish revolution of 1916–23 has been to organise conferences of academics to debate the matter. In the case of the Easter Rising centenary year, the Irish Government's Expert Advisory Group on Commemorations, under its Chair, Maurice Manning, encouraged all universities and institutes of higher learning to mount programmes to explore and reflect on the 1916 experiences of their cities and regions. The Group also decided that there should be 'one major and overarching national event to draw together the multiple academic, cultural and creative strands'. NUI Galway was tasked with the organisation and delivery of this, the 'ultimate' academic conference of the centenary year and Emeritus Professor Nicholas Canny and his colleagues duly obliged, under the title 'Ireland 1916–2016: the promise and challenge of national sovereignty' in November 2016. Those attending, while representative of all elements of higher education plus the arts and the media on the island of Ireland, included what one might describe as a selection of Irish-born 'good and great' of the academic world, who delivered six plenary 'addresses' to stimulate panel discussions.

The conference was duly opened by the then Taoiseach, Enda Kenny TD. The conference volume, published by the Four Courts Press, largely consists of the six plenary addresses (some in revised form), supported respectively in two cases by 16 and 11 statistical graphs, diagrams and tables. The appendices include the EU-related provisions in the Good Friday Agreement and the British-Irish Agreement (1999), European Convention of Human Rights provisions in the Good Friday Agreement, biographical profiles (with photographs) of the six plenary speakers (all holding senior positions in some of the world's leading universities) and the full programme for the event (10–12 November 2016). A video record is available on-line. In the best David Lodge tradition, no doubt a good time was had by all!

Given that this was a multi-disciplinary conference, the historical focus on the actual events of 1916–23 was at a fairly high level and indeed the conference title's emphasis on the whole century after 1916 made this inevitable. So for readers of *Familia,* or specifically those whose main interest is historical, the pickings here are largely restricted to only one of the six chapters. Indeed, all six main speakers had been briefed to encourage reflection on 'how the generations of Irish people who have succeeded the women and men involved with the Easter Rising in 1916 have responded to that event'.

Professor Philip Pettit of Princeton University is an expert on political philosophy and so his paper, 'European republicanism: the past and the potential', traces the trajectory of republican political philosophy from its origins in ancient Rome onwards, including its influence on the American Revolution, the French Revolution and specifically on Wolfe Tone and the United Irishmen.

Professor Roy Foster (at that point still in post at Oxford University), drawing on his recent research and publications on W.B. Yeats and on the revolutionary generation in *Vivid Faces,* highlights the range of voices that were to be heard during the years 1912–23, arguing that events in Ireland were part of 'a wider dislocation' that, as the late Keith

Jeffrey also pointed out in 2015, were 'decisively shaped by the Great War, indeed as a theatre of that war'. Foster also echoes the conclusions of Robert Gerwarth and John Horne that the First World War did not in fact end in 1918 but that the break-up of empires it set in motion created continuing theatres of war and revolution all over Central and Eastern Europe, with paramilitary activity, the shifting and changing of borders, and inter-communal conflict. So what was happening in Ireland from 1919 to 1923 was very much in line with events elsewhere.

Foster, building on *Vivid Faces*, argues that 'early twentieth-century Ireland saw a period of destabilization in all sorts of areas' – labour relations, religion, gender relations and the family, in addition to the dynamics of nationalist politics. However, he concludes that soon after the events of 1916, what he refers to as the rhetoric of radical nationalism gained a dominant position and succeeded in dislodging 'those other rhetorics', which included secularist, feminist, social-democratic and socialist 'tropes'. Thus, many promises withered on the vine as independent Ireland, during its first half-century of existence, settled into being a deeply conservative, culturally narrow and socially deprived country, dominated by a hegemonic, institutional, Catholic church and with partition 'the elephant in the room'.

Indeed, Foster speculates as to the extent to which partition not just reinforced the Catholic Church's dominance, but even enabled it. He references the recent work by David Fitzpatrick and Andy Bielenberg on the disproportionate exodus of Protestants from the Irish Free State after 1918, but concludes, like Terence Dooley and Conor McNamara, that those who remained were still able to play a role in Irish life disproportionate to their numbers and so fared better than the large Catholic minority in Northern Ireland. Foster, like others, also points to the persistence of much of the British colonial inheritance in Irish society and to the slow and at times painful progression towards a more open and more equitable society in the second 50 years of independence. As to whether a 'revolution' occurred, as Foster points out, this is 'a complicated matter'. The losers, such as the southern unionists, thought so, the winners were less inclined to use the word, given its association with events in Russia in 1917. Hence, the widespread use of the more seemingly noble phrase: 'war of independence'. For many, what mattered was simply 'liberation from British rule'. As always with Roy Foster, the phrase-making is a model of elegance and style and the whole is argued in the context of the framework of recent historiography, clearly set out in footnotes.

Professor Clair Wills of Princeton University, a scholar of Irish and British literature and culture in the twentieth century, in her paper 'Culture and globalization: contemporary storytelling and the legacies of 1916', is concerned with the 'challenges for Irish art and culture in an era of globalization' and the 'ways in which the current era might differ from, and respond to, previous "world" moments in the history of Irish literature and culture'. She takes as her starting point the poet Paul Muldoon's response in his poem 'Certain men?' to the W.B. Yeats question: 'Did that play of mine send out certain men the English shot?' Muldoon wondered:

> If Yeats had saved his pencil-lead
> Would certain men have stayed in bed?

Muldoon concluded: 'Certainly not'.

> For history's a twisted root
> With art its small, translucent fruit
> And never the other way round.

Professor Kevin Hjortshoj O'Rourke, an Oxford economic historian, tackles Ireland's economic performance over the twentieth century, within an extended comparative analytical framework, in a lively fashion. This comparative approach produces what the editors describe as a 'rude awakening' for any reader who still subscribes to the notion that independent Ireland was a special case. O'Rourke in his robust and pragmatic analysis suggests that the economic history of independent Ireland, 'given the realities of the small, open and highly dependent economy' was not particularly unusual, that Ireland's linkages to the UK economy led to an over-dependence on what in the case of the latter was one of the poorest performing economies in Europe for much of the twentieth century and that Ireland only escaped from its economic 'national death wish' through its membership of the EEC after 1973 and through the intellectual and political leadership provided by the Whitaker-Lemass partnership. He concludes that the UK withdrawal from the EU and an increasingly isolationalist US will provide serious economic survival challenges for Ireland in future years.

The current Irish-born Vice Chancellor of Oxford University, Professor Louise Richardson, historian and political scientist who has specialised on the issues around terrorism and counter-terrorism, argues the case for 'The role of education in addressing the challenges of the twenty-first century'. In practice, as might be expected, this paper mainly concentrates on the role of universities and in particular the relationship between university education and political violence, and the importance of universities in redressing societal inequality. She rather bleakly concludes that while universities 'do not cause radicalization … nor has university education prevented individuals from becoming terrorists'. On the second issue, she makes the argument that in the future there is likely to be a direct causal relationship between the capacity of universities to educate 'a broader section of society and the degree of social instability experienced by these societies'. Richardson makes a passionate plea for a broad, values-based approach to higher education, as opposed to one too narrowly focused on skills and training.

Another distinguished Irish-born political scientist, Professor Brendan O'Leary of the University of Pennsylvania, cast somewhat in the role of the conference Nostradamus, attempts to anticipate how both climate change and especially BREXIT (or UKEXIT, to use his more accurate term) may prove to be external factors which Irish people cannot control but turn out to be serious challenges to the continued existence of the Irish state. He outlines ten possible outcomes in the case of the latter (some positive but most negative) but is reasonably optimistic that Ireland can survive as an independent nation within the EU and possibly even assume the role of a protector and negotiator for Northern Ireland in Brussels, with the tacit agreement of the UK government. But of course the crystal ball remains somewhat cloudy, even as the exit deadline (29 March 2019) approaches.

While this is a handsomely produced record of an important climax to the academic-focused events of 2016, it is doubtful whether at €29.95 for a fairly slim, albeit hardback, this volume will reach too many readers in Ireland or beyond. Given the nature of the content, one even wonders if the publication of a special *Irish Times* supplement, incorporating these six papers, might have better achieved the stated goal of ensuring the widest possible access to the conference proceedings.

REVIEW ARTICLE

Judging nationalism and unionism

RICHARD McMINN

DERMOT HELEADY
John Redmond:
Selected Letters and Memoranda, 1880–1918
Merrion Press, 2018
pp 350   ISBN: 978-1-785371-55-4   hb   €29.99

MARGARET BAGULEY (ED.)
World War I and the Question of Ulster:
The Correspondence of Lilian and Wilfrid Spender
Irish Manuscripts Commission, 2009
pp 568   ISBN: 978-1-874280-12-5   hb   €50

ALVIN JACKSON
Judging Redmond and Carson
Royal Irish Academy, 2018
pp 304   ISBN: 978-1-908996-93-0   hb   €30

On 31 March 1912, Dublin city centre was the setting for a massive nationalist demonstration in support of the impending Home Rule bill, which was introduced in the House of Commons at Westminster on 11 April. Such were the numbers attending that the entire city centre was at a standstill and four separate platforms in different streets had to be provided for the speakers, led by John Redmond and John Dillon. Those attending had travelled from all over Ireland to represent local bodies, as well as the Gaelic League and the GAA. Overshadowed by subsequent events, the meeting merits scant attention now, but it is a timely reminder of just how popular and admired John Redmond was at that time. Indeed, he was viewed by many, including Augustine Birrell, the Liberal Chief Secretary at Dublin Castle, as the leader of the Irish people – the Daniel O'Connell of his day. Six years later, Redmond underwent what should have been a fairly routine operation in London for a blocked intestine. During the subsequent recovery period, he suffered a fatal heart attack on 6 March 1918, aged 61. The temptation to link this tragedy to the bigger political picture and to write Redmond off as a tragic failure, or to suggest that he was broken in mind and spirits, or even that he died of a 'broken heart', has proved irresistible to some writers.

The 'decade of centenaries' has, however, reopened the debate as to Redmond's achievements and legacy. Indeed, the centenary of his death was marked by state ceremonies in Dublin and in the other locations with which he was most associated, notably in Wexford where he was born and in Waterford, which he represented at Westminster for 27 years. Redmond's tomb at St John's cemetery in Wexford has been renovated, and a commemorative event, organised by the town council, took place there on Sunday, 4 March 2018 to mark the centenary of his death two days later.

At the literary level, Redmond has been the subject of two recent sympathetic biographies – Chris Dooley's, *Redmond: A Life Undone* (2015) and Dermot Meleady's *John Redmond: The National Leader* (a follow-up to his earlier *Redmond: The Parnellite)*, which takes up the story from 1901 onwards. The paperback edition of Meleady's second volume of biography was published by Merrion Press in 1918 to coincide with the centenary of Redmond's death, supported by the volume of letters and memoranda under review.

At the public level, John Redmond has also had his champions in recent times, most notably former Taoiseach and Fine Gael Party leader, John Bruton. His recent review article in the *Irish Times* of 10 March 2018, 'Redmond and Carson – It Could All Have Been So Different', surveying the recent work on both of these early twentieth-century Irish political giants by Dermot Meleady and Alvin Jackson respectively, provides an impressive summation of Redmond's many, and not always fully acknowledged, achievements prior to 1914 – the reunification of the Home Rule Party shattered by the fall of Parnell (whom Redmond had loyally stood by), the removal of the House of Lords veto on Irish Home Rule through the skilful use of the IPP's bloc of votes, the enactment of Home Rule for Ireland on 18 September 1914 (a feat neither Isaac Butt nor Parnell had ever come close to achieving) and, therefore, the implicit acceptance by the UK parliament and monarch of the principle of legislative independence long before the events of 1916, never mind 1918. Bruton would also point to the critical and constructive role played by Redmond and his party in transforming the system of agricultural land holding in Ireland, thereby largely ending landlordism and creating a rural middle class, 'which underpinned Irish democracy in the first half of the 20th century'. The establishment of the National University of Ireland, the introduction of old-age pensions and national insurance and the first ever programme of public housing in Ireland through the Labourers Acts, Bruton would also see as major achievements for the IPP in partnership with successive Westminster governments. 'All this was done without taking anyone's life'.

But what, you may ask, about Redmond's handling of the issues of the First World War and of partition? Bruton conveniently ignores the former, other than to state that 'initially this was not controversial'. He admits that Redmond failed to prevent the latter but then, as he astutely points out, neither did the physical force republicans after 1918. Their activities in fact 'entrenched it'. Finally, he makes much of the seemingly lost opportunity of the post-Rising negotiations in June 1916. Redmond and Carson, who were old friends as well as legal colleagues, had allegedly reached an agreement which 'if implemented, could have peacefully resolved the Irish question'. They had even (the Catholic bishops apart) persuaded a majority of their respective followers to agree to it. It would have, Bruton claims, involved the immediate implementation in 1916 (as a war emergency measure, however) of Home Rule but with the six counties excluded for the duration of the war, after which an imperial conference would be called to consider the matter. But it was torpedoed by the political representatives at Westminster of southern unionism – 'a tragedy' in Bruton's view. A more critical analysis might be that this 'solution' was simply kicking the can of partition down the road for a few years and that the subsequent history of the Irish Convention in 1917 indicates that conferences do not always solve problems. It is, however, also true that Sinn Féin, despite its electoral triumph in 1918, found that its methods were equally unsuccessful in relation to partition and that in this instance, lives were indeed lost on all sides.

Dermot Meleady has devoted many years of research to the career of John Redmond. This new supporting volume of Redmond's selected letters and memoranda, presented in chronological sequence, is clearly intended to buttress the two volumes of biography which its editor has already produced and includes some new and rare images of 'Ireland's lost leader'. Two of the most evocative and perhaps revealing of these images show Redmond in an affectionate pose with his second wife Amy (interestingly a Protestant) and, on the rear of the dust cover, Redmond hard at work at his desk in his study (possibly in his beloved retreat at Aughavanagh in the Wicklow Mountains – ironically a former British military barracks).

The latter image reinforces the point, which clearly emerges from the text, that Redmond was like some latter-day Ulysses, chained not to the mast but in his case to the writing desk (wherever his physical location). I would have to agree with John Bruton that Redmond's vast correspondence illustrates 'the huge practical difficulties Redmond faced in holding together and servicing the numerous constituencies he needed to mobilise for Home Rule' – the House of Commons, Liberal constituency meetings throughout Britain, public and party meetings throughout Ireland, regular tours in Australia and the USA. This was a punishing set of commitments in an age of more difficult travel and communications, made more demanding by the factionalised nature of his reunited party and the petty jealousies of his immediate colleagues such as John Dillon, T.P. O'Connor and above all William O'Brien and by the increasing vitriol emanating from William Martin Murphy and his mouthpiece, the *Irish Independent*, not to mention the growth of Sinn Féin.

As Meleady reminds us, unlike some of his lieutenants, Redmond left no diary or memoir behind. His intention through this volume is, therefore, to give Redmond back his voice, to allow him to speak directly to us from a century ago and 'to correct the caricature to which he has sometimes been reduced in the popular memory and academic discourse'. This he does in a most thorough and meticulous fashion, with total attention to the minutest detail, drawing upon correspondence to and from key figures such as Dillon, O'Brien, Lloyd George, Asquith and others.

A succinct ten-page introduction (which is complemented by additional editorial commentary or explanation at appropriate points within the 17 main chapters of text and by excellent endnotes) highlights some of the unfair stereotypes which the correspondence dispels. Although almost always courteous, consensual and business-like, these neatly handwritten letters and memoranda, reveal Redmond's great determination and persistence, as well as confidence in his own judgements, whether with regard to the reunification of the party, land reform, or the 'considerations of honour' which motivated his actions in August and September 1914 following his careful machinations to secure the prize of the third Home Rule bill from Asquith's government. As to his relationship with the Catholic Church, it was not always an easy one and certainly Redmond was by no means in thrall to the bishops, as his own personal life also demonstrated.

Meleady in his introduction stresses that 'while Catholic nationalists would accept the guidance of Rome in spiritual matters, they would not allow it to dictate their politics'. Even then Redmond was appalled by the papal decrees *Quantavis Diligentia* and *Ne Temere* and was determined to resist them. It is also fascinating to discover in the depths of the correspondence evidence of his hostility to anti-semitism both in Russia and closer to home in Limerick and Cork in 1907. Unlike the anti-semitic Fenian exile John Devoy, Redmond publicly condemned the Limerick boycott and the racist sermons of Fr John Creagh. Another stereotype the letters demolish is that Redmond 'cared nothing for the Irish language or culture'. Indeed, he is revealed as a strong supporter, for example of Gaelic as a compulsory subject for matriculation to the new NUI, unlike John Dillon.

On the debit side, it is clear that Redmond underestimated the threat posed by the nationalist militants, ignoring the credible warning from Bernard MacGillian in Chicago, dated 6 March 1916 (see pp 227–8), of 'a dastardly plot to drench Ireland in blood'. This is all the more significant, given that, as Meleady reminds us, 'despite all the obstacles, and notwithstanding certain narratives that argue backwards from 1916 to suggest a revolutionary atmosphere existed, Home Rule candidates … won all six by-elections between August 1914 and April 1916'.

Finally, as Meleady admits, 'every consideration of Redmond's tragedy must return to the causes of his downfall'. He castigates the late Professor Ronan Fanning and Professor Donal McCartney in particular for failing to recognise that while Redmond and the IPP had certainly been slow to come to grips with the Ulster unionist position, since the autumn of 1913, most Unionists had abandoned blanket opposition to the Home Rule bill, on the basis of some form of partition. Meleady is convinced that neither Gladstone nor Parnell could have done any better than Redmond on this issue. 'It was Redmond's bad luck to lead Irish nationalism at the first moment when the conflict between its aspirations and those of Irish loyalism demanded resolution in territorial form'. Redmond's options had been seriously narrowed by 'an armed rebellion in his capital city'. While Meleady (p. 239) does not put the political spin that Bruton does on the post-Rising Lloyd George initiative to implement immediately the Home Rule Act (see also Meleady's comments on p. 10), he does share the view that the refusal to coerce Ulster, Asquith's famous *non-possumus* of 1914, remained in place in 1921 and proved as much of a problem for Michael Collins as for John Redmond. Meleady notes that it took until 1998 for 94 per cent of the Irish Republic's electorate (on a 56 per cent turnout) to accept the reality of the consent principle.

This book then presents a compelling case for the defence on behalf of this often criticised barrister and by 1914, prime minister in waiting. A small caveat might be entered, however, given that these are 'selected' letters and memoranda, clearly designed to supplement Meleady's major biographical project. What other written evidence might a counsel for the prosecution select?

Margaret Baguley's volume, containing the selected correspondence of two quite significant figures in the history of Ulster unionism from the period 1915–19, when this relatively recently married couple were separated by the vicissitudes of war, although published as long ago as

2009, had certainly slipped under my radar and I suspect under the radar of other potential readers. The sheer size of this heavyweight hardback may have been partly to blame, along with its nature as essentially a volume of primary source material with a short editorial introduction of 16 pages by Margaret Baguley, its industrious and meticulous editor. Certainly not holiday beach reading, given its unwieldy size and guaranteed to swell the excess baggage profits of Ryanair or Easyjet, should one be dedicated enough to take it along! The diaries of Lilian Spender (PRONI, D1633) of course have been well known to historians interested in the history of unionism ever since 1973, when Gill and Macmillan published Patrick Buckland's ground-breaking *Ulster Unionism and the Origins of Northern Ireland 1886–1922* and HMSO published his companion volume, *Irish Unionism 1885–1923: A Documentary History*, which included (pp 256–8) Lilian Spender's classic account of her own role in the UVF Nursing Corps and that of her husband Wilfrid as Quartermaster-General of the UVF during the weekend of the Larne gun-running (24–6 April 1914).

However, Wilfrid's more private political correspondence, also in PRONI (D1295), had been used by Buckland largely as a source for the political history of Ulster unionism in the period and to document his crucial role in 1920 in organising the metamorphosis of the revived UVF into the new Ulster Special Constabulary (USC). Margaret Baguley, in her acknowledgements section, makes it clear that she was initially attracted to Lilian Spender (the subject of her QUB postgraduate research supervised by Professor Mary O'Dowd), given Lilian's role as an upper-middle-class married woman with an interest in politics, of which she was an acute observer and as a woman 'of resolution and fortitude', although never an active suffragette. By 2009, Margaret Baguley had spent 12 years working on the two sets of Spender papers and by then she and her publisher saw the importance of making the wartime Spender correspondence (some 2,750 letters in total) available to a wider public, albeit in a selected, edited form.

The size of the archive, of which this correspondence during three and half years of wartime separation is only a part, makes the heavyweight nature of the book understandable. As someone with experience of editing for publication extracts from a rather more manageable PRONI archive, I can only commend Margaret Baguley for the editorial skill and professionalism of this volume. It is clearly a labour of love, and this is reflected in the attention to detail in the footnotes and cross-referencing of documents, the absence of errors, the measured introductory comments, a comprehensive list of abbreviations and useful biographical notes on key players. Some previously unpublished images have also been employed, although their reproduction does not always do them the full justice, which the use of better quality photographic paper for a series of plates would perhaps have ensured.

Captain, and after a considerable delay, Lieutenant-Colonel Spender DSO as a senior staff officer on the Western Front during the entire period, was well placed to observe and comment on the progress of the war and on the capabilities, or otherwise, of his senior officers. Although usually billeted in some comfort in farmhouses and chateaux (e.g., 'here I am in a big chateau with a French cook'), he made regular trips to the front line, where he displayed considerable *sang froid* when under enemy fire. Lilian, resident in London throughout, having accepted the post of honorary secretary of Lady Carson's Ulster Division Comforts Fund (by no means a sinecure) came into contact with the *grandes dames* of the unionist cause, including Ruby, Edward Carson's second wife, with whom she developed a close friendship. These contacts and particularly her *entrée* into the Carson household, 'enabled her to gain insights into British politics at a very high level'. These insights, as well as the political gossip of the day, she shared with Wilfrid on a continuous basis, as they wrote to each other daily. Unlike some situations, the significance of the archive is heightened by the fact that both sets of letters have survived.

What then can the reader discover from this rich source? First and foremost the letters tell us much about the Spender marriage and the conventions of the period with regard to marital relationships. Emotions are kept under fairly tight control, although modern readers may find the animal imagery in the correspondence a little bizarre and at times misleading. Wilfrid is constantly referred to as 'Wolf' or 'Brown Wolf', while Lilian is 'pet rabbit' or 'pr'. Others too were subjected to the same treatment, e.g., Wilfrid's Corps Commander, Major General Sir Henry de Lisle, with whom he did not get on, is referred to as 'the Cheshire Cat'. Edward Carson is regularly described as 'Sredward', the nickname apparently used for him by men of the 36th (Ulster) Division. Baguley is keen to stress that 'pet rabbit' 'had no intellectual connotations, for Wilfrid always treated his wife as an equal' and indeed deferred to her greater knowledge in relation to books and literature and regularly sought her opinion and advice in relation to his career and possible post-war entry into politics.

Wilfrid's family background, like Lilian's, was English not Irish and his opposition to Home Rule was very much based on military and imperial considerations. 'He believed that the granting of a measure of Home Rule to this small island would imperil Britain's security and jeopardize the integrity of the British Empire as a whole' (Baguley). Thus, he became distinctly unhappy, as he indicates in these letters, with the increasing willingness of Craig and even Carson to contemplate partition and in particular the sacrifice of southern unionists, especially those in Cavan, Donegal and Monaghan. His comments on the ultimately unsuccessful attempt at a compromise settlement in 1916 are a good example of this. Thus, there is a significant irony in his eventual emergence as the Cabinet Secretary of Craig's new, partitionist, Northern Ireland government in the 1920s, especially as in July 1916 the Spenders blamed Craig as 'a fatal influence' on their beloved Carson (see document 250, p. 118). Spender was on leave at the time of the Easter Rising, so it does not feature too much in the letters. As supporters of the extension of conscription to Ireland, the Spenders had no time for Sinn Féin and they reveal little understanding even of the IPP and its desire for Home Rule.

While Carson and Lloyd George paid eloquent tributes to Redmond in the House of Commons following his death on 6 March 1918, their views were not shared by the Spenders. 'So poor old Redmond is dead. I find L.G.'s extravagant tribute rather indigestible, and wonder if Sred. *really* associated himself with every word of it, as he says he did' (Lilian). Indeed, Wilfrid at one point referred to 'fat-headed Redmond'! Equally, they had 'no sympathy for the qualities brought to the British premiership by H.H. Asquith' (Baguley). Bonar Law, according to Lilian, was 'no leader' and Lloyd George was 'impulsive and impetuous, you can't pin him down'. On the other hand, she presented her friend Carson as 'incurably modest' and unlike his public persona, an individual with a keen sense of humour – 'full of stories at dinner and mimicking all sorts of people'.

Margaret Baguley notes that 'Wilfrid was a complex man who adopted causes and carried them to lengths, often detrimental to his own advancement'. His military career provides many examples of this and he was not on good terms with some of his superiors such as Sir John French, who had recommended in 1912 that Spender be cashiered, Major General Oliver Nugent, who commanded the 36th (Ulster) Division and, as already noted, Major General Sir Henry de Beauvoir Lisle, whom he blamed for blocking his chances of promotion. Spender was scathing about 'limelighters', 'place hunters' and 'thrusters' and disdainful of decorations including his own DSO, which he dismissed as 'faldals'. A careful man, who took pride in his own efficiency as a staff officer and in his beloved 36th (Ulster) Division, after the Somme disaster he was firmly wedded to caution and the military tactic of 'bite and hold'. 'It is the slow cautious policy which wins a war of this kind. There is no room for "brilliant gambles" of the Winston Churchill pattern'.

Spender was dismissive of the achievements of the 16th (Irish) Division and of the later attempt in 1917 to put the two divisions in the line together, allegedly to promote 'a union of hearts'. This Spender denounced as 'the stupid experiment of the partnership – another of O[liver] N[ugent's] awful mistakes by a man who said that he would have nothing to do with politics'. This he felt was 'all because people refused to face the obvious fact that Ulster is nearer British stock and S. Ireland nearer Celtic than to each other'. But then this was a man whose racial and political prejudices led him to comment: 'Jews and inferiors aping as big people rub me up when I am brought into contact with them like dirt rubs up a pr, and I am too too conservative to accept gladly socialistic principles, however cleverly disguised'. Hardly surprising then that Wilfrid, having initially believed that the Germans must be defeated 'decisively' and that fact made clear to the German people, by September 1918 was advocating that Germany should be starved and rendered desolate for 30 years. 'I do not think this would be one whit, too severe for them' (document 922, p. 448). There are also hints in Wilfrid's letters of hostility to the Pope and the Roman Catholic Church.

However, it is also the case that in later years, as Leo Keohane's biography of Jack White reveals, Spender did attempt to help White, with his anarchistic and socialist connections, to secure his landed inheritance at Whitehall outside Ballymena, by interceding with White's widowed mother on his behalf. But then perhaps loyalty to their shared public school background may lie at the root of this apparently liberal attitude, not to mention a shared antipathy to Roman Catholic clericalism.

Baguley includes in detail perhaps the most significant and indeed controversial letters in the entire collection. These are Spender's three letters to his wife, dated 2 July 1916, describing in heroic terms the advance of the 36th (Ulster) Division the previous day on the Schwaben Redoubt (documents 220–222, pp 103–04), along with her response, dated 4th July (document 224, pp 105–06). As Richard Doherty in *The Somme 24 June–19 November 1916* has noted: 'In a letter to his wife, written on 2 July, Spender laid the foundation for the myth that 29th and 32 Divisions had let the Ulster Division down'. To be fair to Spender, he probably had not anticipated that some of his letters would appear anonymously in the press – 'I should certainly have written very differently had I known' (p. 111). Equally, he had been careful to simply state that 'the Corps on our right and left had been unable to advance'. It was Lilian who added what Doherty calls 'another layer' on 4 July with her comment: 'It seems so cruel a thing to have happened that the flanking Divs should have failed to come up'. As Doherty correctly comments, 'of course, the other divisions had not failed to come up. They had tried manfully to advance but had been stopped in their tracks by machine guns and shells, paying a terrible price for their courage'. But a misleading myth had been born, a significant issue which Baguley strangely does not address in her introduction.

However, it is important to remember, as Baguley stresses, that 'in essence the Spender correspondence is a private dialogue between husband and wife'. Thus, servant problems, financial issues which

Lilian had to deal with in Wilfrid's absence and Lilian's concerns about her sister's dubious relationship with their elderly uncle with whom the sister lived, take up considerable space in their correspondence. These letters were never intended for public consumption by a later generation. We owe Margaret Baguley a significant debt for making them available in such an effortless form.

Is there much more that can be either said or written about the lives and political careers of those two early twentieth-century Irish political giants – John Redmond and Edward Carson? After all, a series of biographers have analysed in great detail their achievements and failures, commencing in Redmond's case with Stephen Gwynn's memoir of 1919 and his son Denis Gwynn's full-scale biography published in 1932, while the same year saw the publication of the first of three volumes of the Ian Colvin/Edward Marjoribanks *Life of Lord Carson*, with its tone of adventure and romance, followed by the rather more reliable H. Montgomery Hyde's, *Carson: The Life of Sir Edward Carson, Lord Carson of Duncairn* in 1953.

Professor Alvin Jackson of the University of Edinburgh is convinced that while the factual details of both men's lives and of the political context in which they operated have been well covered by these and other more recent writers, such as the 'magisterial' work of Dermot Meleady discussed earlier and indeed through the publications of a variety of Irish historians of unionism from Patrick Buckland and A.T.Q. Stewart onwards, not forgetting Jackson's own comprehensive output. But Jackson is convinced that 'what we think we know about these two most visible of Irish leaders is, after a century of learned investigation, still far from complete' (p. 3). In particular, there is a need to 'liberate Redmond and Carson from their respective historiographical silos – and to view them in at least some of the ways, and with some of the illumination, utilised by contemporaries'. No doubt this is why Jackson has persuaded the Royal Irish Academy to produce such a lavishly illustrated and handsomely designed volume, replete with high quality reproductions of a wealth of contemporary photographs and tellingly-placed political cartoons throughout the volume (some in full colour and some which were less than familiar from other publications).

However, his principal tool is that of 'dual or comparative biography', a familiar enough genre in both British and European history but one which is 'remarkably underdeveloped within Irish literature and historiography', in part perhaps because of 'still acute political sensitivities' and 'the burden of recent conflicts'. Jackson is also convinced that comparative history in the Irish context has been underplayed and that there has been 'a marked absence of comparison between Irish unionism and nationalism', despite their 'symbiotic relationship'. These are bold claims and he believes that the 'sustained comparative approach', together with new evidence from both untapped as well as familiar sources (such as the Amery, Hailsham and Murray of Elibank archives and the papers of the New Zealand statesman F.M.B. Fisher and his wife, Lady Wavertree), can not only illuminate the central themes of the lives of Redmond and Carson but also throw light 'on some of the hitherto occluded aspects of their careers' and 'on some of the motifs of their political behaviour and achievement'.

Jackson's methodology in the book is to organise his chapters thematically rather than following a general chronological approach, to enable him to identify and pursue new analytical approaches 'rather than simply cover familiar ground' – so readers looking for a fully detailed narrative of late nineteenth- and early twentieth-century Irish politics in the context of the union with Britain will not find it here, although the actual sequence of the thematic chapters is broadly chronological. The content of each chapter pursues a comparative approach, balancing commentary on the two great men under consideration but the material is organised and presented in a chronological fashion. A helpful chronology of the main events is supplied at the beginning of the book as a guide to assist readers. So does this pioneering approach deliver?

Certainly, the author succeeds in demonstrating something that after the Easter Rising in 1916 and the establishment of Northern Ireland after 1920 had perhaps become forgotten or obscured by the triumph of Sinn Féin or the implementation of partition. Redmond and Carson were of the same Irish generation, were educated at the same university (TCD) and pursued the same profession in the same courts. For many years they lived close to each other in the centre of Dublin and they were fellow members of the Westminster parliament for 26 years. 'They were tireless political opponents, but continually professed a friendship and mutual regard' (symbolised by Carson's attendance at Redmond's funeral mass in Westminster Cathedral). 'They came from different Irish religious traditions, but were personally generous in their respective religious convictions'. Contemporaries of all kinds up to and including Kings Edward VII and George V constantly linked them and indeed both monarchs got on well with them (especially George who had a high regard for Redmond, as Jackson demonstrates). 'Even their own families – Harry Carson and Louis Redmond-Howard – united in producing a number of dual critiques'.

The first substantial chapter of Jackson's book is entitled 'Private Lives'. It explores the roots of both men, their family connections and friends, their health and wealth (quite a crucial issue for both, although Carson turned out to be a wealthy hypochondriac prone to regular bouts of exhaustion and depression, while Redmond never complained of ill-health and died a relatively poor man), their attitudes to marriage (Redmond was a kindly and uxorious husband to his two wives, while Carson was 'an increasingly remote husband and father', also with two wives following the decease of the first), their religious beliefs which were personally moderate although Redmond, educated by Jesuits at Clongowes Wood College, was perhaps more assiduous in his religious observance, and finally recreation and relaxation. Redmond was a man of the countryside, with his rural retreat at Aughavanagh, almost a model of the sporting squire who intensely disliked metropolitan social events, whereas Carson was a man of no hobbies (other than a brief involvement with hurling as a student) entirely focused (apart from his rest cures at English seaside resorts or German spa towns) on parliament and the law courts. Redmond was cautious by nature, whereas Carson was, within limits, a risk-taker as a barrister in the courts, subject to occasional fits of rage and in his earlier years anxious to improve his personal finances. For Redmond politics were all, for Carson they 'were an extension of his court-room performance'.

In his chapter on 'Land and Law 1879–1929', Jackson argues that 'if the story of Redmond's relationship with land was one of personal moderation mitigated by party pressure, then Carson's story was rather one of relative personal extremism tempered by party moderation'. Jackson profitably compares Redmond to Parnell – both from a dynasty of landed gentlemen, leading a national movement which simultaneously exploited rural grievance and discontent while being willing to recruit sympathetic landlords and large farmers, for whom they saw a constructive role in a Home Rule Ireland. However, land was a divisive issue at times for nationalists and land reform, in which Redmond was very much a key player, deprived the movement of a unifying and mobilising agent (e.g. Redmond versus O'Brien).

Carson and the unionists too faced similar difficulties with the emergence of the Russellite land purchase movement in Ulster and as a defender of the landlord cause, befitting his role as MP for Trinity College, 'Carson was on the wrong side of history'. Jackson's analysis of the two men's legal careers (central to Carson's life but peripheral for Redmond) leads him to conclude that whereas Redmond, with his administrative commitment, has frequently been seen as Ireland's lost prime minister, the same could not be said for Carson in a UK or NI context. However, his forensic skills and character were such that 'he may, in fact, have been the greatest lord chief justice that England never had'. Thus, the law provides 'one of the greatest contrasts in the two lives'.

In his chapter entitled 'Unity and Marginality 1890–1910', Jackson intriguingly explores the similarities between Redmond and Carson in relation to their assumption of leadership roles at the head of their respective parties – the Irish Parliamentary Party (reunited in 1900 after the disastrous three-way split over the Parnell divorce case) and the Irish Unionist Parliamentary Party (with Carson elected as chair in 1910). In the case of the latter organisation, land reform had proved to be a divisive issue in Ulster, provoking the emergence of T.W. Russell's land purchase movement, although religious and class discontent had also generated dissent in the shape of the Presbyterian Unionist Voters' Association and also Tom Sloan's Independent Orange Order, which drew on working class and artisan loyalists in northern urban areas, but also, as I demonstrated many years ago, on agricultural labourers in constituencies in County Antrim.

In analysing these leadership issues, Jackson makes useful comparisons between Redmond and also Carson with the dead Parnell.

He concludes that both were initially marginal men in relation to their respective Irish and British political contexts. Redmond's problem was that he was 'a Parnellite, without being Parnell', always under the latter's posthumous shadow. 'In essence, the Parnell Split "made" Redmond: but it would also – looking much further ahead – "unmake" him', especially given his position as 'chairman' rather than leader working with some difficult lieutenants – John Dillon, T. P. O'Connor, William O'Brien and Joseph Devlin – and always open to charges of being a 'Tory in disguise' or 'Shoneen Redmond' (despite supporting the Gaelic League). In the case of Carson, there was no equivalent of the Parnell split to contend with, but he was always an outsider 'both to Belfast and to metropolitan unionism, as was Redmond within a reunified Irish nationalism'.

Leaving Craig to deal with the unity issues, he was more secure as party leader. Thus, 'distant from those whom he led, influential with, but not beholden to, one of the main British parties – Carson himself was not wholly removed from the strategic style and spirit of Parnell and Parnellism'. In addition, while Redmond lacked the boldness and imagination for a complex command, Carson 'carried into politics the culture of the law courts' and 'brought qualities of individuality, theatricality, brinkmanship and boldness'. Thus, his marginality mattered less than that of Redmond's. But both leaders had 'moved from the margins to lead parties that had been characterised, indeed dominated, by profound division' … 'this marginality conditioned an ongoing degree of suspicion among supporters, sometimes restricted their own freedom of political movement, and often induced a high degree of political caution'.

The core chapter of the book, given that the central theme of both men's political careers was Home Rule, is that entitled 'The Dimensions of Home Rule 1911–1925', which examines their roles as competing generals in relation to the great crisis which brought Ireland and Britain to the brink of civil war. Although, to the confusion of their British allies, they sometimes united in sentimental displays of mutual good will (for example, at the Buckingham Palace Conference in July 1914), there appears to be no evidence that they ever 'met privately and on their own to explore, still less to resolve, their differences'. It is difficult in a review to do justice to the many insights which Jackson offers in this masterly chapter. His overall conclusion is that 'the nub of Carson's relationship with the Tories during the Home Rule crisis was that … they came to be politically dependent upon him … Redmond's problem was essentially that, as the crisis developed, he grew ever more dependent upon the Liberal government'.

Indeed, as time went on, Jackson remarks on the diminution of Redmond's influence with Asquith and the Liberal leadership and an increasingly 'wheedling' tone creeping into his correspondence with them. Jackson plays down the traditional view of the significance of the accession to the leadership of the Conservative party in 1911 of Andrew Bonar Law, with his Ulster family connections – 'in some ways the junior partner in his relationship with Carson', who, conditioned by his experience as a successful barrister, believed that only 'big bad boys' could expect to win. Ironically, Jackson, to some degree echoing Stephen Gwynn's 1919 view, believes that for Redmond 'empire' was an essential feature of his nationalism. 'It is possible to argue that Carson's engagement with empire lacked the vision and coherence of Redmond's thought in this area'. However, he does note Colin Reid's recent argument that Redmond's imperialism was, as Reid puts it, 'underpinned by the assumption of white racial superiority' and Paul Townend's research, which has exposed the emergence in the 1870s of a lasting and influential popular Irish anti-imperialism which 'would ultimately help to subvert Redmond and his vision'.

As for Ulster, Redmond seems to have privately envisaged 'Home Rule within Home Rule' as a way of meeting unionist objections but was gradually drawn into the net of exclusion in some form from late 1913 onwards, the point when for Carson exclusion became the end rather than simply a means to dispatch Home Rule. Finally, there is the much debated question as to whether Carson introduced 'the gun' into Irish politics. Patently not, given the United Irishmen, the Young Irelanders and the Fenians! 'What was new about Carson was not so much that he presided over an armed conspiracy, as that he radically adapted the Irish traditions of militant defiance'. He added weapons to the mobilisations of an O'Connell and he added massive publicity, 'photography, film, arc lights, the press corps', to the insurgency pursued by the Fenians. In other words, 'he was the first who deliberately wanted to be seen introducing guns into Irish politics'. So we have Edward Carson, one of the first modern political spin doctors!

Interestingly, Jackson concludes that the sardonic Chief Secretary for Ireland, Augustine Birrell, contrary to the views of some, did not treat the military operations of Carson's UVF as a joke but was pursuing a deliberate policy of 'indifference' in order to annoy Carson. For Jackson, the 'key insouciant voice' in Dublin Castle was Birrell's Under Secretary, the Ulster Presbyterian, Sir James Dougherty, who consistently dismissed the seriousness of the Volunteer movement. Jackson, however, does not mention that Dougherty's view was greatly influenced by his friend and regular correspondent, Rev. J.B. Armour of Ballymoney, whose letters in PRONI clearly demonstrate this.

In his chapter 'The Great War 1914–18', Jackson inevitably argues that 'the war destroyed Redmond', but he also is of the view that it 'permanently damaged the Carson mystique'. 'Each man had become accustomed to operating within a well-defined set of political parameters, and the war largely changed these'. He explores the ambiguous relationship that both leaders had had with pre-war Germany, with Carson even famously lunching with the Kaiser on 23 August 1913 and according to some Redmondites, the Carsonite militancy may have been one of the influences creating a German belief that Britain would not be able to enter a European conflict in 1914. Redmond greatly admired the German constitution of 1871.

The unforgiving pace of the war changed the political landscape for both and ruthlessly exposed the political weaknesses in their characters. 'Just as Redmond's gentlemanly form and caution were clearly limiting, so too Carson's hesitation and caution in office proved to be significant liabilities'. Jackson explores in detail the issues of recruitment, the impact of the Easter Rising and the Lloyd George negotiations which followed in 1916 and, of course, the ill-fated Irish Convention. Like most recent writers, he concludes that the proposed 1916 compromise was wrecked by the southern unionists and their political allies at Westminster, notably Walter Long, Austen Chamberlain and the 'unelected trinity of peers' – Lansdowne, Midleton and Selborne, combined with Lloyd George's inconsistency. This 'exposed both Carson and Redmond to the dissidents within their respective constituencies'. By 1917–18 at the Convention, it was too late.

Despite Redmond's gentlemanly attempt to find another compromise, this time backed by landed southern unionists, his gamble failed and his death on 6 March 1918 was the final act in the political tragedy. Jackson feels that had he been given the opportunity, Redmond had 'an essential skill-set for political office'. Whereas Carson was 'impatient and unhappy when away from the law courts' and his forensic oppositional skills 'were not readily transferable to the corridors of Whitehall'. Indeed, after leaving his Admiralty post in January 1918, Carson was an increasingly marginal figure, out of the political loop, no longer even leading the Ulster unionists after February 1921 and returning to his legal comfort zone as a Lord of Appeal. Jackson notes Carson's political anger at the Conservatives over the Anglo-Irish Treaty and his increasingly radical statements, astonishing dinner companions by indicating that 'we made a great mistake in not accepting Mr. Gladstone's first Home Rule bill'. By 1928 he was even arguing that 'a Republic' would have been preferable to the dishonesty of the Free State 'humbug'! Thus, Jackson concludes that Carson 'was (at least temperamentally) more of a Parnellite than Redmond'.

In his final chapter entitled 'Image, Memory and Commemoration', Jackson assesses the reputations and legacies of both leaders over the decades until the present day. While this is mainly a survey of relevant literature, notably biographies, in the context of both 'the eddies of historiographical fortune' and 'changing political needs', other media from plays and movies on the one hand to commemorative items such as cups, plates, postcards and busts, do also feature, not to mention the brisk trade in 'holy relics' associated with Carson. Alas in the case of John Redmond, Jackson concludes that even in the years of his rehabilitation, no one has fought passionately over his autograph or possessions. I was however surprised to discover that while Jackson (p. 233) mentions Sir John Lavery's 1916 portrait of Redmond, he doesn't refer to Sinéad McCoole's fascinating account of how Lavery had in fact arranged sittings with both leaders, agreeing with them in advance that their portraits would hang side-by-side in a Dublin gallery (they ultimately ended up in the Dublin City Gallery/The Hugh Lane). According to McCoole (*Passion and Politics: Sir John Lavery, The Salon Revisited*), when Redmond heard of Lavery's plan he replied: 'I have always had an idea that Carson and I might someday be hanged side-by-side in Dublin'. Carson apparently thought that Redmond's portrait was better, and given Lavery's Belfast Catholic background, allegedly remarked, 'It's easy to see which side you're on'. Lavery later claimed that this 'was my first attempt to bind up the contending forces in the bonds of holy paint'.

Jackson notes in this chapter that 'Carson had both greater vanity and thinner skin than Redmond', given that his 'life and career were a sustained theatrical performance', which perhaps in the end primarily deceived 'his own, unionist, people'. 'His chosen memorials overshadow and obscure his ambiguities and complexities'. As for Redmond, an individual who was 'pious, propertied and moderate', he had 'spent much of his career trying to persuade the hard men of Irish nationalism that his heart was with them (if not his head). His tragedy was that no one believed him – except those whom he least wanted to convince: the unionists of the north'.

In answer to my opening question, as to whether much more remains to be said or written about Redmond and Carson, given the plethora of earlier biographies, Professor Jackson has provided a dazzling demonstration that indeed there is. His chosen tool of dual or comparative biography proves its worth in the Irish context and may perhaps stimulate other similar work. This book is both a pleasure to handle and to read, written by one of our most distinguished Irish historians at the height of his powers.

The false dawn of 1918 for Irish women

RICHARD McMINN

LOUISE RYAN AND MARGARET WARD (EDS)
Irish Women and the Vote: Becoming Citizens
Irish Academic Press, 2018
pp 280 ISBN: 978-1-788550-1-30 pb €19.99

MARGARET WARD (ED.)
Hanna Sheehy Skeffington, Suffragette and Sinn Féiner:
Her Memoirs and Political Writings
University College Dublin Press, 2017
pp 564 ISBN: 978-1-910820-14-8 hb €35.00

On 18 July 1912 the British Liberal Prime Minister, Herbert Asquith, visited Dublin. Crossing the O'Connell Bridge with his friend and current political ally, John Redmond, in a carriage, they were confronted by three militant emissaries of the British Women's Social and Political Union (the suffragette organisation led by the Pankhurst family). The three WSPU activists succeeded in throwing a hatchet at Asquith, which in fact grazed Redmond slightly. They also attempted to set the Theatre Royal on fire on the same day. The struggle for votes for women on equal terms with men had now been taken to a new level in Ireland. Even the Ulster counties, much preoccupied with the Home Rule issue at the time, were drawn into this more extreme form of conflict. The abandonment by the Ulster Unionist Party of a brief and tentative flirtation with women's suffrage, and a rejection by Edward Carson personally of the idea in the spring of 1914, was the catalyst for an explosion of WSPU violence directed against political and patriarchal targets such as Abbeylands House in Whiteabbey, Bangor Railway Station and the greens at Knock Golf Club, Belfast.

By 1918, however, largely as a consequence of the First World War (which a minority of suffragists in both Britain and Ireland and indeed elsewhere in Europe had opposed), much had changed and the Representation of the People Act, which was passed at Westminster in June 1918 and was quickly followed in November by the Parliament (Qualification of Women) Act, granted the franchise to women over the age of 30 who met certain marriage, property or educational criteria. The companion legislation in November allowed women to stand for parliament, thus enabling Constance Markievicz to win a Westminster seat (which she refused to take, preferring instead to become Minister for Labour in the newly-formed Dáil Éireann). Some feminists at the time celebrated the achievement of the promised land.

They were to be cruelly disappointed and indeed in the short term it was perhaps more significant that the 1918 legislation enfranchised the 40 per cent of men over 21 who had previously been excluded from voting by property qualifications (a great boon to Sinn Féin in achieving the electoral destruction of the Irish Parliamentary Party). While Irish women in the new Irish Free State only had to wait until 1922 to achieve universal suffrage (1928 in the case of the new Northern Ireland jurisdiction), as these two books clearly demonstrate, the achievement of women's rights and female equality still had a long way to go after the apparent victories of 1918, 1922 and 1928. These had indeed represented a false dawn. As Diarmaid Ferriter pointed out in the *Irish Times* of 30 December 2017, it was as recently as 1977 that Fianna Fáil TD, Tim O'Connor, still felt able to express the view that 'in my county the women are doing a great job of work in keeping their homes going and bringing up their families. This I think is just what Almighty God intended them to do'.

However, the legislation of 1918 did represent a signpost to the future and has therefore been understandably deemed to be worth celebrating in the context of a decade, and indeed a very significant year, of centenaries. As Niamh Puirséil has pointed out (*Irish Times,* 10 February 2018*)*, whereas the fiftieth anniversary was celebrated in Britain in the revolutionary atmosphere of 1968, 'it went largely unnoticed and unmarked in Ireland'. While the imperial origin of the legislation may have been a contributory factor, combined with the continuing low status of women in public life (for example, only five

TDs and four senators in an Oireachtas of 204 members were female), Puirséil is surely correct to emphasise that 'women's history was yet to blossom in either teaching or publishing'. In 2018 the same cannot be said, as these two volumes, amongst others, certainly demonstrate.

Irish Women and the Vote, a collection of 13 essays by a distinguished group of scholars working in the area of women's history (including encouragingly one representative of the male gender), which originally appeared in 2007, has been republished as a new edition for the centenary year under the joint editorship of Professor Louise Ryan and Dr Margaret Ward. Both also contribute substantial chapters to the volume. The original Foreword by one of the early pioneers of Irish women's history, Rosemary Cullen Owens, is reproduced, alongside a new Foreword to the revised edition by Professor Linda Connolly and a useful introductory overview by Professor Maria Luddy, which highlights the key issues addressed by the 13 main chapters. Informative brief biographies of all of the contributors are provided, along with nine contemporary satirical cartoons sourced from the *Lepracaun* and the *Irish Citizen* during the 1912–14 period, a chronology of the Irish suffrage movement from 1869–1922 (a boon for readers, given the sometimes confusing multiplicity of overlapping suffrage organisations) and comprehensive endnotes for each chapter.

The first two chapters by Mary Cullen and Carmel Quinlan explore the beginnings of Irish feminism (including Belfast's very own Martha McTier and Mary Ann McCracken in the 1790s) and the successful nineteenth-century campaigns which resulted in women becoming eligible to serve as poor law guardians and those with the required property qualifications being able to vote in local elections. One of the strengths of the volume is that it avoids the danger of being overly Dublin-focused and there are useful chapters by Mary Clancy on the essentially middle-class campaign for the vote in Galway (1911–15) and Leeann Lane on the local frustrations experienced by the Waterford Quaker feminist novelist, Rosamond Jacob, alleviated only by frequent excursions to Dublin to interact with feminists and nationalists there. Denise Kleinrichert and Myrtle Hill survey the fascinating subjects of the relationship between the labour movement and the suffrage issue in the hot, damp, 'sweated' linen mills of Belfast with their dependent and partly teenage female operatives and in Hill's case, the battle for and against the vote in the equally heated Irish political arena, as the debate over the third Home Rule Bill intensified. Hill is led by her research to acknowledge somewhat ruefully that 'whether in early or late twentieth-century Ireland, the common causes on which women could come together often faltered in the face of other aspects of multiple, sometimes overlapping, but often conflicting identities'. For most women, nationalism or unionism overrode everything else.

In a more narrowly focused chapter, Paige Reynolds, analyses the events of Suffrage Week 1913 in Dublin. Louise Ryan, with her background in sociology, is well placed to explore in timely fashion the critique of sexual abuse and domestic violence against women offered by early twentieth-century feminists through their monitoring of court cases and through the columns of the *Irish Citizen*. The fight for suffrage in Ireland was not without its humorous side and campaigners made good use of satirical cartoons and jokes about their opponents, as Cliona Murphy's chapter and its illustrations reveal. Catherine Cousins provides a more narrowly-focused account of the evolution of the suffragist ideology of Margaret Cousins and her interaction with the theosophy movement, with its links to vegetarianism and celibacy, during both her life in Ireland and her subsequent feminist activities in India in the post-1918 years. Margaret Ward contributes a wider perspective with her account of how the outbreak of the First World War in the short-term damaged the cause of suffrage in Ireland, as was the case in Britain and Europe generally. The 'knitting socks for soldiers' mentality became a dominant one amongst many middle-class women. Only the Irish Women's Franchise League (IWFL) retained a degree of what Louie Bennett described as 'stability' and unsuccessfully attempted to send representatives to the 1915 Peace Congress of Women at the Hague. Post-1916, while Irish suffragists mobilised against the threat of conscription, the movement was split over the national question. 'Political ideology challenged gender loyalty', Ward argues, echoing the conclusions of Myrtle Hill.

The sole male contributor to the volume, William Murphy, examines how in Ireland the suffragettes, having stepped up the militant aspects of their campaign, found themselves before 1914 potentially facing imprisonment, first in Mountjoy Prison and then latterly in Tullamore. However, initially they were treated quite well as *de facto* political prisoners but subsequently pioneered the use of the hunger strike, which in turn provoked a harsher response by the authorities, including the use of the so-called 'Cat and Mouse Act'. Murphy convincingly demonstrates that the suffragettes 'introduced to Ireland the tactic which has become synonymous with Irish political imprisonment from [Thomas] Ashe to Bobby Sands: the hunger strike. The novelty of their campaign and its subsequent influence upon political imprisonment in Ireland should not be underestimated'. In footnote 124 (p. 135), Murphy is dismissive of Tim Pat Coogan's suggestion that the hunger strike was 'peculiarly Irish', a Gaelic weapon of honour. For Murphy, the hunger strike was, as Kevin O'Higgins crudely put it, a 'women's weapon' in the first instance.

In the book's final chapter, Catriona Beaumont reviews the issue of female citizenship and gender equality in Ireland after the franchise was granted to women on the same terms as men in 1922. She takes the story up to 1943 and the heavy defeat suffered by four independent women candidates in the general election of that year. The intervening period was largely a rearguard action fought by a vocal but limited number of activists against the attempted erosion of women's rights, for example in de Valera's 1937 Constitution. So the promise of 1918 and indeed 1922 had certainly failed to materialise. However, as Beaumont argues, a small group of women had at least continued to highlight the issue in a largely hostile environment and foremost amongst those was Hanna Sheehy Skeffington, a leading activist in the years of promise and beyond.

Margaret Ward has had a distinguished career in the field of women's history, beginning with the publication in 1983 of what was to become a classic landmark text – *Unmanageable Revolutionaries: Women and Irish Nationalism.* This was followed by impressive biographies of Maud Gonne and in 1997 of Hanna Sheehy Skeffington. The publication in 2017 by UCD Press of this edited and contextualised volume of Hanna's writings, running to 463 pages of text, provides a fitting companion volume to the 1997 biography. It clearly represents both a labour of love and an example of editorial professionalism and academic scholarship of the highest standard. In undertaking the task,

Ward was able to benefit from Hanna's assiduous record keeping and hoarding of documents and photographs, although some items were carried away by a raiding party of British soldiers in the aftermath of the Easter Rising when Hanna's pacifist and suffragist husband, Francis Skeffington, had been ruthlessly murdered on the orders of a British officer, later found to be insane. This treasure trove of source material was subsequently donated to the National Library of Ireland by Hanna's descendants.

Hanna had begun to write her memoirs shortly before her death in 1946 but only got as far as completing in full the first of 14 planned chapters, which deals with her family background (she was the daughter of the middle-class IPP MP, David Sheehy) and early childhood. Altogether, a third of the chapters were written in some form, taking the story up to the establishment of Dáil Éireann. However, Ward has been able to fill in the gaps and extend the coverage beyond 1918 through the inclusion of extracts from Hanna's journalism and her many speeches.

The book, which benefits from an affectionate foreword by Hanna's granddaughter Micheline Sheehy Skeffington and from a detailed timeline of Hanna's life and times, includes no fewer than 30 photographic plates, mainly, but not exclusively, from the NLI archive. As well as the often revealing memoir material written in a very accessible style, there are chapters covering women and education, women and the national movement, votes for women, war and pacifism, the death of Hanna's husband Francis, her propaganda work in the USA after the Rising, her role in the War of Independence (including a somewhat optimistic account of the work of the unofficial Sinn Féin courts), her opposition to the Treaty (Hanna was never a fan of Michael Collins – 'had a touch of the dictator-to-come about him' and while he 'had a boisterous humour of the barracks type' ... 'had the usual soldier's contempt of civilians, particularly of women'), her public row with Séan O'Casey over *The Plough and the Stars* which Hanna saw as an attack on the men of the Rising, accounts of her travels in Europe (including Stalin's Russia, which like many fellow left-wing intellectuals she seems to have been uncritically impressed by), her memories of Countess Markievicz, her increasing disillusion with both Fine Gael and the IFS ('rapidly becoming a Catholic statelet under Rome's grip') but ultimately with Sinn Féin and de Valera also ('Well meaning, of course, better than Cosgrave, but really essentially conservative and church bound, anti-feminist, bourgeois and the rest'), her prison experiences including a spell in Armagh Prison, her feminist push-back against the male domination of the new Ireland, including through standing in the 1943 general election, noted previously. Even a selection of her book and theatre reviews and of the obituaries on her death are included. Each of the 17 chapters has a useful introduction by Ward, incorporating an overview of the contents and its highlights. Hanna is a skilful writer and even when dealing with grim aspects of her life (for example, her hunger strike in Mountjoy in 1912) summons up the realities of such an experience. 'The sense of smell becomes acute – I had never smelt tea before. A dying woman craved for a rasher, and it was fried somewhere nearby (perhaps to tempt us?). That was tantalizing'.

However, Hanna, like all human beings, had her blind spots and inconsistencies. While impressed by women's release from 'the tyranny of the pots and pans' on her visit to Soviet Russia in 1930, as Ward notes, Hanna and her companions 'were not shown Soviet prisons, so took on trust the assurance that prisoners were not punished but trained for citizenship'. Ward lets her off rather too easily perhaps on this issue. 'While delegations such as this were criticised for their naivety and blindness to the growing totalitarian state, what comes out of her jottings is her hope for the future, and her enjoyment of escaping for five weeks from the consumerism of the West'. It is also clear that Hanna's pacifism, when it came to the issue of Ireland's future, had its limits, unlike colleagues such as Louie Bennett. 'If I saw a hope of Ireland being freed for ever from British rule by a swift uprising, I would consider Irish men justified in resorting to arms in order that we might be free, and I should still be radically opposed to war and militarism' (1915). She had no time for unionism and partition.

Equally, in her 1927 *Irish World* article contrasting the funerals in the same week of her friend Countess Markievicz ('Ireland's Joan of Arc') and the assassinated Free State Minister for Justice, Kevin O'Higgins, Hanna does not hold back in lauding the former and condemning the latter, showing no apparent concern for the brutal manner of his demise. 'The love and loyalty of one's own people are a better armour than all the machine guns ever made, a securer protection than all the treason and safety acts ever devised' (p. 300). Indeed, as Ward acknowledges (p. 68), in her draft memoir Hanna even 'glosses over internal divisions in the [suffrage] movement; perhaps the passing of the years rendered them less important in her eyes'.

However, in the final analysis, when it came to the biggest personal crisis in her own life, the murder of her beloved husband Francis in 1916, one can only admire the determination and dignity with which she handled the episode and her success in securing the Simon Inquiry which, despite its limitations, vindicated her stance. Margaret Ward is to be congratulated for making more accessible this fascinating and diverse range of evidence about the life of one of early twentieth-century Ireland's most important female pioneers.

REVIEWS

LEO KEOHANE
Captain Jack White:
Imperialism, Anarchism and the Irish Citizen Army
Merrion Press, 2014
pp 288   ISBN: 978-1-908928-92-4   pb   €22.50

As one of only a handful of genuine Irish anarchists/syndicalists, Captain Jack White DSO has 'remained, till now, a hugely under-researched and enigmatic figure', with only 'a walk-on part in Irish folk memory', as Professor Emmet O'Connor eloquently put it in his review of the above book in *Irish Historical Studies,* vol. xl, no. 158, December 2016. Even in his native Broughshane area, he has largely been air-brushed from history, unlike his father, General Sir George White VC, the so-called 'hero of Ladysmith' during the Second Boer War. There is, however, no danger that his son Jack will also end up adorning a local Orange Lodge banner!

Indeed, the only revolutionary act for which Jack is remembered locally is that he was allegedly the first male ever to be seen wheeling a baby in a pram in the village, albeit the pram (although hopefully not the baby) was sometimes parked for considerable periods outside a local pub. Indeed, Keohane recalls a similar kind of Broughshane folk memory of the ageing White (born 1879) in the wartime 1940s, making his lonely way slowly home on horseback in the early hours to the family's house and small estate, Whitehall, in nearby Cooreen (see Keohane, p. 41). By that time Captain White and his younger second wife Noreen (Shanahan) were living in genteel poverty in a fairly large house with only primitive facilities, dependent on selling vegetables at the local market. On his death from prostate cancer in February 1946, Captain White's entire estate came to only £81 19s. 5d.

Jack White published *Misfit: My Autobiography* in 1930 and along with a number of pamphlets, it has until now remained the principal source for any account of his career. However, White's biographer, Leo Keohane, a lecturer in Critical Theory at NUI Galway, having completed a doctorate on anarchism as an alternative perspective in political philosophy, has been keen to explore the philosophy of its relatively few adherents/admirers in early twentieth-century Ireland. James Connolly, with his links to syndicalism, was one obvious choice and White, given his unorthodox life and career despite his establishment background, another.

White was the only son of Broughshane landowner General Sir George White. He received his military training at Sandhurst, where he claimed to have learned about 'fortification and fornication', won a DSO for bravery in the Second Boer War, served as an *aide-de-camp* to his father, now Governor of Gibraltar, where Jack dined with both King Edward VII and Kaiser Wilhelm II, but resigned from a subsequent military training role following a crisis of political conscience in 1907. His 'innate anarchism' (Emmet O'Connor) and his admiration for Leo Tolstoy led him into various short-term odd jobs and ultimately the 'hippie' Whiteway colony in the Cotswolds. He also entered into a controversial marriage with the glamorous, half-Spanish and Roman Catholic Dollie Mosley, against the wishes of both families. This tempestuous union, blighted by White's restlessness on both the political and romantic fronts, was doomed to failure. White is perhaps best known as a co-founder and first commandant of the Irish Citizen Army during the 1913 Dublin Lockout, and as an associate of O'Casey, Connolly, Larkin and Markievicz, with all of whom he had difficult relationships. Keohane has been able to provide additional detail on the ICA phase of White's career and on his subsequent dalliance with the Irish Volunteers in Derry, despite his suspicion of both nationalism and Catholic clericalism. Numerous other causes and campaigns followed – driving an ambulance on the Western Front, attempting to organise a Welsh miners strike in protest at the executions of the Easter week leaders, participation in a number of left-wing groups in Ireland in the 1920s and 1930s and the inevitable 'homage to Catalonia' in 1936 (a disillusioning experience for him as for others, given the realities he experienced of Stalinism at work in Spain).

These career moves were all marked by acrimony, arrogance and perceived slight, an abrasive military manner and a quirky belief system – anarchism laced with a dash of Protestant theology! They were also punctuated by occasional spells in prison and ended, as noted above, in relative poverty in Broughshane in the 1940s. A colourful character certainly, but not easy to live with, as his second wife Noreen discovered.

Keohane has been able, unlike previous researchers, to add to the existing sources through tracking down White's descendants, now living in Edinburgh, notably his sons Alan and Derrick and his grand-niece, Katy English, who 'made available to me a vast haul of family papers' and a series of photographs, which enliven the text. One can only envy him the generosity of the White family – 'not once was there a suggestion that I should alter matters that might feature unflatteringly'. As I have noted in this journal before, custodians of family records are not always so happy with a 'warts and all' approach by academic historians. So this account of White's life is certainly the fullest to date, although given his interest in political theory, Keohane does interweave the biographical material with periodic passages analysing anarchism and syndicalism both in an Irish and a wider context. Although he acknowledges and exemplifies White's character faults and weaknesses, Keohane is not an unsympathetic biographer. Despite his subject's immaturity with regard to relationships and his bravado (which is much on display in *Misfit*), Keohane sees Jack White as 'a man who stuck to his ideals … in different circumstances with different opportunities he may have made a far greater mark' (p. 7).

My own interest in Jack White relates to his involvement in the organisation of the celebrated Ballymoney Town Hall Meeting of 24 October 1913 of Protestants opposed to 'Carsonism' and in favour of Irish Home Rule, at which a 'New Covenant' was launched by Captain White, supported by Sir Roger Casement and others (see *Familia,* no. 29, 2013, pp 20–43).

Keohane's account of the Ballymoney meeting, its significance and White's role as its prime initiator, very much echoes the views expressed in my *Against the Tide* (PRONI, 1985), which is fully acknowledged as a key source in the endnotes. The other political heavyweight involved was Sir Roger Casement, and Keohane rightly notes (p. 61) that 'from the very beginning White's talent to exacerbate and disconcert was evident'. Indeed, White himself acknowledged that there was a 'rival messiahship' between them and Keohane argues that Casement, although a charismatic character, had his share of critics as well, in particular as regards his temperament. However, as Rev. J.B. Armour, who in 1913 played a behind-the-scenes organisational role, put it in one of his letters to his son: '[Casement's] explanation of the matter is that there is a slate off. Certainly, White is peculiar'. One nugget of new information which Keohane produces is that while White was occupying an adjoining cell to Casement in Pentonville Prison in 1916 (the former serving three months for sedition), these two prickly individuals were still arguing about the organisation of the Ballymoney meeting, even on the very night before Casement was hanged!

For all of Keohane's diligent research work, White remains an enigmatic figure, full of contradictions. His personal papers, alas, have still never been found. The man who had claimed to be a pacifist of sorts also favoured active self-defence, as his training role with both the ICA and Irish Volunteers demonstrated and indeed Tony, his eldest son, later recalled his father threatening that if the Nazis came up the avenue at Whitehall, 'he would take out his shotgun and get a few of them first'. Writing in a pamphlet in 1937, White declared that 'a Christian Anarchist, which, if I am to have a label at all, and I hate all labels, is the nearest label to fit me'. Indeed, it is extraordinary to discover in Keohane's fair and balanced biography that the man who at various times claimed to have been attacked and beaten by the Dublin Metropolitan Police, the RUC, the Blueshirts, the IRA and the Orange Order was also a regular correspondent of the workhorse of the Craigavon Unionist government, 'William [sic] Spender'.

Perhaps Armour's description of him as 'peculiar' was an apt one and certainly less dismissive than Casement's view that he had 'a slate off', or the even more sweeping opinion expressed to Keohane by 'a very eminent local historian' (unidentified) that Captain White 'was a bit of an eejit'! Leo Keohane has given us much food for thought in this thorough analysis and while White may remain something of an enigma, it can no longer be claimed that he is under-researched.

RICHARD McMINN

ALAN F. PARKINSON
Election Fever:
Groundbreaking Electoral Contests in Northern Ireland
Blackstaff Press, 2017
pp 368   ISBN: 978-1-780731-20-9   pb   £14.99

My dictionary defines 'fever' as 'any illness characterised by high temperature'. Dr Parkinson may have had an alternative meaning – 'intense nervous excitement' – in mind when choosing a title to attract readers to a 360-page volume giving detailed accounts of eight Ulster elections – by-, general, and provincial. But this catalogue of rising hopes and dashed expectations is the history of a chronic illness as well as a record of exciting politics.

To the eight chapters dealing with selected polls, from the North Belfast by-election of 1905 to the 2003 Assembly election, the author adds a short postscript, two appendices – the first with short summaries of all major elections in NI from 1905 to 2017, the second containing potted biographies of some of the politicians of the period.

An introduction of almost 50 pages sets the overall context. This is about as good a summary of the Northern Ireland problem as I have read. Dr Parkinson maintains an admirably balanced perspective throughout. Extensive use of opposing analyses and opinions found in the *Irish Press* and the *Belfast Telegraph* help do this, and they also add the immediacy of eye-witness accounts of past events.

The Rt Hon. Karen Bradley MP, Secretary of State for Northern Ireland (at the time of writing) would benefit from reading this book and learning all she never knew about how people here vote and why.

The book documents the various attempts to create a middle political ground that was neither Catholic/nationalist nor Protestant unionist, and the obstacles in the way. This tribal division was there in the North Belfast by-election in 1905, the year the Ulster Unionist Council was formed, and almost two decades before Northern Ireland came into being.

What was different was the strong challenge to Conservative/Unionist domination by a candidate, William Walker, who was both a left-tending radical and a Unionist who was targeting the votes of Catholic and Protestant workers. Another difference was the participation of leading figures from 'across the water' in support of Walker – Ramsay MacDonald was his election agent, and Keir Hardie and Arthur Henderson campaigned for him on the streets of North Belfast.

The ease with which an effort to appeal to both sides can be sabotaged, then as now, is shown in an episode recorded by Dr Parkinson. On the run-up to polling a right-wing Protestant group sent a set of questions to the candidates. Walker, foolishly, and honestly replied, giving his unionist opinion on such questions as the ban on Catholics succeeding to the throne, or being appointed to the post of Lord Lieutenant of Ireland. These were hardly burning issues in North Belfast, but served to reheat Catholics' sense of not-belonging.

Despite occasional flirtations with optimism, in the end Dr Parkinson is realistically pessimistic. Much has changed – the dominant Unionist Party has been eclipsed by the Democratic Unionist Party (DUP), nationalism, including, almost, the Social Democratic and Labour Party (SDLP), has been swallowed by Sinn Féin.

His final comment in the book is that Northern Ireland, politically, 'remains a place apart where elections represent periodic opportunities to manifest tribal loyalties shaped by history and tradition, rather than the expression of pragmatic voter choices relating to the modern world.'

Where did it all go wrong? Probably at the beginning; the partition envisaged in the Government of Ireland Act and the ensuing Treaty Agreement was very different from the chasm that opened almost immediately. Dublin sought to prevent it by boycott and use of force against the new entity, northern nationalists both wished and believed that partition would either not happen at all, or would soon collapse, and refused to recognise Northern Ireland or participate in its institutions.

So from birth the northern statelet was unionist, and Unionists failed to recognise that it could not succeed long term if a significant majority of the people withheld their consent from being in it.

The Council of Ireland, meant as a gesture towards a common Irish dimension if not identity, was wrecked by Dublin's refusal to nominate to it, to the relief of the Belfast government. Within a very short time the common name of Irishman had little meaning in political circles.

The chapter on Bobby Sands' win in the Fermanagh-South Tyrone by-election of 1981 helps us to understand just how strong the pull of community, some call it tribal, loyalty can be. The SDLP, John Hume, in particular had been sharply critical of IRA violence, condemning it both as evil, and as working against the long-term interests of Irish nationalism. But not even Hume could bring himself to insist that the SDLP put up a candidate against a convicted IRA bomber. Sands did not run as a Republican hero but as a victim; he stood as an 'Anti H-Block/Armagh Political Prisoner' and his campaign was focused on the Maze hunger strikers, on their treatment in prison, on Mrs Thatcher's 'intransigence'. Some nationalists may have felt that the election of Sands would end the hunger-strike without loss of life.

As the author notes, this was the strategy of the 'Armalite and the Ballot Box' before the term was coined. (IRA killings continued during the election campaign.)

The last election under Dr Parkinson's microscope is the Assembly poll of 2003, after the implementation of the Belfast Agreement, which saw Sinn Féin and the DUP overtaking the SDLP and the Ulster Unionists. There is no attempt in the book to pronounce judgment on the Agreement or its success or failure, but the author's final comment written presumably in 2017, and quoted above, that elections in Northern Ireland are still little more than opportunities for voters to declare their tribal loyalties says enough.

This is hardly surprising. The Belfast Agreement marked the end of any attempt to bring peace and stability by strengthening the middle ground and isolating the extremes. Mr Blair's primary objective was to get an IRA ceasefire, and the wording of the Agreement repeatedly shows deference to Sinn Féin sensibilities. Blair wanted Sinn Féin and hard line unionists on board, and did so by institutionalising the tribal divide as Irish or British and promising 'parity of esteem' to each competing set of demands.

Dr Parkinson does have one or two Homeric nods. Several times he asserts that Lord Brookeborough was Terence O'Neill's uncle; not so, they were not related. It also says Dame Dehra Parker was O'Neill's grandmother. They were related, but she was the grandmother of O'Neill's cousins, James and Robin Chichester-Clark, but not of him. These are minor slips in a lively and important book

DENNIS KENNEDY

DOUGLAS BARTLETT
An Illustrated History of Limavady and the Roe Valley:
from Prehistoric to Modern Times
Privately published, 1st ed. 2010, 2nd ed. 2017
pp 196 ISBN: 978-0-9565683-1-1 pb £15

This book is ambitious. It sets out to survey the history of Limavady and its surrounding area from pre-historic times to the early twentieth century. It succeeds admirably and, in doing so, exhibits a combination of qualities found only rarely, even in local histories judged to be successful.

Written in a style pleasing both to the specialist and to the general reader, it is generous in its chosen ground, dealing not just with Limavady and the Roe Valley but also with neighbours who impinged on their history (Coleraine, Derry, Dungiven, and various locations in Donegal, for example); and, where appropriate, setting developments in a still broader context, whether Irish, British, European, trans-Atlantic or Antipodean. Also, while providing a continuous narrative, it lingers on those aspects of local history where significant physical evidence has survived: chambered graves, Beaker pottery, the King's fort at Drumsurn, jewellery like the Broighter gold, townscapes in plantation maps, contemporary and later statues and memorials, and notable contributions to the built environment – so that, while much more than this, the book acts as a field guide to the area. From time to time the author encourages enthusiastic readers to get out and about themselves. The Martello Tower at Magilligan, for example, 'is conveniently placed for a quick visit, as passengers wait for the ferry to Donegal which docks only a few metres from it'. And this friendly approach is richly complemented by over 100 illustrations: while these are of the highest relevance and quality, they are never allowed to drown the text. Only occasionally as a reviewer have I come across a general work worthy of an unqualified recommendation. This is one such: a splendid local history by a local man.

This is not to suggest that a greedy reader could not ask for more: to give two examples. In general the British context is handled well, except in the case of James II, whose high-handed and controversial appointments were not confined to Ireland but were an extension of his actions in England. The author is clearly more comfortable with people, events and artefacts; less so with the continuum of economic history. Here the linen industry is less satisfactorily dealt with than any other element in the book. There are, however, great strengths elsewhere, in particular a confident description and analysis of the region's experience during the Ulster Plantation; extended treatment of the career of the blind harpist, Denis O'Hampsey; an explanation of the fundamental role played by the locality as the site of the 8-mile-long baseline used in the first Ordnance Survey mapping of Ireland between 1824 and 1846; and a balanced, indeed carefully nuanced, treatment of the Famine years in the area. There are also mini-biographies of individuals who, though born in the far north of Ireland, built their reputations elsewhere. Chief among these are John Mitchel 1815–75, the journalist and political activist; William King 1812–95, one-time slave-owner in the United States, but later a leading abolitionist in Canada; and William Ferguson Massey, born in Limavady in 1856 and Prime Minister of New Zealand 1912–25.

Physically, this is a most attractive book, designed by April Sky Design of Newtownards and printed by a leading Ulster firm, W.&G. Baird of Antrim. It has been privately published, which may make it difficult to locate. Yet it is certainly worthy of a most diligent search.

PETER ROEBUCK

MARIANNE ELLIOTT
Hearthlands:
A Memoir of the White City Housing Estate in Belfast
Blackstaff Press, Belfast, 2017
pp 272   ISBN: 978-0-856409-97-4   pb   £12.99

Alfred Cobban's claim, quoting Albert Schweitzer, that the French revolution came as 'a fall of snow on blossoming trees' might come to mind when I completed this book: could it also be attributable to the onset of the Northern Ireland 'Troubles'? I had been lulled by the title and the cover image of this intriguing book into expecting a personal story. It is much more than this. If anything it amounts to a three-dimensional history. At its core is the author's personal story complemented by oral history of neighbours on one of the first mixed housing estates in Northern Ireland after the war and set in context by the social history compiled by a professional historian. The White City can be seen as a microcosm for post-war Northern Ireland.

It is remarkable how the UK carried on waging the Second World War while simultaneously making preparations for its aftermath. In Northern Ireland the dereliction of society before 1939 when added to the war damage, particularly in Belfast, made remedial action unavoidable. The post-war agreement between Westminster and Stormont of parity of taxation aligned to parity of benefits enabled the populace here to benefit from the new Welfare State and created a bigger pool of resources available to the devolved administration. Professor Elliott considers the impact of the rolling out of that Welfare State and the burgeoning of social life in Belfast in the 1950s and 1960s. She relates the major stories of the era such as the *Princess Victoria* disaster and the 'Curran Murder' to life in White City without the connection appearing contrived.

Jonathan Bardon (*A History of Ulster*, 1992, p. 532) has commented on the 'dismal housing record' of the government and particularly of Belfast Corporation. Within its devolved authority the post-war Unionist government made housing a clear priority. A new minister was appointed to a newly-created ministry and a new institution, the Housing Trust, was given statutory powers, becoming a catalyst for major change. The author is surprised that there has been so little focus on this institution and proceeds to redress some of that deficit here. She rediscovers for us a ministerial working-class champion in William Grant, a Unionist doppelganger of Paddy Devlin, and emphasises the significance of the first two Chairmen of the Housing Trust, Sir Lucius O'Brien and Herbert Bryson. Their representations resulted in the first ever survey of housing conditions in 1944, highlighting the need for 100,000 new homes and a further 80,000 in need of repair.

The author depicts Unionist ministers like Grant being prepared to support ideas of selection based on need, to eliminate the 'putting in a word' culture and to anoint unorthodoxy in persons like O'Brien, a Quaker and social reformer, and Bryson, dedicated to social change, to the Board of the Housing Trust but could not get around to appointing a Roman Catholic despite the wish of that board to have one third Catholic representation. Marshall McLuhan's idea that 'the medium is the message' did not filter through in time to save liberal unionism. Nevertheless, Grant was successful in standing up to considerable opposition from within Unionist ranks and particularly from the border counties, as he had the support of the Prime Minister. Brookeborough is portrayed here telling a UUC delegation that he would not be responsible for discrimination against the minority.

The establishment of the new Housing Trust is a story of mostly but not entirely strong men, including some civil servants, but the induction and maintenance of stable communities in the new estates transforms into a story of strong women. The unorthodoxy continued into the elevation of the importance of housing management. On the frontline in this role was a phalanx of women managers trained in the system of Octavia Hill, a Victorian social reformer who pioneered the development of tenants' self-esteem and their caring for their neighbourhood. They set out to demonstrate and maintain a new partnership between landlord and tenant from selection through to advice on housekeeping.

This is where the book's strength of being a personal, family and neighbours' history as well as an historian's comes into play. Moving into the newly built White City, Orlit-built estate in the Whitewell area on the cusp of north Belfast in 1949, Elliott is able to bring her own experience and that of her mother and their neighbours to their feedback on the Housing Trust. Overall praise for the Housing Trust was virtually unanimous despite the poor quality of the experimental Orlit build material. It set a standard for the local authorities to be measured against and for the Housing Executive to sustain.

In line with her earlier work Elliott does not play to the Nationalist/Catholic victim v Unionist/Protestant perpetrator axis. In respect of education she asserts that the northern government's 'record on education was as good as it could have been in such a divided society'. The Education Act (NI) of 1947 authorised free school places for all and allowed for the extension of compulsory schooling until the age of 15. The advance in provision throughout the 1950s was marked by new schools in north Belfast, Graymount and Dunlambert at secondary level and later Ballygolan and Throne at primary level. Progress was slower on the Catholic side. Elliott, while recognising the campaign of some Protestants to resist concessions to the Catholic authorities, emphasises that the Church's resistance to perceived government interference and subsequent refusal to accept two Ministry of Education representatives on school management committees, subjected Catholic parishioners to finding 35 per cent of the capital cost of new schools until 1968. The Unionist hierarchy moved more quickly to conciliatory positions than the Catholic clergy. Under the 1947 Education Act an impressive array of three grammar schools, 15 state, six Catholic secondary intermediate and one technical college emerged in Belfast. Is trust our constant fault line?

The final strand of the book tries to link the White City experience to indicators for the future. All the Housing Trust estates around Belfast were socially mixed. I grew up on one and remember the range, from civil servant to labourer. The White City is an example of one that was religiously mixed from the beginning. Catholics composed about 27 per cent of the households and surprisingly maintained that level of around a quarter in the 1971 census. The proportion declined to 5 per cent in the 1991 census. This book tracks the course and causes of that change. In the end it asks the question, 'Does mixed religion (social) housing work?' Herbert Bryson in his evidence to the Cameron Commission in 1969 thought that it did. The oral histories here provide positive reinforcement.

She then entwines a question about the effectiveness of integrated education. She quotes from one survey – as long ago as 2002 – among Hazelwood Integrated College pupils which was positive about relationships inside the school but notes that some retreated into sectarian rioting in the area when away from the school community. It is disappointing that she treats integrated education as little more than an afterthought. I do not think that it is by accident that the Hazelwood Integrated Schools at primary and secondary level – which occupy the former Graymount and Throne sites on the edges of White

City – have been so successful since their creation in 1985. Indeed, this work helps those of us who were involved in that creation to understand better the foundation that had already been laid. A more pertinent question may be – what kind of citizens will those pupils become as adults? Having learned to bring their full identities to the school community and find accommodation in a context of mutual respect and understanding, can they contribute to that fuller integration in the housing communities of the future?

Hearthlands is a well-written challenging read. I lived through the same period as the author and it caused me to re-appraise my own positions. Others, of whatever age, should find its hybrid format an entertaining medium for that history. The notes and bibliography provide an invaluable Satnav for those who wish to follow the author's example.

BRENDAN FULTON

MARK EMPEY, ALAN FORD AND MIRIAM MOFFITT (EDS)
The Church of Ireland and its Past:
History, Interpretation and Identity
Four Courts Press, 2017
pp 360   ISBN: 978-1-84682-637-5   hb   €49.50

This book makes for very interesting reading which will appeal not only to those with an interest in the Church of Ireland but also to those with an interest in how church history or ecclesiastical history has changed over the centuries. It is concerned not so much with the history of the Church of Ireland as how authors over the last four centuries have sought to write this history. It provides a valuable insight into the new ways historians today approach church history, something that applies to all churches and not just the Church of Ireland.

In the opening chapter Alan Ford explains how with the spread of the Reformation across Europe in the sixteenth century Protestant writers produced church histories which sought to justify the current position of their national churches. He points out: 'The rise of Protestant church history naturally stimulated the growth of its Catholic twin, giving birth to the centuries-long rivalry between Catholic and Protestant historiography'. In subsequent centuries, until relatively recently, church history was usually written by clergy or lay persons with a strong attachment to their own denomination.

Attention first focuses on James Ussher, Archbishop of Armagh, 1625–56, and the seventeenth-century Irish historian, Sir James Ware, who established an important basis for future historians of the Church of Ireland. In his study of Ussher, Alan Ford describes how he claimed that the beliefs and practices of the early church, going back to St Patrick, were in harmony with the contemporary Church of Ireland. He argued that St Patrick established an independent Celtic church, which fell under the control of the papacy only in the twelfth century, but re-established its independence with the Reformation.

In his chapter on Ware, Mark Empey looks at how he drew up lists of Protestant episcopal succession through the Reformation back to the early church. The purpose of these two seventeenth-century historians was to make exclusive Protestant claims on the early church, especially the role of St Patrick. Their work did identify and use important primary source material but their interpretation was selective, in order to promote the cause of their contemporary religious beliefs.

In 'Writing the history of the Church of Ireland in the eighteenth century' Toby Barnard looks at the work of a number of clergy who wrote histories of Ireland, often repeating the claims of Ussher. In addition to his historical work, Ussher was widely recognised as a great scholar with numerous publications and an extensive correspondence. In October 1825 the board of Trinity College Dublin appointed C.R. Elrington, Regius Professor of Divinity at the college, to edit and publish all his writings. Jamie Blake Knox examines this publishing project, which ran to 17 volumes, and shows how Elrington sought to orientate Ussher's biography in a high church direction.

The nineteenth century witnessed the publication of a number of histories of the Church of Ireland. Richard Mant, Bishop of Down and Connor, was the author of a two-volume, nearly 1,700 page history (1840). Sean Farrell looks at Mant and this work in the context of religious politics in early Victorian Belfast. Mant's high-church emphasis led him to stress the episcopacy and to give a critical view of Presbyterian concerns in the seventeenth century, which caused some tension in Belfast.

J.H. Todd, appointed Regius Professor of Hebrew in Trinity in 1850, was a leading scholar of Irish. His study, *St Patrick, Apostle of Ireland*, was published in Dublin in 1864. This work has been subsequently criticised for Todd's perceived 'ecclesiastical bias', but Dáibhá Ó Crónín in a chapter on Todd and the volume pays tribute to the exemplary way he describes the early Irish episcopal and monastic system. Thomas O'Loughlin considers the work of another scholar of Irish, William Reeves, Bishop of Down, Connor and Dromore, 1886 to 1892, and a president of the Royal Irish Academy, who was responsible for an edited study of the seventh century *Adomnan's Life of St Columba* (1857). He praises the detached scholarship Reeves brought to this task.

Interest in the historic origins of the church took on a new relevance before and after disestablishment of the Church of Ireland in 1869. James Golden examines how supporters of the church, writers and spokesmen, sought to emphasise their links to the early church as a way to promote their legitimacy and sense of Irishness. They were keen to reject any idea that they were just a branch of the Church of England with sixteenth-century origins. Ruari Cullen studies the writings of George T. Stokes, Professor of Ecclesiastical History at Trinity. Among his historical work, *Ireland and the Celtic Church* was probably the best known. He not only argued for a continuity with the early church but also claimed historical Irish connections with Christianity in the eastern Mediterranean rather than with Rome. Such claims are not now given serious credit and must be seen as part of the rivalry with other churches, Catholic and Presbyterian, to stake out exclusive claims on the religious past.

This interdenominational rivalry over ownership of the Irish past reached a peak in the 1930s. The year 1932 saw widespread celebrations concerning the 1500-year anniversary of the arrival of St Patrick in Ireland, with all the churches making proprietorial claims about St Patrick. At the request of J.A.F. Gregg, Archbishop of Dublin, W.A. Phillips, Lecky Professor of History at Trinity edited a three-volume multi-authored history of the Church of Ireland. Miriam Moffitt looks at the background to this project and the publications produced. Some essayists wrote neutral accounts of the past but others remained attached to a more exclusive, traditional version. This decade witnessed the beginning of efforts to take a more objective view of Irish history, but this did not yet extend to religious history. In a follow up chapter Miriam Moffitt considers Church of Ireland historians, 1850–1950, and how they treated twelfth-century reform of the Irish church. Alan Ford explores divisions within the church with a study of history writers in the Jacobean and Caroline traditions in the Church of Ireland, 1600–2000.

Developments in the writing of the history of the Church of Ireland since 1950 are examined in a chapter by Ian D'Alton. He points to two changes which have influenced this recent work. First, there has been 'professionalisation' with a growth in the number of academics, students and general public members researching and writing on church history. Besides general histories we now have collections of essays on aspects of church life, as well as local studies. Secondly, there has been a move from a narrow denominational concern to a broader more neutral approach. This is well brought out in the subject of the Reformation in Ireland and the role of the Church of Ireland in these events, a topic previously viewed in narrow confessional terms. In the last four decades, however, there has been a more dispassionate debate on the matter, which began with the early publications of Brendan Bradshaw. A chapter in the book contains essays on this debate by Nicholas Canny, Karl S. Bottigheimer and Steven Ellis. This is followed by a chapter by James Murray who brings the Reformation debate after Bradshaw up to the most recent publications on the subject.

In the final chapter David Hayton provides a general survey of the writing of the history of the Church of Ireland, as described in this book. He discusses the new approach found in recent decades to the subject of church history, affecting all denominations. This work now attracts the attention not just of church members but also those whose interest in religion is entirely academic. Study of church institutions has been joined by interest in belief and cultural practices, as well as inter-church relations. The emphasis on more objective historical scholarship in Irish history writing has brought a new level of objectivity to church history.

Of course, this change in approach is influenced by the more ecumenical age in which we live. On St Patrick's Day 1981 Archbishop Robin Eames declared: 'St Patrick belongs to us all', while on St Patrick's Day 1988 Cardinal Tomas O'Fiaich stated: 'His name should be the special rallying-cry for all Christians of Irish birth or descent'. Today we may be critical of the exclusive nature of earlier church history writing. However, we should remember that the authors were responding to the dynamics of their religious, social and political world, as we do today.

BRIAN M. WALKER

TANJA POPPELREUTER (ED.)
Glamour and Gloom:
1930s Architecture in Belfast
The Ulster Architectural Heritage Society, 2017
pp 272   ISBN: 978-0-900457-81-4   pb   £18

The Ulster Architectural Heritage Society has an honourable history of publications which are models of panache and style. *Glamour and Gloom: 1930s Architecture in Belfast* is a recent excellent example. This stylish publication, with its attractive faux dust jacket design and distinctive Elephant frontispiece, is a treasure house of informative text, excellent photographs and meticulous diagrams and detailed building plans as should be expected from talented architecture students and their tutor.

Dr Poppelreuter makes it clear that the 1930s was at once a period of innovation, modernism and technological advance – 'The Glamour' – but also a time of political and, above all, economic uncertainty – 'The Gloom'. This still has reverberations in the twenty-first century. The range of essays and 19 case studies cover a wide range of aspects of the architecture of this exciting period.

The contributions on the new iconic temples of finance and commerce in central Belfast are full of new insights into how the city attempted to come to terms with the changing nature of western capitalism in the 1930s. The strong association between our now somewhat neglected Bank of Ireland steel framed Portland stone-cladded mini 'skyscraper' in North Street and the monumental temples of capitalism in downtown Manhattan as envisaged by the architect Joseph Vincent Downes is truly thrilling.

The book also draws our attention to a number of 1930s and 1940s Belfast buildings we rather take for granted today such as the Whitla Hall at Queen's University Belfast and the charming Masonic Hall on the lower Crumlin Road. These are clearly identified as Modernist steel-framed structures which helped bring the innovations of 1930s modern architecture into our public space.

The contributions on the 1930s cinema construction boom are illuminating and entertaining. Doubtless influenced by Dr Poppelreuter's own insights, the authors of these case studies show the clear links between the technological innovations of synchronised sound and the 'talkies' and our own local cinema boom. It is a pleasure to read the descriptions of these glamorous palaces of escapism which were affordable havens for ordinary Belfast people who at the time were often living in damp overcrowded terraced housing. It is heartening that the book gives so much exposure to the work of John McBride Neill, Northern Ireland's foremost cinema architect at the time. His output was prolific. No less than six new cinemas were constructed in 1935 alone (The Strand, the Majestic, the Troxy, the Curzon, the Regal in Larne and his masterpiece, arguably *the* icon of local 1930s architecture – the Tonic in Bangor.

1930s innovations in the north of Ireland were not just technological and architectural but also extended to the social sphere. In this respect *Glamour and Gloom* does great justice to the pioneering work of Reginald Sharman Wilshere, Belfast Corporation's education architect. He married the best contemporary principles of pedagogy to design and produced bright, airy, child-centred schools for a whole generation of Belfast pupils. Examples include Avoneil, Strandtown, Cliftonville, Carr's Glen and Botanic public elementary schools as well as the McQuiston Memorial School which later assumed a new lease of life as the School of Music.

Finally, the book illuminates some of the hidden gems of modernist suburban housing. These crisp white painted, mainly flat roofed, metal window framed dwellings were the epitome of modern 1930s chic. Generally, however, they were a step too far for the tastes and expectations of the local middle classes and their builders.

Glamour and Gloom is not the first book to deal with 1930s architecture in Northern Ireland. Paul Larmour gives us a good overview in his chapter 'Bricks, Stone, Concrete and Steel: The Built Fabric of Twentieth Century Belfast' in Boal and Royle's *Enduring City: Belfast in the 20th Century.* However, Dr Poppelreuter's publication really turns up the spotlight on many of the details and the philosophy behind much of this remarkable period of local building innovation.

Ironically, *Glamour and Gloom*, a book dealing with architecture and design, has some in-built structural weaknesses of its own. Dr Poppelreuter's introduction sets the scene and explains that the book consists mainly, though not exclusively, of case studies of her M. Arch. students in Ulster University. Inevitably perhaps, this gives the book the feeling at times of being an archive of extracts of Masters theses. The result is the occurrence of some repetition and a stifling of any real sense of narrative and continuity.

The main themes of the book – city centre commercial buildings and banks; examples of suburban modernist public buildings; the cinema building boom; the innovative school building programme masterminded by R.S. Wilshere titled 'Individual and Pedagogy' and a final set of texts dealing with innovative suburban domestic architecture – could well have benefited from more editorial intervention with perhaps clear introductions and separations for each of these themes. This would have given the reader an easier voyage across the sea of 1930s modernist architecture in Northern Ireland.

These quibbles aside, *Glamour and Gloom* is to be strongly commended as a beautiful illumination of a fascinating period in our architectural heritage. It is a mine of scholarship and a beacon for further work in this area.

GERRY CLEARY

JOHN KIRWAN (ED.)
The Chief Butlers of Ireland and the House of Ormond:
An Illustrated Genealogical Guide
Irish Academic Press, 2018
pp 424   ISBN: 978-1-9110-2404-0   hb   €50

This is an invaluable and superbly-illustrated compendium of Ormonde history, comprising: the lives of the Chief Butlers of Ireland (subsequently earls, dukes and marquesses of Ormonde), *c.* 1185–1997; the building history of their principal seat, Kilkenny Castle, *c.* 1207–*c.* 1870; the Ormondes' contentious inheritance from the Wandesford family of Castlecomer, County Kilkenny, 1793–1885; and the last decades of the Ormondes and Kilkenny Castle, 1922–94.

The book begins with four slightly overlapping preliminaries: 'Foreword', 'Preface', 'Acknowledgements' and 'Introduction'. These are followed by the 'Lives', the core of the book, which occupy over 250 pages; the majority of them are reprinted, with acknowledgement, from the *Dictionary of Irish Biography* (RIA/CUP, 2009), the entries for the more obscure Butlers, particularly those of the twentieth century, being written by John Kirwan himself. Next comes 'Kilkenny Castle: an outline of its history, architecture and archaeology', an accomplished and informative account by Ben Murtagh, who explored and documented the Castle's archaeology during the Office of Public Works' building operations in the 1990s. Finally, there are three appendices. The first two, both of them significant and original contributions from Kirwan, are based on his work as a freelance archivist engaged by Kilkenny Castle Archives Ltd, and are respectively entitled: 'A family settlement [of 1792] – a family row: the history of the inheritance of Lady Frances Susannah Anne Wandesforde, Countess of Ormond and Ossory [1754–1830]'; and the second 'Kilkenny Castle – its last days as a family home: an account based on the surviving papers at Kilkenny Castle'. The third is a transcript by Kirwan of the will of John Butler of Kilcash, dated 1764.

There is a sense of *déjà vu* about many of the contents. On the other hand, what would be the point of re-inventing the wheel which runs pretty smoothly through the 'Lives' section of the book (and where is the polymath to be found who would comfortably span the period 1185–1997?). The history, architecture and archaeology of Kilkenny Castle sits happily as a separate entity, and its content could not intelligibly have been distributed among the 'Lives'. Appendices 1 and 2 may have come 'out of stock', but they are important sidelights on the main story. Appendix 1, in particular, documents a classic case of 'cadet inheritance': the Wandesforde wealth, mineral and landed, ultimately did the Butlers no good at all and only involved them in litigation; instead, the Butlers served as a stud farm for the Wandesfordes, regularly supplying them with male heirs and ensuring that the Wandesforde estate stayed independent. Kirwan's elucidation of these complexities is masterly.

Where he is less successful is in integrating the disparate parts of the book. Numbered endnotes are provided for the Introduction, 'Kilkenny Castle' and the appendices. However these are not numbered straight through, but follow five separate sequences. The same system does not, and could not, apply to the 'Lives'. Those taken from the *DIB* are referenced as they were in that publication – i.e. a block of 'Sources' cited at the end of each entry, not individual footnotes or endnotes pinned to precise points in the text. However, the conventions, and particularly the abbreviations, used in the *DIB* are not the same as those used in the endnotes, and nowhere is there a 'List of abbreviations'. It would have made things clearer and more uniform if the 'Sources' for the 'Lives' had been re-cast in the form in which the endnotes appear. The convention of full title first and short title thereafter might then have been applied throughout the book. Another peculiarity is the way in which the authorship of all the 'Lives' is stated. At the end of the 'Sources' a forename and surname appear, and the realisation eventually dawns that this denotes the author of the 'Life' concerned. Instead of being buried in this way, he or she should have signed off the entry in a conspicuous space at the foot of the text, and it would have done no harm to cite, under the signature, the volume and page reference of the *DIB* original.

Kirwan's individual contribution to the 'Lives' introduces further problems. Basically, he seems to have written five of those which fall between the mid-eighteenth century and 1820 and almost all of those which feature thereafter (two 'Lives' are unattributed, but must be by him). These are all lives of Butlers who have not made the grade of the *DIB*, particularly the personally undistinguished twentieth-century marquesses. Throughout the book, as he explains in the Preface (pp xvi–xvii), he adds to the main text of many of the 'Lives' what he calls 'Editor's notes', 'Further editor's notes' and even additional 'Further editor's notes'! Most of these notes relate to matters genealogical and are a guide to those researching their Butler descents; they are mainly drawn from *The Irish Genealogist*, *The Journal of the Butler Society* and, to a lesser extent, *The Old Kilkenny Review;* but they often fill gaps in the sources cited by the authors of the *DIB* 'Lives' and add useful historical information. These clumsy series of editor's notes ought to have been amalgamated into one note per 'Life'. Moreover, even the

'Lives' written by Kirwan himself are followed by 'Editor's notes', a practice which casts doubt on the identity of the author of the main text. Also, there are instances where it would have been better to transfer into his main text material which did not deserve to be relegated to the 'notes'.

It should be stressed that these comments relate purely to matters of presentation. Kirwan consistently describes himself merely as 'editor', even though this does less than justice to his original contributions to the book. He never attempts to attribute to himself the work of others – quite the contrary. But it is a failing in a multi-authored book to make it less than clear who is responsible for what.

There is no 'List of the illustrations', so it may simply be said that they are countless. Locating them has been a feat of research in its own right and a demonstration of Kirwan's long involvement with Butler family history. If in colour in the original, the illustrations are reproduced in colour in the book and, instead of being corralled into clusters printed on art paper, are distributed in different shapes and sizes in different parts of the book; and in places the frequency of the illustrations, and the length of some of the captions, interrupt the text. But this may be regarded as a good fault. The appositeness of their positioning and the quality of their reproduction make them a distinguished feature of this book. It is that rarity, a coffee-table book of weighty substance.

Remarkably, many of the family portraits reproduced are from the OPW collection in Kilkenny Castle, and for the most part hang in the famous picture gallery there which is illustrated on p. 249. There are several references, notably in Appendix 2, to the dispersal of pictures and other contents, notably in a ten-day clearance sale in 1935. Many other pictures reproduced or referred to are still in family possession, though divided among the various surviving branches of the family. But – though this is not actually discussed – the 'heirloom' portraits and tapestries on display in the Castle at the time of the 6th and last Marquess's death in 1997 were not split up and sold to the highest bidder but instead at a moderate valuation to the OPW, which means that they remain *in situ* as an entity. This decision on the part of his executors is characteristic of the sense of history, heritage and family which has animated the last three marquesses, who gifted and preserved Kilkenny Castle and demesne to the people of Kilkenny in the most public-spirited manner, and who endeavoured, when selling was unavoidable, to sell the Ormonde deeds and other heritage contents on easy terms and in a way which kept them together and transferred them to the care of the State. The same spirit of benevolence is still extant in present-day Butler descendants, whose financial sponsorship of the book is acknowledged on pp xxi–xxiii.

These present-day descendants, and the wider Butler family connection, are currently without a family head. The Chief Butlerage was sold back to the Crown in 1811; the marquessate of Ormonde would appear to be extinct since 1997; and it is far from clear that a claim to any of the subsidiary honours will be substantiated or even made. However, the Ormonde name still counts for much, in Kilkenny and beyond, and having in their days of greatness been more Irish than the Irish themselves has helped them to weather the storms of the twentieth century. Their ancient compeers and competitors, the FitzGerald earls of Kildare, 'rivals in power and equals in renown' (p. ix), have fared less well. Although they stepped over the Ormondes to a dukedom in 1766 and enjoyed a greater share of influence than them for most of the nineteenth century, they suffered the catastrophic misfortune of the 7th Duke of Leinster (1892–1978), who was not even a FitzGerald by birth, and whose career of irresponsibility, waste and destructiveness reduced the FitzGeralds to ruin and insignificance. Not for them the dignified decline of the Ormondes. Today there is a flourishing Butler Society, of which by no coincidence John Kirwan is Hon. Secretary, and no FitzGerald equivalent. What was lacking for decades in the case of the Butlers (p. xiii) was 'a comprehensive overview, under one cover, of the "Lives" of the Chief Butlers of Ireland and their senior agnatic heirs, the earls, marquesses and dukes of Ormond(e)'. That gap has now been more than filled by Kirwan's *Chief Butlers of Ireland and the House of Ormond*.

A.P.W. MALCOMSON

PETER GILMORE, TREVOR PARKHILL AND WILLIAM ROULSTON
Exiles of '98:
Ulster Presbyterians and the United States
Ulster Historical Foundation, 2018
pp 240   ISBN: 978-1-909556-62-1   pb   £14.95

Ulster Presbyterians in the late eighteenth century retained a strong consciousness of the trans-Atlantic New World to which they had been regularly advised to migrate since the 1720s. The powerful myth of this 'promised land' shaped a public discourse which contrasted all of the ills of Ireland with the freedoms and allure of this thriving experiment in independent democracy, known after 1783 as the United States of America. The tumultuous 1790s and particularly the failed Rebellion of 1798 created a fresh expulsive impetus for Protestant dissenters of a radical bent who for one reason or another found it impossible to remain at home. This handsome new volume focuses attention on these migrants and the variety of contexts which fashioned their departure, crossing and arrival in this Revolutionary era.

The book might be thought of as containing four central elements – firstly, four short introductory essays which help flesh out the broader context to this migration episode; secondly, thirteen (one for each colony perhaps?) pen portraits of individual migrants; thirdly, three considerations of specific groups and finally a biographical directory (or prosopography) which seeks to identify and record as many migrants who fit this categorisation of whom something is known. In fact, the differentiation between individuals and groups is in some ways deceptive in practice as the vast majority of these migrants were usually strongly connected one with another and often made the most of connections in their host society with speed and skill. One of the key terms which is repeated throughout the text is 'networks' and reconstructing these variable networks, often across the Atlantic, is central to the task of historians trying to understand their experience. Family, political allegiance, business interests and religious identity wove webs of connection and association which appear on almost every page. Although trans-Atlantic correspondence was becoming increasingly regular and influential in Ulster at this time, the book serves to remind the reader that actual return migration from America to Ireland was perhaps more regular than might be assumed in the later eighteenth century. And, although migrants might be framed as 'exiles', there are frequent references to return trips east across the ocean. In the spring of 1798, the intrepid Margaret Duncan at the advanced age of 75 completed a return trip from Philadelphia to Stewartstown, County Tyrone, to visit relations and old acquaintances.

Religious identity was very much centre-stage for large numbers of these migrants, many of whom were practising clergy or probationers in search of a pulpit in the New World. The prosopography compiled here certainly reminds us that it would be foolhardy indeed to underestimate the seriousness with which religion was taken in the late eighteenth century. What is immediately apparent to any reader is the advanced capacity for heated debate and fissuring amongst Presbyterians and the dizzying array of churches and sub-sects on offer in America reflected that. Perhaps, it would have been useful to have specifically dedicated one of the introductory essays to mapping out the theological and ideological backdrop to navigating through the world of evangelical Protestant churches on both sides of the ocean.

Peter Gilmore colourfully recounts the scene on board the ship *Peggy* crossing the Atlantic in May 1799 with several '98 exiles on board. Here he tells us how John Caldwell observed that the Rev. James Simpson, the strict Calvinist Newtownards Old Light minister 'grumbled so incessantly' about the New Light views of the Rev. William Sinclair that other passengers strove to keep well out of his way. As Gilmore points out in a footnote elsewhere, the older idea that New Light notions were strongly associated with the fomenting of the Rebellion are in something of a retreat and that orthodoxy was believed by the bulk of those studied here. Making choices in the New World about religious identity could offer paths to Americanisation for immigrants and for some like the Rev. James Hull it might lead to an unlikely journey from dissenting preacher, through a legal career to ordination in the Episcopal Church. Might this theological migration have proved more difficult in Ulster?

In pre-O'Connellite Ireland no section of Irish society was as politically conscious as Ulster's Presbyterians and not surprisingly many of those studied here projected a fervent sense of an international radicalism stretching back for at least a generation. Upon arrival in

America the majority of exiles lent their support to the Democratic-Republican Party and many made every effort to cultivate a relationship with Thomas Jefferson himself. Jefferson's Federalist opponents were generally suspicious of immigrants, immigrants from Ireland in particular. Whilst a fresh dynamic was clearly detectable, there was also some continuity – well before the American Revolution migrants from Ulster such as Francis Allison acted as New World disciples for the political ideas of enlightenment thinkers including Francis Hutcheson of Saintfield. The work presented here usefully augments that of David Wilson (1998) in highlighting the roles of immigrant radicals in the political organisation and ideological development of early American republicanism.

The emigrants of the late eighteenth century, unlike those of the early eighteenth century, left a thoroughly dynamic Ulster with trade, economic development and population all surging ahead. Ulster's Presbyterians had long demonstrated a particular calling to the world of commerce and by the 1790s very strong trading connections tied merchants in Belfast and Derry to ports on the eastern seaboard of America. Although their departure may not always have been entirely voluntary, most seem to have rapidly embraced commercial opportunities. The younger you were the easier adjustment to the New World seemed. Developed mercantile networks facilitated trans-Atlantic movement and thus return trips in the age of sail should not entirely surprise us. One of the commodities both consumed and manufactured was spirituous liquor and the profiles here paint a picture of citizens quite different from the respectable image of late nineteenth-century Presbyterians. Of importance too, no doubt, were social and fraternal connections such as those of freemasonry that spanned the Atlantic.

In eighteenth- and nineteenth-century Ulster the strongest factor serving to predict the likelihood of emigration was the already existing presence of a family member in the diaspora. Most migrants, even at times of crisis like 1798, did not go blind into the unknown. It would be very interesting to see the geographical patterns of migration mapped according to the place names referred to in the text. The close, intimate relations of the family networks reflected in the Directory of Ulster exiles was compounded by a tendency to cluster in quite tightly-knit neighbourhoods on both sides of the ocean. Family bonds compounded local identities and the sense of familiarity evident in so much of the correspondence generated helps us reconstruct the mental maps of the historic migrants. What does appear to be the case is the centrality of urban settlement in the New World amongst the departed, foreshadowing the predominant pattern which would emerge in the next generation as Ulster-American migration transitioned to mass migration from the 1820s onwards.

Prosopographical studies are rarely comprehensive but this work, particularly through the biographical directory, offers an excellent stem database which can be augmented in the future as fresh evidence is unearthed. Comparative analysis with those radicals who stayed or went elsewhere in the diaspora may reveal much about the perspectives of those living through these intense times. Understanding the mind set of those like Robert Simms or William Tennent, who resisted the pressure to 'get out', is as important as studying the trajectories of the migrants themselves. All in all, this is a very welcome and timely addition to the literature and a good example of the benefits of transnational scholarly team work. The authors contribute a huge wealth of vital scholarly experience in the field and are to be congratulated and thanked profoundly for their efforts.

PATRICK FITZGERALD

MARGARET GRAHAM AND JEAN ORR (EDS)
Nurses' Voices from the Northern Ireland Troubles:
Personal Accounts from the Front Line
RCN Harrow-on-the-Hill, 2013
pp 220   ISBN: 978-0-9574308-7-7   hb   £25

Twenty-four years after the first official cessation of violence, 20 years after the Good Friday agreement and over seven since the eventual establishment of a power-sharing executive in Northern Ireland, there are a number of unresolved issues that stand in the way of a society fully at peace with itself (and its neighbours) in Northern Ireland. One of these is the extent to which the several services – medical, social, law enforcement, probation, etc. – who were closely involved with the after effects of 3,670 fatalities and some 16,000 bombing incidents, can now have their stories told (and listened to).

Nurses Voices from the Northern Ireland Troubles: Personal Accounts from the Front Line serves as a forum for relating the experiences of the medical services – nurses, student nurses, health visitors, midwives (but not paramedics, doctors and administrators) – during some 35 years of what *The Times* of London called 'a suppressed civil war', commonly referred to (as in the title) as 'The Troubles'.

This is very much a book where the evidence does speak for itself. A recently-qualified health visitor tells of her time on Springfield Road, Belfast in the late 1960s when it was the focus of much panic-stricken movement of population as Catholics and Protestants, all living on the road, sought the 'security' of living with co-religionists. 'Sometimes I saw and heard things which it would have been better that I had not … The fear of travel out of people's safe zones was endemic and … was an underlying factor in the increased depression rates … people shared their "nerve" tablets with others during moments of crisis' (pp 24–5).

A student nurse, only 18 years old, relates being sent to a cubicle in an emergency situation during a particularly bloody night of sectarian violence and her horror at what she found. 'I had never seen such wounds … My uniform and apron were covered in blood and tissue … he grasped my hands and begged me to say a prayer. There we stayed, he and I, and spoke together to a higher being, each … in our own way asking for divine intervention' (p. 36).

The section 'major events' is a reminder of the emotional as well as physical havoc wrought by a litany of atrocities that marked the Troubles, not least the Enniskillen War Memorial bombing in 1987 where 'many of the dead were their [the nurses'] friends' (p. 148). Of particular interest is the nurse who later joined the WAVE trauma centre which has done such sterling work in helping Troubles' victims come to terms with their mental and physical damage from a whole range of perspectives (pp 186–7).

The tone of the evidence that is reproduced throughout this attractively-presented publication is very much matter-of-fact and intrinsically professional, even in the most intimidating of circumstances. In another regard it is interesting that the initiative to make an official record of memoirs of the practising medical world was not initiated until 2011, a useful reminder of an observation well known to most genealogical searchers – ask the questions and obtain people's stories now before it is too late. Just as David McKitterick's monumental *Lost Lives* serves to outline the damage inflicted on society in Northern Ireland since the late 1960s, this welcome publication amply confirms the extent to which the nursing professions contributed to helping victims cope.

TREVOR PARKHILL

GEORGE WEAY OF PLEAN AND ROMILLY SQUIRE (EDS)
Scottish Clan & Family Encyclopaedia
St Kilda (Holdings) Glasgow, 3rd ed., 2017
pp 508   ISBN: 987-1-9997567-0-3   hb   £45

How many of the more romantically inclined of us would revel in having the appendage 'of that Ilk' associated with our surname? There are many instances of just such a genealogical flourish in the endlessly absorbing information available in a book that can justifiably call itself, as this one does, an 'encyclopaedia'. This is the third (2017) edition of the *Scottish Clan & Family Encyclopaedia*, first published in 1992 and then in 2007 (and how nice to see 'encyclopaedia' in the title spelled thus). The editors have assembled an authoritative cast of contributors who have compiled what is by any standards a very useful resource for research into Scottish clans and families, many of which have had and continue to have strong nine-county Ulster even all-Ireland connections since the sixteenth- and seventeenth-century plantations.

The main considerations of the individual families is preceded by a series of chapters which provide more-than-useful information on a series of related topics. 'Clanship an Historical Perspective' traces the establishment and development of the clan system, the basis of the fabric of Highland society, until the middle of the eighteenth century and finishes with three paragraphs on 'The Aftermath of Culloden'. 'Heraldry' by George Weay of Plean, Romilly Squire and Patrick Barden describes the system of personal and clan identification that has been in operation since the twelfth century and which continues to operate. It is in this learned section that the illustrations that characterise the book are seen to most impressive effect. 'Genealogy in Scotland' by the late Kathleen B. Cory, updated by D. Richard Torrance, outlines the principal repositories and the accessibility of the sources they curate. The Clan Map of Scotland (p. 66) located at the end of this chapter is a particularly helpful guide to the spatial distribution throughout Scotland of the respective families that feature in greater detail in the rest of the book.

There then follow some four hundred pages of family details, alphabetically arranged, from Abercromby to Young, most with a coat of arms, tartan or family motto, and in some cases all three. The information contained in these entries gives rise to any number of 'I didn't know that' instances. An almost-at-random selection will suffice:

> p. 74, Thomas Aikenhead the last person to be hanged (at Leith, in 1697) for blasphemy, the grisly result of this young student decrying the validity of the texts found in the Old Testament.

> p. 128, The traditional hero of the Carmichael family is Sir John de Carmichael of Meadowflat who fought in France with the Scottish army sent to the aid of the French in their resistance against an English invasion ... at the battle of Beauge Sir John rode into battle combat against the English commander and unhorsed him, breaking his own spear in the action. His victim was the Duke of Clarence ... brother of Henry V ... To commemorate this deed the Carmichaels bear the broken spear as their crest.

> p. 244, In 1342 at the Battle of Drumoak the Irvines slaughtered the invading Keith warband. The third Laird of Drum ... was a knight of almost legendary prowess who later fought at the Battle of Harlaw in 1411. This battle marked the last challenge by the Lords of the Isles to royal authority ... Sir Alexander de Irwune engaged in single combat with Maclean of Duart, the famous 'Red Hector of the Battles' and after a legendary struggle both died of the wounds inflicted on the other.

> p. 384, The most famous of the name [Napier] is the seventh Laird of Merchiston, John Napier, who developed the system of logarithms.

p. 387, The most celebrated episode in the history of this family [Paterson] occurred during the Jacobite rising of 1745 ... Sir Hugh Paterson of Bannockburn ... entertained Prince Charles Edward Stuart ... the prince met Sir Hugh's niece, Clementina Wilkinshaw, who became his mistress and bore him a daughter, Charlotte, Duchess of Albany.

p. 399, John Pitcairn, a major in the Royal Marines, was in command of the unit which fired the first shots in the American War of Independence.

p. 441, The Stewarts, who were to become monarchs of the Scots, were descended from a family who were seneschals of Dol in Brittany.

The appendices contain useful sections on a chronology of dates in Scottish history from 400AD, a list Scottish monarchs up to the Union of Scotland and England in 1707, and a glossary of heraldic terms.

What is perhaps most striking is the wealth of nations that have contributed to settlement and development of society in Scotland over the centuries – Gallic, Norse, Norman, Welsh, Scandinavian, British to name but a few, and all this before the Scots settled in Ulster!

TREVOR PARKHILL

MAIRÉAD CAREW
The Quest for the Irish Celt
The Harvard Archaeological Mission to Ireland, 1932–36
Irish Academic Press, 2018
pp 320   ISBN: 978-1-7885-5009-3   hb   €24.95

In the late nineteenth century Herbert Spencer led the charge in applying Charles Darwin's theory of natural selection to human society. This distorted interpretation of the concept of the survival of the fittest failed to get legislation to support it at Westminster, despite sustained lobbying, by Winston Churchill amongst others. But Social Darwinism found much favour in official circles in the United States and the outcome was the forced sterilisation of tens of thousands of those considered 'inadequates', social and physical deviants in danger of polluting the nation's gene pool. Earnest Hooton, a prominent physical anthropologist and a member of the American Eugenics Society, got his opportunity to put his convictions to the test when he was invited to lead an expedition to Ireland in 1932.

Mairéad Carew tells the story of this remarkable Harvard mission with admirable clarity and zest. She has striven hard to ensure that this book, generously illustrated with photographs, is compelling reading, indeed, downright arresting in places. The government of the Irish Free State, headed by Eamon de Valera, gave enthusiastic backing to Harvard University's five-year archaeological research programme in Ireland in the 1930s. This was to determine the racial and cultural heritage of the Irish people. The mission included the examination of prehistoric skulls, complemented by the physical examination of thousands of volunteers who came forward to have their skulls and nose shapes measured and their hair colour graded. The chief adviser to the Harvard mission was the Director of the National Museum of Ireland, Adolf Mahr, an Austrian archaeologist who had joined the Nazi Party in 1932, a year before Hitler came to power in Germany. Mahr declared that Ireland 'is not the cradle of the Celtic stock, but she was its foremost stronghold at the time of the decline of the Celts elsewhere'. 'Ireland is now the only self-governing State with an uninterrupted Celtic tradition', he continued, 'the last refuge' of the Celtic spirit, 'pre-eminently *the* Celtic country'. Those on both sides of the Atlantic who funded this mission considered it politically and economically important to confirm the identity of the Irish as white, Celtic and northern European.

There were three strands to this mission. The first, an investigation of a rural community in County Clare, was carried out by Conrad Arensberg and Solon Kimball. Since *Family and Community in Ireland*, the highly-regarded outcome of this study by this pair is well known, Mairéad Carew concentrates on the other two: the physical anthropological programme; and the archaeological programme.

Hooton, who managed the Harvard Archaeological Mission, was certain that Ireland was the country most likely to have preserved the characteristics of the Celtic race. 'We believe that the mysticism, artistry, and the other peculiar gifts of the modern Irish can be understood only by fitting their prehistory into their modern civilization', he wrote. Ireland was selected because it was 'politically new but culturally old' and that it was 'the country of origin of more than one fifth of the population of the United States'. Most of the funding was raised in the USA, with wealthy Irish Americans well to the fore, but the Free State government made its own contribution by providing the labour force (as part of an unemployment relief scheme) needed for archaeological digs and the like. For de Valera and his colleagues, here was the unique opportunity to show that the Irish were white European Celts, part of the Aryan race, a very superior sort of people. The idea of a Celtic race had long been evident in literature; now modern science would be reinforcing that concept – along with the inhabitants of Scandinavia, the Irish would emerge as the purest of Celtic descendants because their ancestors had been beyond the reach of Roman conquerors carrying Latin genes.

The physical anthropological expedition was led at first by C.W. Dupertuis, an advanced Harvard student. He explained to the *Irish Times* that 'Ireland being more or less an isolated country, was probably not so mixed racially as Continental countries, and he felt that in certain parts of the country the descendants of more or less pure racial types which came in from across the waters would be found'. Now began the collection of anthropometric samples from thousands. Dupertuis's energetic wife, Helen Dawson, gathered data from no fewer than 1,800 women. It was important to get a representative sample of the population and so members of the Dáil, monks, travellers and members of the landed gentry were persuaded to take part. Along with other body dimensions, the skull was carefully measured. Seasamh Ó Néill, Secretary of the Department of Education, was particularly active in cajoling civil servants to submit themselves for examination; Colonel Éamon Broy, the deputy Garda commissioner, wrote letters of introduction to his superintendents; and in Northern Ireland, Sir Richard Dawson Bates, the Home Affairs minister, gave his official sanction. Ancient skulls from archaeological sites (Knockast in particular) were filled with mustard seeds to assess cranial capacity. The results were pleasing: brain size was found to be 'well above the average' for modern Europeans.

Today we have no difficulty in finding this obsession with eugenics to be, at the very least, wrong-headed and embarrassing. But the

Harvard mission did have some impressive achievements. Thanks to generous funding from the other side of the Atlantic – at a time when the world's economy was undergoing acute contraction – Ireland benefited from the most professional and extensive archaeological investigations the island had yet experienced. Indeed, it would be another half century before the like was seen again. Unlike their Irish predecessors (and not a few contemporaries), the archaeologists strove to avoid damage and to restore monuments as carefully as possible to their original structures. The sites included midland lake dwellings at Lagore and Ballinderry, a burial cairn at Poulawack in County Clare, and the megalithic tomb at Creevykeel in County Sligo. In Northern Ireland E. Estyn Evans, then just a lecturer in geography at Queen's University (which at that time had no archaeology department), and the venerable antiquarian from Ballymena, W.J. Knowles, were well to the fore. Excavations were carried out at Glenarm, Cushendun, Curran Point at Larne, Rough Island in Strangford Lough, and Newferry on the Lower Bann.

Some of the artefacts unearthed gained a great deal of publicity, including a bronze hanging bowl, a gaming board and a dug-out boat. These finds Mahr had no hesitation in labelling 'Celtic'; but years would pass before radiocarbon dating would prove him almost entirely wrong. To their credit, the Harvard archaeologists hesitated to give positive backing to Mahr's pronouncements. The gaming board had, in fact, been made by ... a Viking.

JONATHAN BARDON

JEFFREY DUDGEON

H. Montgomery Hyde:
Ulster Unionist MP, Gay Law Reform Campaigner and Prodigious Author

Belfast Press, 2018

pp 62   ISBN: 978-0-9539287-9-8   pb   £4.99

Born in Belfast in 1907 the son of a linen merchant, at a time when the linen industry had catapulted Belfast to being the fastest growing city in the United Kingdom of Britain and Ireland, Harford

Montgomery Hyde (1907–1989) was educated at an English public school, then at Queen's University Belfast where he obtained a first class honours degree in history (1929), and at Magdalene Oxford, where he was awarded a law degree. Called to the Bar in 1934, his first salaried employment was as private secretary and archivist to the seventh Marquess of Londonderry, who earlier had been the first Minister of Education in the first Northern Ireland government and whose innovative and far-sighted scheme to educate Catholic and Protestant children in the same schools had come mightily unstuck. He went on to have a good war as a Lieutenant Colonel specialising in intelligence work, mostly in Europe. Prior to that he had married an artist, linguist and society girl and at their fashionable London wedding the toast was proposed by the Dublin politician and raconteur Oliver St John Gogarty. Hyde in the end was married three times.

Dudgeon has provided a more than useful catalogue of Hyde's unusual, to say the least, career in politics. This is particularly apt for the period (1950–59) when he was Member of Parliament for North Belfast, all at a time when he was involved in several issues relating to the liberalisation of laws on and public attitudes to homosexuality as well as slightly quirky topics, such as retaining the right of Trinity College Library to remain as a copyright library.

In this context, Dudgeon adroitly addresses the burning question: given this pedigree, why did such a beacon of propriety become immersed to the extent that he did in the campaign to legalise homosexuality? 'Why did he take up this deeply unpopular struggle. Did he have a political death wish?' He dryly offers the view that, despite Hyde's upright and exemplary society profile, 'the classic markers of gayness were there: an interest in history, archives, genealogy and spying, an affection for [the] aristocracy, the ownership of two marmalade cats and a tendency towards Rome. Only church music was absent'.

This timely short biography of H. Montgomery Hyde – as he was usually known – is written, as the sub-title would indicate, principally from the perspective of his courageous campaigning work on behalf of the gay community and the long struggle to legalise homosexuality in Northern Ireland. Jeffrey Dudgeon, who subsequently assumed Hyde's mantle in this regard and who campaigned, often at great cost, over the last half century for the same cause, has provided a well-documented account of that part of Hyde's career. The other several and, to my mind, equally interesting aspects of Hyde's career, as war hero, Member of Parliament and above all, resourceful researcher and writer on Irish history – there are over 50 titles to his credit – are to a large extent only touched on. There is only a nod in the direction of 'his most enduring work', *The Rise of Castlereagh*, published as long ago as 1933 and which continues to be regarded as something of a classic.

Dudgeon has called on the archive which Hyde entrusted to PRONI where there well may be sufficient material to provide the more expansive biography this Belfast-born author, historian, politician, rights campaigner, deserves.

TREVOR PARKHILL

MARTIN SHEPPARD (ED.)
For the Fourth Generation
Matador, 2017
pp 298   ISBN: 978-1-785893-31-5   pb   £9.99

IDEM
Love on Inishcoo, 1787:
A Donegal Romance
Matador, 2018
pp 330   ISBN: 978-1-789010-23-7   pb   £15

Archivists operate on the assumption that they are working for eternity and need expect no results or acknowledgement until then. It has therefore been a surprise and a bonus to the team led by the Public Record Office of Northern Ireland who, in 1995, catalogued *in situ* and subsequently microfilmed (MIC597) the archive at Templehouse, Ballymote, County Sligo, to be greeted less than 25 years later by two publications based party or wholly on sections N and P of that archive. It was deliberately called after the house where it is located, rather than the Perceval family who own and inhabit Templehouse, because it represents a coming-together of the archives of a number of inter-related families, among them the Hardcastles, the Hurrys, the

O'Malleys, the Metcalfes, the Clive-Bayleys and the de Hamels, in addition to the Percevals themselves. The link figure in most of this is the current Mrs Perceval, *née* Debonnaire Hardcastle. The editor of the two books under review, Martin Sheppard, is also part of the family network.

The first book, *For the Fourth Generation*, takes its less than self-explanatory title from the 'Reminiscences of childhood' with which it begins. These were written in 1954 by Eva O'Malley (1884–1960), younger daughter of Sir Edward Loughlin O'Malley (1842–1932), a British colonial judge and latterly a British consular judge in the Ottoman Empire, and his wife, Winifred, *née* Hardcastle. Although the O'Malleys are an ancient and important County Mayo family, the reminiscences relate wholly to the upper middle-class life which the children of this branch lived in England. The same is true of the biographical and other material relating to adult O'Malleys, notably Peter Frederic O'Malley QC (1804–74), grandfather of Eva, who unsuccessfully fought a bitter and violent parliamentary election for Finsbury in 1868, and George Hunter O'Malley (1844–1908), colonel of the Royal Artillery, the adored but feckless younger brother of Eva's father, Sir Edward.[1]

Unsurprisingly, the sections of the book which derive from the Hardcastles and their connections (including Mary Hardcastle, Lady Monkswell, 'whose diary is a remarkable record of Victorian society'), also refer exclusively to family and personal affairs in England. This applies, too, to the section of the book (pp 69–131) which derives from the Templehouse archive, since these families had no connection with Ireland until the marriage of Deb Hardcastle and Sandy Perceval of Templehouse in 1967 (or, strictly speaking, until her grandfather, Joseph Alfred Hardcastle, came to Armagh as Astronomer Royal at the Observatory in 1917, where he died in the same year).

The book is somewhat scrappy and episodic, and Martin Sheppard admits as much in his summary of its contents. His description of it is that it 'brings together fourteen items of family interest to those descended from Joseph Hardcastle, MP (1815–1899) and Peter [Frederic] O'Malley, QC (1804–74) … [i.e. the fourth generation of the title and beyond]'. He adds that the chapters other than Eva O'Malley's 'Reminiscences' 'are about individual family members or their houses. Each one tells a story, based on original sources, set in context and annotated.' The footnotes are in fact very informative and apt, and he also provides an alphabetical list of individuals, grouped according to surname, and an exhaustive table of family descents. The index is comprehensive. So, as he has taken pains to make the complicated connections accessible to the general reader, he hardly does himself justice by describing the book as only 'of family interest'.

The second book, *Love on Inishcoo*, has all the cohesion, indeed intensity, which the first one lacks. It is a love story, told in 51 letters written between July 1787 and August 1788 by the lovers, Edmund Cobb Hurry (1762–1808) and Eliza Ann Liddell (1762–99). These are all transcribed and edited by Martin Sheppard, who also draws information from 250 further letters, written between 1789 and 1796 (when the correspondence inexplicably ceases), and from letters to or from either Edmund or Eliza written by or to third parties. The source, in almost all cases, is the Templehouse archive.

Edmund was the eldest son and heir of one of the partners in a Great Yarmouth firm of 'Russia merchants'. He was on his way to the Baltic in June 1787 when he put in at The Rosses, County Donegal, to assess the investment potential of the fishing enterprise recently established on Rutland Island by the landlord of the entire district, William Burton Conyngham. Edmund was unimpressed, and judged rightly. However, his detour was not in vain, as he was introduced on arrival to his future wife, Eliza Liddell. She was living in Inishcoo House on the small island of the same name, between Burtonport and Arranmore, which was the residence of Conyngham's agent, Robert Corbet, Corbet's wife and their five daughters. Eliza's role in the household was as governess to the daughters – one of the few avocations open to a gentlewoman with no fortune who needed a job which would not entail loss of caste.

The couple were mutually attracted from the start and soon became mutually attached. But the budding relationship was tempered by Eliza's fears of being thought a fortune-hunter and her well-bred, maidenly modesty; also, and to a much lesser extent, by Edmund's fear that religion – specifically his Unitarianism – might prove an obstacle. When Edmund sailed from Donegal in July 1787, first to Kirkwall, then to Elsinore, Riga and beyond, their correspondence became 'agonisingly slow' and uncertain. In October, with the imminent collapse of Burton Conyngham's over-ambitious enterprise, the Corbets, with Eliza and the five children (whom she described impatiently to Edmund as 'a troop of sick and troublesome brats'), sailed for Dublin and thence to Chester. Edmund headed north to conduct her from Chester to London, then had to sail away on another Baltic voyage, and finally returned to marry her in August 1788 in St Mary's Church, Putney.

The book reads like an eighteenth-century epistolary novel, so unusual is it to find a real-life expression of the passion coupled with uncertainty experienced by two 1780s lovers. The main introduction, and the introductory remarks which precede each section, are well judged – informative but not overwhelming. The footnotes are reduced to a bare and unobtrusive minimum. The letters are left to speak for themselves. As Martin Sheppard remarks, they are 'not the letters of aristocrats or celebrities, but of an ordinary, if intelligent and well educated, couple, who happened to have fallen in love'. The Irish element in the story is, in spite of the title, pretty limited, since neither of the lovers was Irish, and for them and all the other protagonists Inishcoo was actually a short-lived, away-fixture. But the human interest is overwhelming, and is beautifully presented in this book.

A.P.W. MALCOMSON

1 The biographical notice of Peter Frederic on pp 132–40 is taken from an unpublished history of 'The OMalleys, 1820–1860' by his grandson, Sir Owen O'Malley (1887–1974), Eva's brother, a British diplomat who retired to live at Rockfleet, Burrishoole, County Mayo. In his retirement he pursued genealogical and historical research, partly to prove that his branch of the family, the O'Malleys of Belclare and Lodge (Castlebar), were the chieftains of the clan, and partly to achieve the publication of a highly contested family record, the manuscript narrative of Captain George O'Malley (1786–c. 1865), a famous smuggler. In the latter pursuit, Sir Owen's best endeavours were defeated by the disappearance of the original and by disputes over the ownership of the copyright in various typescript versions which still exist and which remain unpublished. These complex issues have been addressed by L.M. Cullen in an article in the *Journal of the Galway Archaeological and Historical Society*, vol. 67 (2015). It would be interesting to know if any documentation in the possession of the English O'Malley descendants listed by Martin Sheppard throws further light on them.

FRANCES McGEE
The Archives of the Valuation of Ireland 1830–1865
Four Courts Press, Dublin, 2018
pp 240   ISBN: 978-1-84682-136-3   pb   €17.95

The archives of the valuations of Ireland that took place between 1830 and 1865, and the subsequent re-valuations and revisions that are also available in Dublin and Belfast, comprise the single most thorough and reliable source that is of equal interest and usefulness to family, local and academic historians. This well-organised publication considers in accessible detail 'the archives created by the initial valuation between 1830 and 1865, which established the facts about property and occupation'. It outlines the often complicated logistics of a technically-skilled process that is still ongoing. In this 35-year period, spanning the trauma of the Great Famine, every piece of property in the 32 counties was valued: town- and farm-houses, tiny plots of land and great demesnes are all logged. Additionally, the names of the heads of households that are listed, for the first time on an all-Ireland basis, have been the coping stone of many a genealogical search.

Frances McGee's long-term – over 40 years in the National Archives, Dublin – archival experience has given her the authority to say (p. 19 of this very timely book) 'The valuation archives have a unique importance as a research source on nineteenth-century Ireland', a claim that is almost certainly echoed, and gratefully, by the many researchers who have called on this vast array of records, either in the original manuscripts or as the printed Griffith's Valuation. Moreover, the historical significance of the archive is highlighted by the modest claim that 'the archives date from a period from which there are relatively few other sources'. In other words they are that rarest of sources, a pre- and immediately post-famine survey of the entire country that, because it continues during and after the disaster, enables a 'before and after' picture to be compiled from consistently-recorded evidence that has been collected by trained professional observers and practitioners.

One of the strengths of the book is the economic explanation (pp 32–3) of the difference between the early, 'Townland', valuation, in which only properties valued at £3 or more were recorded and where lessors are less-frequently named, and the later 'tenement' valuation, undertaken from 1852, which is altogether more comprehensive. This arose from the introduction in the 1840s of the Poor Law and the observed need for its financing based on a countrywide property-by-property valuation. It is this infinitely more sophisticated and thorough valuation that is the basis of the printed Griffith's Valuation which has been the ready reference manual, and has often provided the first 'Eureka' moment for thousands of searches.

For those areas covered whose valuation was undertaken during the years of the worst impact of the Famine, 'the books paint a picture of economic conditions in the late 1840s that is stark, with evidence of poor living conditions, eviction and abandonment'. There is also a great deal of what might be termed 'accidental' information that has found its way into the valuers' notebooks, including helpful detail on family relationships – for example, where a tenant is described as 'mother to the lessor' (p. 108).

Given the scale of the resource and, even granted that it falls outside the scope of the book (whose end date is 1865) it might be thought that the valuation archives held in PRONI are given relatively short shrift (pp 196–7), more particularly as their additional value, recognised here, that 'the valuation books relating to Northern Ireland 1864–1930 that are held there are digitized and can be searched [online]' is a boon for those seeking to link the successive post-1865 generations as far as the first quarter of the twentieth century.

This book is not a user's guide to the archive and does not, other than generally, indicate the essential relationship between the valuation books, printed or manuscript, and the maps on which the tenements are numbered as they are in the books. For rural areas the maps are based on the 6-inch Ordnance Survey maps, produced from the early 1830s; for town tenements they are based on the 60-inch town plans that are such a feature of the legacy of the early Ordnance Survey. It is in this regard that the combined sources, valuation books and maps, are at their most helpful, something that can best, perhaps even only, be learned from a hands-on use of the combined sources, maps and tenement lists that have formed the basis of a townland or parish study throughout the island.

Frances McGee has adroitly used her professional archival experience and writing expertise to bring us a carefully-considered and illuminating account of the crucial early valuations of property in Ireland. Moreover, in detailing the manner in which these records were meticulously compiled, leaving us with an irreplaceable source for research right to the townland level, she has provided a valuable research aid that ought to benefit family, local and academic historians alike. A word of appreciation need also to be said about the generally consistent quality of the series in which the publication features, the Maynooth Research Guides for Local History.

TREVOR PARKHILL

ELIZABETH RUSHEN & KATHLYN GIBSON
Anastasia:
From Callan to Stockyard Creek
Anchor Books, Australia, 2017
pp 180   ISBN: 978-0-9924-6719-7   pb   AUD$34.95

The Anchor Books press has over recent years produced a succession of titles on migration to Australia from Ireland throughout the nineteenth century, principally on the theme of female emigration, some of which have been reviewed in earlier issues of *Familia*. Elizabeth Rushen and Kathlyn Gibson, in this latest Anchor Books production, outline the intrepid story of Anastasia Burke, born in the parish of Callan, County Kilkenny, in 1827, survived (unlike some of her family) the Great Famine, made her way to Australia in 1855 and eventually, after a brief marriage, found herself managing the not-inconsiderable business interests she inherited from her deceased husband in Stockyard Creek, a goldfield in South Gippsland, Victoria, until her death in early 1907.

When Anastasia was just six years old her mother Judith died while giving birth to the eighth child in the family. Her father Patrick was thus left with the rearing of seven children, in the parlous circumstances faced by the generation prior to the Great Famine, an era which saw mounting economic, population and political pressures, all preceding the catastrophic successive potato crop failures of the mid-1840s. In setting Anastasia's family and personal circumstances in context, the authors have made adroit use of a relatively limited range of pre- and post-famine sources, including the townland valuation and Griffith's valuation records, marred only by a reference (p. 1) to the Land League in 1829, 50 years before its time and a slightly more misleading miscalculation (p. 12) that 'more than 4.5 million died or emigrated as a consequence of the Famine'.

Having survived the tempestuous 1840s and with her grown-up siblings no longer her responsibility, and faced with the increasing limited married prospects experienced by the post-famine generation, the authors take Anastasia (and us) through the steps by which the Colonial Land and Emigration Commissioners offer of free passages for eligible women, one of the steps taken to address the gender imbalance in the colony, enabled her to make the journey to the Antipodes. Following her arrival in Adelaide in October 1855 there is a ten-year period when, although Anastasia does not feature in the available records, the authors use their considerable research experience to construct a credible account of what she may have been engaged in. Anastasia arrived just at the end of the free passage for single females initiative and had in fact, because it had attracted unfavourable publicity as being a drain on local resources, created something of a controversy. Of the 2,800 who arrived in the first eight months of 1855, 2,047 were from Ireland, and 75 per cent of the total were listed as 'domestic servants'.

Ten years after her arrival, Anastasia Burke decided to depart South Australia and move to Victoria. The authors entertain the notion that it was the lure of gold that was behind the move because 'by 1871 she was in the centre of the latest [gold] rush in a small corner of South Grippaland, at Stockyard Creek' (p. 35). By January 1873 she had met and married William Thornley, a hotel proprietor, who died only four months later, the authors' conjecture of a form of tuberculosis. Thereafter 'Anasatsia was catapulted into a number of new roles ... as a widow, publican and shareholder in several goldmines' (p. 58).

Among the projects she concerned herself with was the development of the Exchange Hotel, which had become her responsibility and where she would die, aged 80, in 1907. And, although the gold rush in the immediate vicinity of Stockyard Creek tailed off in the 1870s, the hotel remained something of a social fulcrum and became 'a central gathering place of celebration after community events such as wood chopping contest, successful cattle sales and the local races ...' (p. 71). Anastasia herself became a major shareholder in at least one other gold mine and by 1883 she owned the Foster Gold Mining Company. She also purchased and developed land and was very much an influential figure in the district, allowing her hotel to be used for issues of community concern. In the best successful emigrant tradition she returned to Ireland in 1901 aged 74 and erected a sizeable Celtic cross containing the names of her mother, father (who had himself been a stone mason) grandparents and brothers and sisters, all of whom she had outlived.

There is a handsome selection of associated images between pages 98–99 (including some in colour) of the remains of Callan Workhouse, County Kilkenny, and some of the sources on which the story is based.

This absorbing tale of a redoubtable woman, a young single female migrant to Australia whose story, exceptional in every sense, outlining her personal experience, her business exploits and her community profile, deserves to be heard.

TREVOR PARKHILL

DAVID STEERS (ED.)
First World War Roll of Honour of the Non-Subscribing Presbyterian Church of Ireland
First Presbyterian (Non-Subscribing) Church Downpatrick, 2018
pp vii & 50   ISBN: 978-0-9993154-0-5   pb

Rev. Dr David Steers had assiduously researched and now made available what may be regarded as the definitive list of members of the Non-Subscribing Church in Ireland who served in the First World War. It is (p. iii) 'an alphabetical list of members of each church who are known to have served ... (p. iv) with a separate list for female members where possible. Where a member gave their life ... that name is highlighted'. In all there are 588 names from 34 churches, including 98 fatalities.

Most poignantly of all, and this is where Dr Steers' research is seen to best effect, are the obituaries relating to each of the church members killed during the four years of the conflict. These provide absorbing information on their family background, the regiment in which they served, where they died, whether or not there is a known grave and the jobs and careers they had prior to enlisting, among much else. For example, Sergeant Edward Reid, 'son of Gregory and Mary Ann Reid', members of the Non-Subscribing Church at Templepatrick County Antrim, is recorded as being buried at Aeroplane Cemetery, West Vlanderen, Belgium, in August 1917, having served in the Royal Irish Rifles from the early days of the war until his death at the crucial (for the Allied cause) Battle of Messines, and having been awarded the Military Medal.

Members of the Non-Subscribing Church, Unitarians, are known for their on-the-whole-liberal and humanitarian sympathies. Many who enlisted did so not necessarily to fight but to help the Allied cause in a number of non-combative roles. The list includes the names and details of some 25 females who served. Foremost among these was the nursing profession, including those who served both at home (Great Britain and Ireland) and abroad, particularly in France, in the Voluntary Aid Detachment and Queen Alexandria's Imperial Military Nursing Service. In the case of the latter, Margaret C. Reid, of the Templepatrick, County Antrim, congregation, served in Malta. (It is not noted but it could well be that Margaret was the sister of Sergeant Edward Reid, also a member of the Templepatrick congregation, noted above). Non-Subscribing women also served as telegraphists and ambulance drivers.

Equally striking is that, of the nine names recorded as having served from the Glenarm, County Antrim congregation, no fewer than five were killed, one in the Canadian Infantry and one in the New Zealand Rifle Brigade, itself a reminder of the extent to which the Commonwealth contribution to the war effort included Irish immigrants. Included in the list are the names of those in the Non-Subscribing congregations in Dublin and Cork. Of the 16 who enlisted from Dublin, seven were killed: evidence, if such were needed after four years of commemoration throughout the island, of the all-Ireland context of the First World War.

TREVOR PARKHILL

Tracing your Irish Ancestors

Family history conferences • 10–15 June 2019, 04–11 September 2019

Ulster Historical Foundation is pleased to announce details of our family history conferences and programmes to be held in 2019. Don't miss out on a superb experience.

The Foundation is famous for its hugely popular family history events which comprise archival research, lectures, tours and visits to Ireland's rich and diverse heritage attractions.

In 2019 the Foundation will be hosting two events which will appeal to family historians interested in their Irish roots regardless of experience.

Irish Family History Experience: Introduction to Irish Genealogy, 10–15 June 2019

This brand new, six-day programme will offer you the opportunity to spend three days learning from the experts and researching in the Public Record Office Northern Ireland (PRONI) followed by the option of three days of touring Ireland's famous historic sites or further research in PRONI.
www.ancestryireland.com/family-history-conference/summer/

Tracing Your Irish Ancestors Family History Conference, 4–11 September 2019

Our classic 8-day family history programme (10 days if you include the genealogy essentials course), includes research in the archives in Belfast and Dublin, lectures, and tours to famous historic sites and cultural attractions, including Kilmainham Gaol, Giant's Causeway and Brú na Bóinne. Crucially, for the research enthusiast, you can spend all your time in the archives if you wish to do so – the choice is yours! Throughout the week we will be there to offer advice and help point you in the right direction.
www.ancestryireland.com/family-history-conference/autumn/

Testimonials

The time I spent in Northern Ireland with the group organized and led by the Ulster Historical Foundation was among the very best holidays I have ever enjoyed. It is very difficult to imagine how it could have been better. – Murray Barkley, Canada

I thought it was an excellent conference, well organized, interesting tours, knowledgeable and friendly staff. A great way to explore and learn about Ireland while researching my family history. – Julie Connelly, Canada

The Ulster Historical Foundation's Family History Conference was very well organised. The staff were very helpful in what can be a very frustrating exercise. – Joyce Edmonds, Australia

Great conference UHF! It was very Informative, well organized, friendly, and fun. Looking forward to my next one – Suzanne Billing, USA

So many little touches added to the quality of the conference experience. It was a brilliant idea to list attendees' research interests in the program booklet. – Martha Kaiser, USA

If you're wondering whether to engage UHF's services or attend one of their conferences I can assure you that you'll experience absolute quality. I attended the June 2016 UHF conference and to sum it up – I attended a genealogy holiday … My only complaint is that it ended! But, I've already decided that I'm going to attend another one in a few years' time. Yes, it's that good! – Davina Hughes, New Zealand